PLANT LORE
—— OF AN ——
ALASKAN ISLAND

foraging in the Kodiak Archipelago

PLANT LORE
—OF AN—
ALASKAN ISLAND

foraging in the Kodiak Archipelago

FRAN KELSO

AND THE OUZINKIE BOTANICAL SOCIETY

Technical editor EVELYN WISZINCKAS
Photography by EVELYN WISZINCKAS
Illustrations by BARBARA BURCH & SANDRA COEN

Copyright © 2022 Fran Kelso.

Illustrations by Barbara Burch and Sandra Coen
Illustration facing the title page by Janet Quaccia
Drawing of two plant foragers: Linda Getz
Photography by: Evelyn Wiszinckas, Timothy Smith, Norman Smith and Kevin Smith

All rights reserved. No part of this book may be reproduced, stored, or transmitted by any means—whether auditory, graphic, mechanical, or electronic—without written permission of both publisher and author, except in the case of brief excerpts used in critical articles and reviews. Unauthorized reproduction of any part of this work is illegal and is punishable by law.

ISBN: 979-8-88640-505-7 (sc)
ISBN: 979-8-88640-506-4 (hc)
ISBN: 979-8-88640-507-1 (e)

Because of the dynamic nature of the Internet, any web addresses or links contained in this book may have changed since publication and may no longer be valid. The views expressed in this work are solely those of the author and do not necessarily reflect the views of the publisher, and the publisher hereby disclaims any responsibility for them.

One Galleria Blvd., Suite 1900, Metairie, LA 70001
1-888-421-2397

Dedicated to the memory of
Jenny Chernikoff, Sasha Smith, and Jennifer Griffin
Three women who loved the work of nature

OUZINKIE BOTANICAL SOCIETY
EDITORIAL STAFF

Fran Kelso: Editor

Barbara Burch, Sandra Coen, Linda Getz, and Janet Quaccia: Artwork and Illustrations

Evelyn Wiszinckas: Photographer and Technical Editor

Georgia Smith: Researcher

Angeline Anderson: Oral Researcher

Jenny Chernikoff: Local Use Consultant

Alexandra (Sasha) Smith: Local Use Consultant

Rosemary Squartsoff and Linda Getz: Foragers

Greg Wolfer: Research Professor

Chris Quick, Sheila Anderson, Carl M. Smith, Thelma Anderson,
Nell Tsacrios, Claudia Torsen: Past-Year Class Members

Marian Brown, Nina Gilbreath, Father Gerasim, N.V.A.: Russian Language Consultants

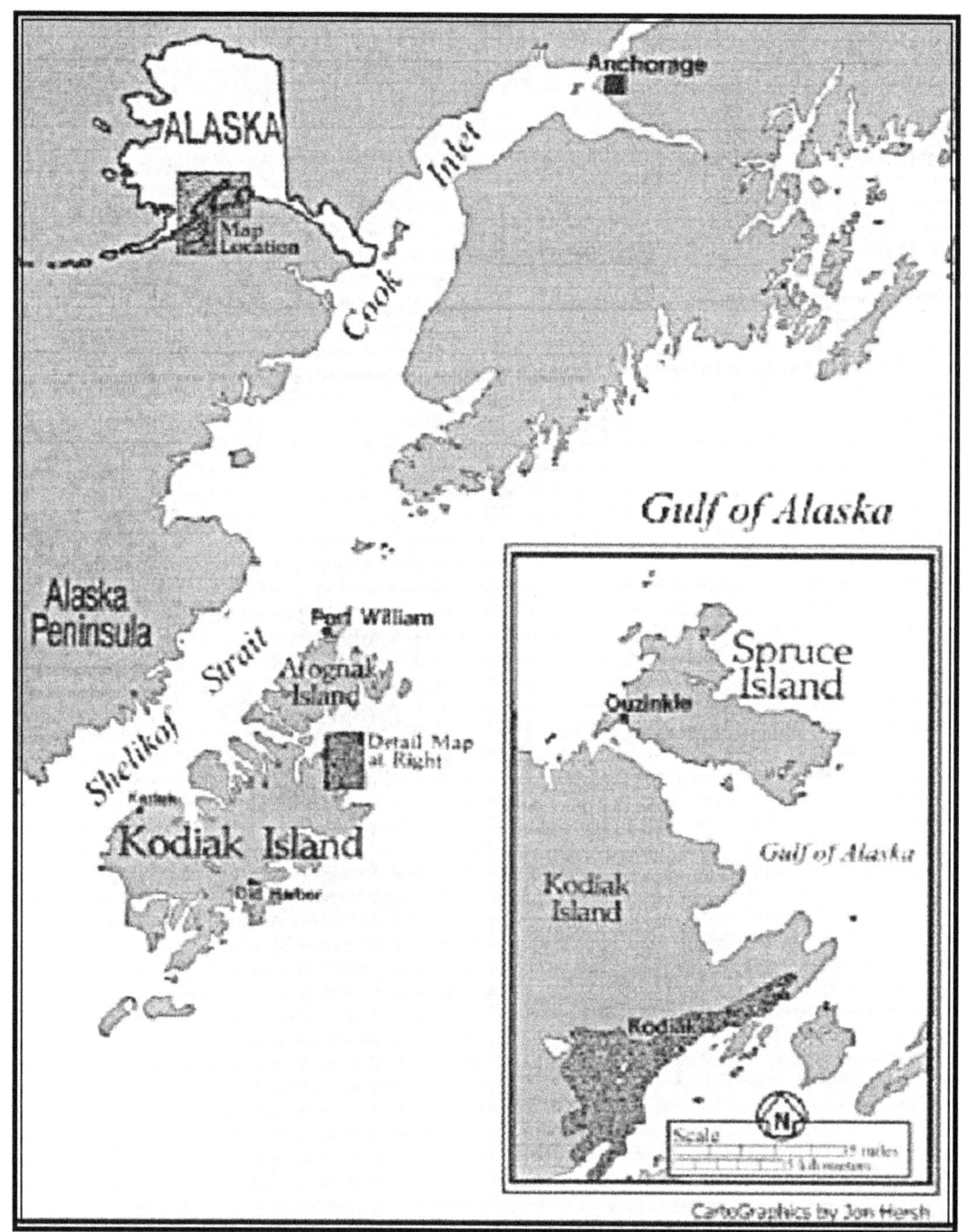

TABLE OF CONTENTS

Preface 1
Ouzinkie, Then and Now 6

THE PLANTS, by habitat

Introduction: How To Use This Book 23
Seashore And Beach Marshes 29
Bogs, Pond Edges, Damp Terrain, Or Alpine Slopes 59
Grassy Meadows And Forest Clearings 87
Stream Banks; Moist, Sunny Hillsides And Rocky Places 115
Open Woods And Forests 149
Gravel Bars And Riverbeds Or Dry Slopes 179
Cultivated And Disturbed Soils; Along Roadbeds 189

THE INDEXES and supplemental information

Plant Family Index 217
Color Index 261
Medicinal Index 273
Berries, Low And High 297
Hints On Cooking Wild Edibles 301
Dyes From Wild Plants 307

WRAPPING IT UP...

Glossary 317
Bibliography 325
Index 331

PREFACE

It has been 24 years since I first presented my manuscript of *Plant Lore of an Alaskan Island* to Mr. Bob Henning at Alaska Northwest Publishing Company. First edition published in 1985; second edition in 2011, to the delight of all of us who were part of the original "Plants Class" (Ouzinkie Botanical Society), an outgrowth of my job as an Adult Education teacher in Ouzinkie.

For nearly 24 years I lived on my homestead on Spruce Island, close to Kodiak Island. Spruce Island is approximately seven miles long and three miles wide at its widest point. It is densely forested with Sitka spruce. The central part of the island is a high ridge, which culminates in Mt. St. Herman, its highest point. This mountain rises above the bays and beaches of Monk's Lagoon at the eastern end of this lovely northern paradise. St. Herman, a Russian Orthodox monk, who was the first saint to be canonized on North American soil, lived for many years in a small cabin at Monk's Lagoon.

My transition from the town of Kodiak, the "population center" of Kodiak Island, to Spruce Island was made by degrees. I first came to Ouzinkie with my husband in the early 70's. In 1977, after he and I chose separate paths, I enlisted friends to help me to build a small cabin on the land we had claimed through the Bureau of Land Management's "homesite claim" program. In 1979, I moved to my homesite to stay. That fall I started my job as the village ABE (Adult Basic Education) teacher.

Ouzinkie is a Russian-Aleut village of approximately 250 people, depending on the year. It is located on the west coast of Spruce Island. The island itself lies adjacent to Kodiak Island, and is separated from it by Narrow Strait. We often call this mile-wide channel of ocean water between the two islands "the freeway", as it is a main thoroughfare for boats heading for the fishing grounds. Indeed, as no road connects Spruce Island and Kodiak Island, boats or planes are the normal mode of transportation.

As the adult educator in the Native village of Ouzinkie, (pronounced "you-zinc-ee") I started a study group with the purpose of learning together about wild, edible, and medicinal plants growing in our area. We held a weekly class, went on a hike to forage or to observe what was growing nearly every weekend, and had a monthly potluck prepared from the foods native to our island. ("You eat it first, Fran – if you don't keel over dead, we will try some too.") Our weekend hikes continued for the next few years; after four years of learning about plants by searching them out in their native habitat and studying them, I compiled the information we had gathered into the first edition of this book.

I have had an ongoing relationship with wild plants in the years since that first edition. Our group continued our foraging trips at fairly regular intervals during all the years that I lived on Spruce Island. In 2001, when I moved to Kodiak to live, I started a small business called "Backwoods Botany". My intent was in part selfish: By acting as guide and teacher to folks who wanted to go on a hike to learn about plants, I was able to learn more – and to relearn what I had forgotten – about many of my wild friends of forest, field, and shore.

Thus, this new edition of *Plant Lore* includes information from the original book plus new material gathered over these past 23 years. A few new plants have been introduced into the text as well. The choices of the plants presented in this text were based on first-hand knowledge. These were the species we studied as a group or found regularly on our hikes in our area. Their habitat was our habitat.

Some new learning tools have been added to this edition. The series of the indexes at the back of the book present in-depth information about identifying, using, or avoiding these plants. Also, the book has been organized by habitat, to make it easier to know what you might find in a specific type of landscape. Our choicest recipes for wild edibles have been included, as well as some of the fish and game recipes found in the first edition, to complete your meal.

The purpose of this book is two-fold. The first is to offer you a tool to aid you in identifying the species presented here. The second, more personal purpose is to give you a feel for the island and the people who shared the same natural habitat, and through quotes from the elders and small anecdotes about some of our "Plants Class" adventures, to take you with us on a vicarious trip through our bit of the Alaskan wilderness.

The first edition of *Plant Lore* included a charming interview with Alexandra (Sasha) Smith and Jenny Chernikoff, the two elder members of our group of plant enthusiasts. In this second edition, I have dissected their conversation and partnered their remarks with the specific plant we were discussing.

JENNY CHERNIKOFF
Photo by: Fran Kelso

ALEXNDRA (SASHA) SMITH
Photo by: Fran Kelso

These two women were, for me, icons of their culture. Their connection to the earth was still a vital part of their lives. From them, we as a group learned, and enjoyed the learning. The two of them were in their late 70's when the plant interview that appeared in the first edition was conducted. They were cousins who had been friends since childhood and had lived all their lives in Ouzinkie. They saw the old ways change, and new ways that were not always better ways come to stay. Still, they held intact their love for the world of nature, and willingly shared both that love and their knowledge with us.

This book is dedicated in part to them. They were our connection to the ancestors who had come before, and who had been their teachers. It became our honor to learn, and to share with them, in the time-honored oral tradition of women passing along their knowledge of the world of growing things, to be used and enlarged upon by the next generation.

I am also dedicating this book to a young woman who shared our close connection to nature – my daughter-in-law, Jennifer Griffin. The plant outings we shared were far too few. During the last 4 ½ years of her life, she struggled with cancer. Still, she lived her life as fully as she could, and kept a positive attitude in spite of the war she was waging. During her last several months on earth, she volunteered to help me with the "Plant Family Index" for this book, and contributed some of the research for that index. I am so glad to be able to include a part of her work in this book, and am pleased to be able to dedicate this endeavor to honor her unquenchable spirit.

In our first edition of *Plant Lore*, Sandra Coen, a fine artist with an outstanding ability in plant identification, did all the drawings of plants. Some of her drawings appear in this edition as well. However, Sandra is no longer in the area, so I asked local artist Barbara Burch to do the drawings for the new plants included in this text. I was very pleased with these drawings, and wanted a chance to show off a bit more of her talent. Therefore, I asked her to replace some of Sandra's drawings with her own and to do the landscape drawings for the seven plant habitat divisions. She also furnished the two copies of illustrations by Hannah T. Croasdale, Dartmouth College, from the book, *Botany*, Third Edition, written by Carl L. Wilson and Walter E. Loomis. These show the parts of a vascular plant and the parts of a flower, and may be found in the introduction to the plant family index. Included there as well is her drawing of 3 types of root systems, taken from an original by Bonnie K. Walters that appears in *Vascular Plant Taxonomy*, Fourth Edition, written by Dirk R. Walters and David J. Keil. Barbara has also utilized a drawing from Dr. Eleanor Vierick's book, *Alaska's Wilderness Medicines,* to make us a copy of the root structure of angelica and water hemlock. I have admired Barbara's talent as an artist for around 30 years, and am very happy to be able to present a sampling of her art for you to enjoy.

It is a treat for me to be able to offer you some color photographs of local plants in this edition as well. I was pleased to ask Evelyn Wiszinckas, a favorite Kodiak photographer, to furnish me with the necessary pictures. We ended up including a few of her black and white pictures at the beginning of book sections as well. Evelyn's large collection of photos, her original ideas, and her willingness to experiment to reach a desired end made our photo selection adventure a memorable one. She has done far more than required, chalking it all up to a worthwhile new learning experience.

There are two extra-special pieces of artwork in the first few pages of this new book. The first is a repeat of a drawing done especially for our original book by Janet Quaccia, who lived for some time on Spruce Island. I had asked her if she could do a drawing that captured the essence of Spruce Island, and she drew the round picture that appears facing our title page. You will also find a new art selection which appears immediately after the Table of Contents. Linda Getz, who joined our "Plants Class" as a forager and plant enthusiast, is also a very fine artist. Presented here is her whimsical drawing of two of us focused on a new plant discovery. It is my treat to share the work of these two talented women with you.

As with the first edition, Eric Hulten's *Flora of Alaska and Neighboring Territories*, copyrighted in 1968, was an indispensable asset. Information on genus, species, and known presence of the plant on Kodiak Island came from his encompassing work.

I also gained an unexpected asset when I was able to persuade Carolyn Parker, botanist at the University of Alaska in Fairbanks, to check my work on the new "Plant Family Index" for its botanical accuracy. In spite of her own over-full schedule, she agreed to read the completed section and offer corrections or suggestions. Without her help, I don't think I could have met the challenge provided me in the writing of that section. Not only did she read and offer corrections to the pages I sent her, but she also answered every one of the several emails I sent her with "just one more question". When I started this project, I had no idea I'd learn so much! Thank you, thank you, Carolyn!

Thanks, too, to Verna Pratt, who took the time to go over the drawings in the original book very carefully, and to make recommendations as to how we could improve them.

With a new edition come other new people who are deserving of thank-yous. One person to whom I am especially grateful is Janice Schofield. Her excellent book, *Discovering Wild Plants*, was published four years after my first edition of *Plant Lore*. All of us in "Plants Class" benefited from that book, as Janice's thorough discussion of wild plants of Alaska taught us a great deal. Then, in the summer of 2004, I finally had the chance to attend a workshop taught by Janice, here in Kodiak. What a memorable weekend! After I began work on this book, Janice graciously gave me permission to include a few of her recipes and remedies. You will find the appropriate credit to Janice in the text. Some notable examples are her basic tincture recipe (sundew), her "Spring Tonic" recipe (devil's club), her Balm of Gilead recipe (cottonwood), and her "Seasonal Herbcakes" recipe (beach pea). Janice, you are now an honorary member of "Plants Class".

Two people, Nicholas Pestrikoff and Timothy Smith, helped me tremendously when I was putting together the "Ouzinkie, Then and Now" section that follows this preface. It was my enjoyable experience to listen to some of their stories and reminiscences. Nicholas, who was born in Ouzinkie and lived there most of his life, is now 72. He has a treasury of stories to tell about his village. Timothy moved to Ouzinkie as a boy, when his parents, Reverend Norman and Joyce Smith, were sent from the village of Larsen Bay to Ouzinkie by the Baptist Ministry. At present, Tim maintains a very nice website, www.tanignak.com. On this site, he has articles about Ouzinkie and a collection of priceless old pictures of the village and its people. He has graciously agreed to furnish a few of his pictures for the "Ouzinkie, Then and Now" article. Two of his pictures also appear in the book text as well.

Kevin Smith, life-long Ouzinkie resident, also furnished a picture of "dory knees" for us, as well as two aerial shots of the present village and a Ouzinkie map. You can view more of Kevin's fine photography among the pictures on The Ouzinkie Tribal Council website, www.ouzinkie.org.

I gained some insight into the cod-fishing industry from Ed Opheim, Sr., dory builder and long-time resident of Spruce Island. On many visits to his home, I have enjoyed tales of his experiences that have certainly added color and drama to my vision of a way of life that is no more.

His son, Ed Opheim, Jr., helped me with some of the history of cattle raising in Ouzinkie. I am most appreciative of his willingness to share his memories. My thanks go, too, to friends in Ouzinkie, who have told me of their experiences over the years. Some of these are included in this brief history.

I would like to offer a note of explanation regarding Native language: In my short history of Ouzinkie that follows this preface and in the body of this book, I have referred to the language spoken by the Native people of the area as "Aleut". I realize that it is currently more correct to use the word "Alutiiq" instead of "Aleut". However, old habits die hard. When I first moved to Banjo Beach, I was told that I was living close to a Russian-Aleut village. The villagers themselves taught me that their language was the "Aleut language". Therefore, in the first edition of this book, my references were to the "Aleut" people and plant names. For consistency, I have kept to this usage. My apologies to anyone whom I may have unintentionally offended by doing so.

Over the years since the first edition was sold out, I have talked of reprinting it. A handful of years ago I was approached by a lady named Loretta Stoltenberg, who was then working in the State Parks office in Kodiak. Loretta began a one-woman campaign to get my book back in print. Over a period of two years, she managed to get the whole book plus all the illustrations onto a C.D. Between us, we proofed and corrected. Now that I had the book on a disk, I could no longer delay in trying to get it republished. And, indeed, if it weren't for Loretta, I might have given up the project.

I chanced to meet another friend shortly after the book was finally completed and on the disk. Robbie Townsend-Vennel helped me run some copies that I could sell in 3-ring binders, and then also urged me to look for a publisher.

In the process of readying the book for resubmission to a publisher, I discovered that it was easy to get bogged down in the paperwork of preparation. My excellent photographer, Evelyn Wiszinckas, changed hats from time to time and helped to educate me in the mysteries of computer magic. She has been a great teacher! (I have learned far more about computers than I ever wanted to know!) Volunteer assistance from faithful friend, Chris Lund, helped me through a few clerical nightmares. Both she and Evelyn also offered their share of "you can do its" and "atta girls". Thank you, ladies!

Writing this second edition has certainly been a learning experience for me! It is my hope that you, too, may gain knowledge and pleasure from our new version of *Plant Lore of an Alaskan Island*.

OUZINKIE, THEN AND NOW

MAP OF SPRUCE ISLAND

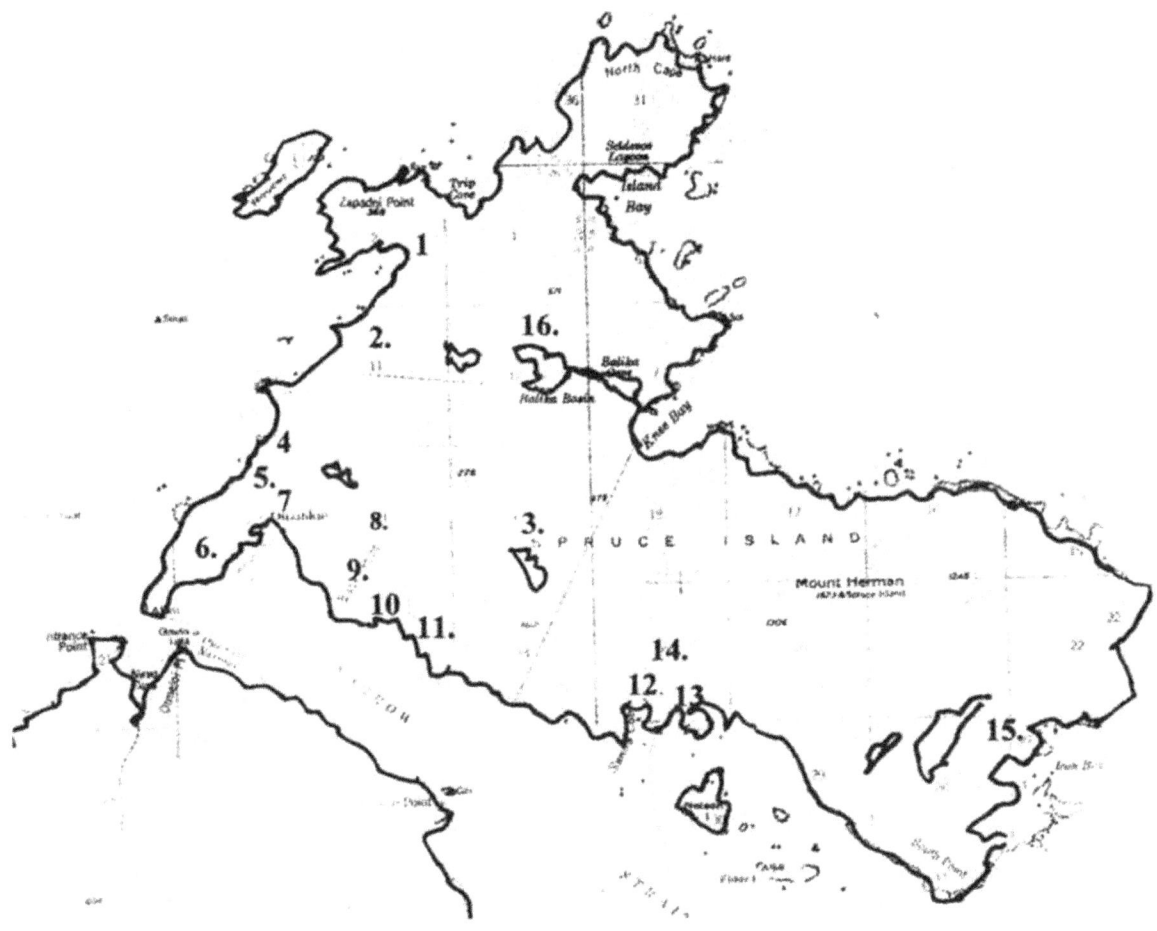

MAP LEGEND

1. Pineapple Cove
2. Garden Point
3. Lake Mahoona
4. Runway
5. Otherside Beach
6. Sourdough Flats
7. Ouzinkie
8. Pumphouse
9. Dump/Sawmill
10. Eskimo Cove
11. My house on Banjo Beach
12. Sunny Cove Lagoon
13. Pleasant Harbor
14. New Valaam Monastery
15. Chapel at Monk's Lagoon
16. Big Lagoon

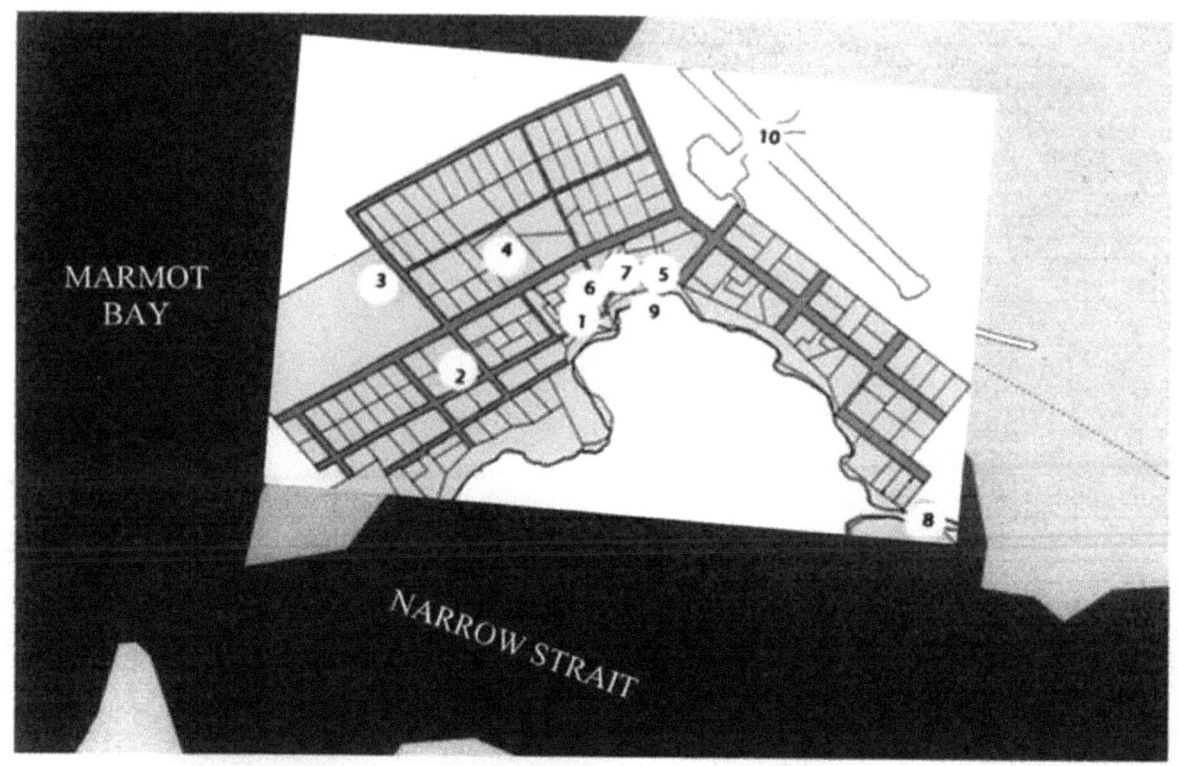

MAP OF CITY OF OUZINKIE

MAP LEGEND

1. Store
2. Mission
3. New school
4. Old school
5. Location of old post office on beach
6. New post office
7. Russian Orthodox Church
8. Katmai Creek
9. Sandy Beach
10. Runway

OUZINKIE, THEN AND NOW

Before we take a botanical hike across Spruce Island, I would like to place you in the proper setting. Therefore, let me introduce you to the people who live in this habitat and relate to you a bit of their history. These are the people from the village of Ouzinkie or from the Opheim families at Pleasant Harbor, about 4 miles down the coast from the village. Though the Ouzinkie lifestyle was undergoing changes when I arrived there, the villagers were still close enough to their past to give me a clear view of where they had come from.

Only a few Native families made up the village of Ouzinkie until the mid-1800s. At that time the tiny settlement was chosen as a retirement community for the Russian American Company in Kodiak. I asked Nicholas Pestrikoff, who is 72 and has lived in Ouzinkie all his life, if he knew if the Russian retirees all arrived *en masse*. He explained that they came a few families at a time. He said that many of the Russian workers had married Native women and had families. "When it came time for them to retire", Nick said, "The company found it much cheaper to relocate the families to Spruce Island and other village communities than it would be to send them back to Russia."

Early villagers raised cattle. I asked Nick how cattle first got to Ouzinkie. The question prompted him to tell me an interesting story. He began by telling me that, in his father's day, fishing was done by a sailing fleet. Small sailing dories, sometimes double-ended, from an average of 16 feet long up to larger 24-footers were used to fish salmon, halibut, and cod in the Kodiak area. Nick's father often built the small vessels, both rowing skiffs and sailing dories, which made up the local fishing fleet.

(As a side note, Nick mentioned that his wife, Lilly, had grown up in the village of Karluk on Kodiak Island. Her father, Larry Ellanak, who later moved his whole family to Ouzinkie, started fishing as a young man with the sailing fleet that was fishing in Bristol Bay. It is interesting that Nick's father built small sailing dories and his wife's father fished in the same type vessel.)

I was wondering what this story of sailing dories had to do with cattle, when Nick began telling me about the large sailing schooners that also fished, and undoubtedly served at times as tenders, delivering supplies to fishermen or taking their salmon when they could not reach a cannery. Schooners also delivered needed supplies to the local canneries. To these sailing vessels went the job of delivering large numbers of live cattle, which were used as milk cows or butchered as needed at the cannery for meat to feed their work crews.

Nick surmises that there were times when the small Ouzinkie boats came to the cannery to deliver their salmon, and captain and crew sat down for an excellent meal in the cannery mess hall. When they saw how well the workers were fed, they decided that raising cattle for their own use in the village would be a good idea. Soon everyone wanted to have a milk cow and some stock for winter beef, and the villagers' small herd was started.

Ed Opheim, Jr., who was born in 1939, told me that he thought the Russians might have brought the first cattle to Ouzinkie and to Afognak Village. He said his grandfather, Chris Opheim, started raising cattle in Sunny Cove near Pleasant Harbor shortly after he came to the island in 1923. Ed said they kept a good-sized herd of cattle for many years in the Sunny Cove area or nearby. He told me that at one time their herd numbered around 70 head. These cattle were raised both for home use and for butchering to sell in Kodiak.

Ed recalled that most families in Ouzinkie had from one to several head of cattle in the old days. Ed, who lived in the village in his youth and went through 4th grade at the BIA school there, told me that all of the Ouzinkie cattle hung out together, and when they all came down to the beach in front of the village, the whole wide expanse would be covered with cattle. Interestingly, the town herd and the Sunny Cove herd might occasionally leave their own territory and journey far enough to meet and mingle, but they would not trespass on their neighbors' turf past a certain point.

Jenny Chernikoff told me that the villagers used to butcher cattle for winter meat or for beef to sell in Kodiak every fall on the beach where my house now stands. When I first came to the village, Jenny and the Opheims were the only ones who still had any cattle. When the fishing industry and the canneries began providing employment for many villagers and cannery stores began selling ready-cut, packaged meat, cattle raising became less popular, and gradually the herd dwindled.

If one wanted fish, it wasn't necessary to go far from home to find them. Native fishermen often used a beach seine or went out in their dories and set a gill net. Gene Anderson told me one time about an experience he had as a boy. He went out with his uncle to set the gill net. When they returned some hours later, they couldn't find the net! They cruised the area slowly for some time, and finally found it, completely submerged: anchor; line; floats; the entire gill net. When they pulled it up, they found that there were so many salmon caught in that net that the weight had pulled all the gear underwater. As Ed Opheim, Sr. explained, "In those days there were more fish and fewer fishermen." He used to tell about going by dory, motorized by that time, to Kitoi Bay on Kodiak Island, and leaving a bloody trail behind the boat because so many fish were packed together in the bay.

Because of high demand, boat building became an important craft in the earlier days when wooden boats made up the entire fleet. At his sawmill, Ed Opheim, Sr. cut and sold lumber to be used both for dories and for other island building projects. Ed himself, who was still building wooden dories when I reached Spruce Island, became renowned around the state and even outside Alaska for his fine craft. Nicholas Pestrikoff told me that his father, builder of so many of the sailing dories, had built around 1300 rowing skiffs and sailing dories in his lifetime.

I learned of the senior Pestrikoff's occupation in an earlier conversation when I asked Nick what he did in the winter when there was no salmon fishing. He replied, "I looked for dory knees. When I found good ones, I cut them." It was customary for the dory builders to look for spruce trees with roots that were curved in just the right way to form the framework for the dory's hull. These curved pieces were used for both the bow stem and for the side framework. The side pieces were used in pairs, and were known as "knees". If you walk through Spruce Island forests, you will come upon trees with a flat-sided piece about three feet high, where a root section has been cut away from the lower trunk of the tree. You will know then that a dory-man had walked the woods years before you, and he had found his perfectly curved root on that tree.

The canneries that operated in Ouzinkie over the years did not always process salmon. There were times when they would process crab or shrimp. Most years, however, the cannery then in operation would take in salmon only, and this fishery became the most important source of income for the village. The Opheim family, however, chose a different direction. They fished for cod from their wooden dories and from their larger boat. The cod were salted in barrels. These were sold by the ton in Kodiak, then put on a freighter and sent to Seattle for processing.

Ouzinkie's parade of canneries was run by a series of companies. These commercial operations were located at varying times on either side of Ouzinkie's horseshoe bay. The large complex of buildings that housed the Grimes Packing Co., and later the Ouzinkie Packing Co., was completely destroyed by the tidal wave in 1964. No new cannery has ever been built on that side of the bay.

Across the bay near Katmai Creek, another cannery was opened after the tidal wave and went through an interesting history of owners and uses, only to be destroyed by fire in October of 1975, while my ex-husband and I and a group of friends worked on our proposed home at Banjo Beach, down the coast from the village.

According to Nicholas Pestrikoff, more than one floating processor had tied up in Ouzinkie over the years. In fact, the famed "Kalakala" (www.kalakala.org) was moored in the village for about a year. Nick explained that all of these floating processors had the same problem: fresh water. When it became apparent that there wasn't enough water for the villagers and the processor, the latter had to go. Since that 1975 fire, there have been no more canneries or floating processors in the village of Ouzinkie.

The severe destruction created by the tidal wave of 1964 changed the face of Ouzinkie forever. Timothy Smith (www.tanignak.com), who was ten years old at the time, offers an excellent eyewitness account and many pictures of this disaster. Here are some highlights from his story:

The 1964 quake measured 9.2 on the Richter scale, the largest quake ever recorded in North America. The quake and the tidal wave that followed did severe damage in Kodiak. All the low-lying buildings in the Kodiak channel were destroyed, and most of the fishing fleet was damaged or destroyed.

In Ouzinkie, the actual damage to the village from the earthquake was minor, but the ensuing tidal wave more than made up for this small blessing. The complex of buildings that formed the Ouzinkie Packing Company was totally destroyed. Houses on the Ouzinkie shoreline were gone, floating off with the tides. Of all the buildings that floated off their foundations, only two small storage sheds were salvaged. An entire section of the Ouzinkie store was sheared off and deposited miles away.

Fishermen scrambled to move their boats to deeper water. However, one boat, the "Spruce Cape", was caught in a shallow passage of water when the largest wave hit, and the boat and all aboard were lost.

Down the coast, the Opheims lost their sawmill and a new boathouse they had just completed. They saved their house from floating off by tying it to some trees. I remember Anna Opheim telling me that they had just installed new carpeting in the living room. Of course, this was ruined. The Opheims later rebuilt their home on the high ridge overlooking the beach.

Tim told me that the BIA school (now known in the village as the "Old School") was the only place that still had reliable electricity after the quake. Says Tim, "It became the headquarters for a bank of old marine band radios, as Ouzinkie tried to keep in touch with the outside world. It was hard to study with all those radios blasting…"

Due to the earthquake, the entire northern end of the Kodiak Island Archipelago had sunk six feet lower, thus completely changing the high and low tide lines. Consequently, acres of beautiful meadows and forested lowlands on Kodiak Island and on Spruce Island were lost due to these changes.

There are two places of worship in Ouzinkie: One is the Russian Orthodox Church and the other is the Baptist chapel in Baker Cottage (commonly called "the Mission" by Ouzinkie residents).

The Russian Orthodox religion actually came to Spruce Island before it came to Ouzinkie. In the early 1800s, Father Herman, who was the last of the original monks sent as missionaries from Russia to Alaska, moved to the eastern end of Spruce Island to a spot now called Monk's Lagoon. He called his place of habitation "New Valaam". There, near the beach and amid the spruce forest, he built an orphanage, a school, and a chapel, taking in children from Kodiak who needed a place to go. Father Herman died on Spruce Island in 1837. In 1970, he became the first saint to be canonized on North American soil.

In 1906 the Russian Orthodox Church was built in Ouzinkie (Jenny Chernikoff proudly told me it was built the year she was born.) The church soon became an important focal point for Ouzinkie village life.

In the mid-1900s, Father Gerasim Schmaltz moved to Monk's Lagoon at the eastern end of Spruce Island, where he lived in a tiny cabin near St. Herman's chapel. Fr. Gerasim's reason for coming to Spruce Island was to preserve and protect the ministry and legacy of St. Herman. This exceptional man interacted regularly with the Orthodox community in Ouzinkie and was much loved by them.

Fr. Gerasim's work to preserve St. Herman's spiritual writing and personal letters is not too far removed from the work done by nuns and monks who came to our island while I was living at Banjo Beach. On the high hilltop above Pleasant Harbor, they built the New Valaam Monastery, named in remembrance of St. Herman. Those who were my down-coast neighbors did a lot of translating, writing, and in general preparing research for publication. Meanwhile, they were observing their church regimen daily and living a simple yet labor-intensive lifestyle.

In 1938, the Kodiak Baptist Ministry built Baker Cottage in Ouzinkie. Says Tim Smith, "It was originally built as an orphanage, with other missionary work a secondary task." Baker Cottage was a large 3-story white building with an abundance of bedrooms, spacious living quarters, and a little chapel built into the ground-floor area.

Children from the orphanage at Baker Cottage were moved to the Kodiak Baptist Mission in the mid-50s. In 1958, Reverend Norman Smith, who ran the Baptist mission boat, the "Evangel", was relocated to Ouzinkie. He and his wife, Joyce, and their four children moved from their tiny cabin in the village of Larsen Bay to the spacious Baker Cottage. Tim Smith recalls that, to him, it was like moving into a mansion after residing in their little tarpaper shack.

The Baptist Mission and the Russian Orthodox Church served their community side by side, and Ouzinkie villagers interacted with both. After all, Joyce taught kindergarten at Baker Cottage for 42 years, until her retirement, and served as village health aide for most of that time as well. Norman did everything from minding the city generators to delivering mail from plane to post office, besides providing his Sunday services in the chapel. For several years after their move, Norman still took the "Evangel" on its trips to outlying villages as part of his ministry.

Among the advantages of having two religious sects represented in the village were the benefits of celebrating two sets of holidays. The Russian Orthodox Church still bases its year on the Julian calendar, as opposed to the Gregorian calendar, which is the most widely used calendar in the world today. Therefore, it became the custom in Ouzinkie to celebrate first an American holiday, then a Russian holiday, approximately two weeks apart. It appears to me to be a sound philosophy to celebrate both. Why choose only one celebration when you can have two?

In the early years of the Americanization of the educational system in such remote areas, schooling could be a challenge for young villagers. Until the 1980s, when Ouzinkie's school program added 11th and 12th grades, the village did not furnish schooling past a certain year, and the youngsters had to go off-island to boarding schools. Nicholas Pestrikoff's school experience provides a good example. Young Nicholas started kindergarten in Ouzinkie in 1941 in the waterfront building that had housed the school before the new BIA school was completed. He then attended first and second grade in the BIA school, and then was transferred to a Kodiak grade school. At that time, when a village student came to Kodiak to school, it was the policy to put him back one year. Consequently, Nick repeated second grade in Kodiak. For seven school years he lived at the Kodiak Baptist Mission and went to grade school in the Kodiak school system. For his 9th through 12th grade years, he was sent to the boarding school, Mt Edgecumbe, in Sitka, where he obtained his high school diploma. Nicholas said he was the exception rather than the rule. It was more common for village students to drop out after 8th grade because they didn't want to leave home again for high school.

The BIA school was completed in 1939. Then, in the late 1970s the first portion of a newer, more modern school was built. The old BIA school became the Ouzinkie city offices. That new school has been enlarged over the years, until now it has a gymnasium and up-to-date facilities to handle grades K - 12.

Prior to the 1980s it was common for young village people to leave their families, perhaps for the first time, to attend a boarding school much as Nick had done. Jenny Chernikoff, born in 1906, had fond memories of her boarding school years in Oregon, where she attended classes and also helped with farm chores and learned such skills as needlework, which remained a passion of hers for the rest of her life. In Nicholas' time, high school students were sent to Sitka's Mt. Edgecumbe. Then, a dormitory for village students was finally set up in Kodiak, near the high school. Students were still spending the last two years of high school at the "dorm" in Kodiak and attending classes at Kodiak High School when I moved to Spruce Island.

Ouzinkie finally got its first grocery story in the '30s, when the first cannery moved in. Early stores were cannery-operated. Before that time, people lived off the land and the ocean. They raised their cattle for beef, enjoyed fresh milk, and often made their own butter and cheese. Nicholas explained to me that, in the early years long before the cannery stores, housewives would have to put in an order for staple grocery items in Kodiak. Their order would be delivered from Seattle by an ocean-going tender. As the tender only came to the village once a year, the village customer would have to order in sufficient quantity for the whole year. Nicholas said that butter was sold in barrels then; oil was sold in large tins; flour in 100# sacks.

Later the Alaska Steamship Company began coming to the village every couple of weeks. Nick recalls that the arrival of that freighter was an event greatly anticipated by the village children, as the freighter had a ship's store that would open as soon as the boat docked. The store sold bulk candy, a popular item with the young customers.

Before the tidal wave of 1964, the grocery store had been moved to the spot that is its approximate location today. The store changed hands as the canneries changed owners, until finally the Ouzinkie Native Corporation bought the building in which it was housed from Columbia Ward Fisheries. For some time they leased the store portion of the building to Alaska Commercial. When there was no other choice, ONC would run the store themselves, to insure that the villagers could enjoy at least a limited grocery availability.

In the days when Nicholas was growing up, the village had no need of roads, as there were no vehicles. People lived in small hand-built houses. Paths, frequented by cattle and people on foot, wound among them. The only wheeled vehicles used in those days were perhaps a wheelbarrow or a small hand-pulled wagon or cart. However, there came a time when village residents desired the new housing units being offered by the Alaska State Housing Authority and funded by the Federal government. In order to acquire these houses, the village had to agree to allow government-funded roads to be built. This decision to allow roads in the village was a momentous one, and, indeed, it was the start of the process that would turn the village of Ouzinkie in a new direction. The advent of the roads and the new houses changed the appearance of the village, and soon the lifestyle began to change as well.

When I first came to Ouzinkie in the mid-70s, it was a village in transition. Remnants of the old ways lingered, but new ways came swiftly. I could still see glimpses of the old village, yet I could see it changing to fit a newer time. The following paragraphs give short descriptions of the changes I observed.

As already mentioned, the residents of the old village lived close to nature; theirs was a subsistence lifestyle. They had abundant fish, wild game, and often cattle. Some families raised chickens for eggs and meat. Some grew vegetables and ate wild greens. Several families had garden spots at the end of the island, in a fertile area known as "Garden Point". When I first arrived, the Anderson family and Jenny Chernikoff still cultivated their garden plots. I remember Jenny's hiring Georgia Smith's two boys, Carl and Kevin, in the springtime to help her haul kelp from the beach in front of Garden Point to her plot, to use to fertilize her potato bed. This kelp was placed at the bottom of long trenches dug in the garden area; then covered with a bit of soil; then planted with potatoes.

Some habits persist. Though the old garden spots have been abandoned to a prolific nettle crop, fishermen still provide their families with fresh fish, making sure the village elders get their share. Hunters still bring home wild game to enhance their winter larder.

A few of the hand-built Ouzinkie houses were still in use when I first moved to the island. To me, these older places carried the charm of individuality. However, after the first government housing came in, the list of those wanting their own new house grew. Now, new roads and houses have appeared on three sides of Ouzinkie. Only on the bay side, where houses line the ridge top above the beach, does the place look much the same as when I arrived, as all building spots were already in use.

There were still just a few roads in Ouzinkie when I first arrived. I remember walking with Jenny to the top of the ridge behind the houses facing the bay. There was no road there then – just a two-lane wagon track that led to the Ouzinkie water pump house. Jenny used to call that primitive wagon track "the highway". Later Jenny's "highway" would be a real road, ending at the pump house. A few years after that road went in, the village fathers determined that a new dumpsite was needed. A road was built past the pump house for an additional mile out of town, to the top of the hill above Eskimo Cove, and a short half-mile from my house. There a much larger dump facility was established. There, too, Ed Opheim's original sawmill equipment from before the tidal wave found a new home. It had been purchased and refurbished by Dan Soderberg, who cut and sold lumber for a wide assortment of village projects.

One charming remnant from the old village still remains: There has never been a road built along the beachfront. Instead, there is a wooden, high-railed boardwalk, designed for foot traffic only.

When village children began attending public schools, they were not allowed to speak their Native language, and in some cases they were punished if they did. Many of the older residents spoke both Russian and Aleut at one time, as they interacted and intermarried with Russian people. As the younger generation began attending American schools, they learned English out of necessity. However, when I first moved to Spruce Island, the elders still remembered much of both the Aleut language and Russian. It used to fascinate me to listen to elders chatting on a street corner, conversing in a mix of Russian and Aleut, certainly understandable to only their generation. When I began learning Native plant names from the older generation, I found that they used an Aleut name for some plants, and perhaps a Russian name as well, and occasionally they used a name that appeared to be a combination of both languages. As this knowledge of plant names was passed on orally and not in writing, it is not surprising that some names were changed in the process.

The fishing industry in Ouzinkie underwent its process of modernization along with the rest of village life. Shortly after I'd moved to the island, I remember standing on the ridge above "Otherside Beach", at the back of Spruce Island, and watching Zack Chichenoff and his crew in his little wooden seiner, the "Faith", setting their net, and then hand-pulling it into the boat with no hydraulic machinery to make the job easier. Zack was the last fisherman in Ouzinkie to do his fishing all by hand, in the old way. Now powerboats and modern hydraulics make the job much easier.

During my first years at Banjo Beach, there were still a couple of people in the village who liked to row their small dories from place to place. Old-timers would recall the days before outboards, when they would think nothing of rowing long distances if necessary. Perhaps there would be a wedding in Kodiak or a dance in Karluk, or a special feast-day in Afognak Village. If they wished to go, they rowed. Nowadays, a powerful outboard or two runs the skiff to its destination in a short time (weather permitting, of course!).

There were only a couple of motorized vehicles using the limited road system when I reached the village. My ex-husband, Les and I moved all our belongings from Kodiak to Sandy Beach in front of Ouzinkie via Grumman Goose floatplane. (We originally moved to Ouzinkie because Les had been offered a job at the cannery.) A miniature tractor, small enough to look like a toy, and towing a narrow cart, met us there. Our goods were loaded into the cart and the tractor towed it along the front wooden boardwalk. The vehicle just fit between the rails flanking the walkway. At the cannery, everything was lowered into a skiff by a crane on the dock and taken to our new quarters in Eskimo Cove.

Then, as more roads were built, villagers brought in 3-wheelers; then the more stable 4-wheelers. Soon after, small cars and pickups began to arrive at the beach on landing craft. People who once walked everywhere found it much easier to ride.

In the "Good Old Days", the city generators went off at 10:00 p.m. and came on again at 7:00 a.m. I had occasion to enjoy a few special celebrations in the village when someone would "buy the lights" for $75.00, and the generators would run all night. These were rare occurrences.

Now a hydroelectric project helps to supply 24-hour power for electricity and for the city water pump house. In a high bowl in the island's central mountain ridge is Lake Mahoona. A dam was constructed at the end of the lake nearest Ouzinkie, and a new pump house was built inland, closer to the base of the dam site. There is sufficient fall from this dam to fill one-third to one-half of the village's power needs. This system is supplemented by diesel generators, as needed.

In my early years at Banjo Beach, technology had only a toehold in the lifestyle of the island. There were no private phones, so everyone used a CB radio (I used to call this communication system the "Ouzinkie soap opera"). There was one radiophone in the village, but even that conversation was not private, as various community members picked up the phone band on their scanners and listened in.

Private phones and TV reached the village at the same time, as the two technologies pooled resources to put up the necessary reception dish in order to get started. Soon everyone in the village had a telephone and a TV. At times I had to reschedule an Adult Ed tutoring session because my student wanted to watch a favorite TV program.

With the advent of TV and VCRs for watching movies, the type of entertainment enjoyed by the village changed. Instead of playing card games such as cribbage, rummy, pinochle, or spades, or board games (a favorite used to be Yahtzee), folks watched TV. Before TV, it was common for villagers to make up some popcorn and walk to the community hall to watch a movie once a week. The movie was played on a screen that was enlarged by a sheet. In the "new Ouzinkie", people rented, purchased, or traded movies to watch at home on the VCR.

Village youngsters, not unlike many city youngsters, seem to have an aptitude for things technological. When computers and computer games came to the village, the youngsters gobbled up these new innovations. Now, the village's new media center houses a combination library and computer room that is always full of enthusiasts, one at every machine.

Mail delivery still remains an important village event. Before planes flew to the village, mail and other cargo arrived once a month on a "mail boat" named the "Shuyak". By the time I moved there, the mail was brought in by floatplane. The little post office was conveniently located at Sandy Beach, the long beach at the front of the village, close to where the floatplanes landed. Mail time was a good time to visit with the villagers, as the front porch and small lobby of the tiny post office was usually full of waiting people. In the winter, floatplanes could not fly if the temperature was below 17 degrees because of the danger of icing up the pontoons or wings. After a long cold spell with no mail delivery, a large crowd would be gathered at the post office when the mail plane finally arrived.

Once the new runway was in place, the old community hall was torn down, and a larger modular post office was erected on the site. This building was located right on the road system and could be accessed easily by whoever was delivering mail. In the years when I lived there, this person was usually Norman Smith, with his 3-wheeler and cart.

After the post office was moved, a new community center, a clinic, and a new fire station were all built on the road system. A state-of-the-art meat processing facility was added, with an area to prepare game, cold storage, and freezer lockers. Later, the Ouzinkie Tribal Council moved their offices into part of that building. Since I moved from the village, a new, larger clinic and a new tribal hall (also the location of the popular media center) have been added, along with several more new houses. Though there is no longer a cannery near Katmai Creek, there is now a new breakwater and small boat harbor at that site.

Thus, the new road system became a starting point for changing a small subsistence village into a much more modern community. The Ouzinkie I first knew has changed since those early years. I am so glad I met and formed friendships with those who were still close enough to the old ways to take great interest in the plants that grew around them and to wish to share knowledge. Now that you have learned a bit about Ouzinkie people and their history, let's begin our hike across the island to learn about the plants that have grown there through all these village changes.

Ouzinkie from Bay Side, 1957
Photo by: Norman Smith

The "Shuyak", Mail Boat
Photo by Timothy Smith

Russian Orthodox Church Winter, 1967. Photo by: Timothy Smith

"Old School". Photo by: Timothy Smith

Baker Cottage, Fall, 1959. Photo by: Norman Smith

The "Evangel". Photo by: Norman Smith

A "Dory Tree". Photo by: Timothy Smith

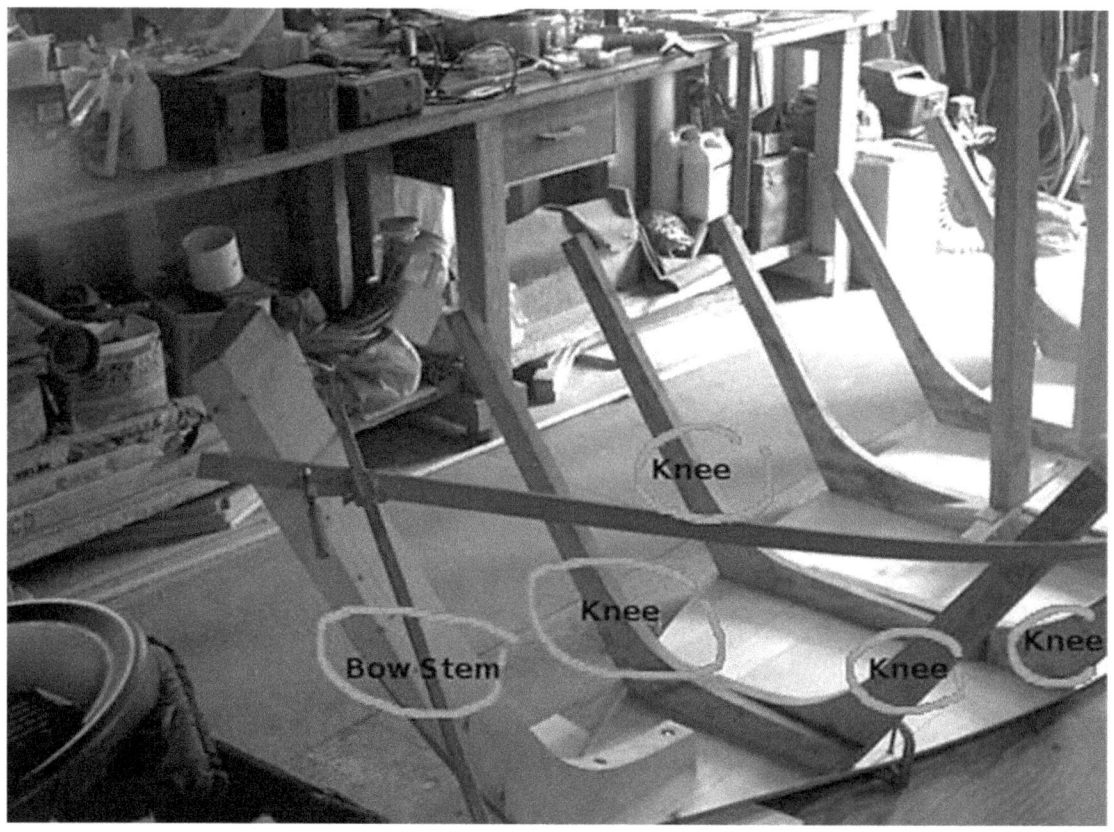
Dory Frame, Showing Bow Stem and "Knee". Photo by: Kevin Smith

One of Ed Opheim, Senior's Dories. Photo by: Timothy Smith

Ouzinkie Paking Company, Pre-1964. Photo by: Norman Smith

Ouzinkie from the Bay, 2007. Photo by: Evelyn Wiszinckas

Aerial View of Modern-Day Ouzinkie. Photo by: Kevin Smith

Aerial View of Modern-Day Ouzinkie. Photo by: Kevin Smith

INTRODUCTION: HOW TO USE THIS BOOK

In this book, we invite you to take a walk with "Plants Class" for a unique foraging experience. This one-of-a-kind plant guide provides a series of informational tools to help you identify and use the wild flora you collect.

How do you use the tools in this book? Let's say you are hiking your favorite Alaskan trail. You find a plant you'd like to identify, so you pull out your *Plant Lore of an Alaskan Island* guide. Your first step in using the guide is to look around you to determine in which of the 7 habitats your plant is growing. Peruse that section of the book to see if you can find a drawing and description that fits. To gain a more in-depth view of the botanical characteristics of your new wild acquaintance, look for its family in the "Plant Family Index" and read that description.

Many plants can be found in a variety of habitats. Perhaps it is shown in a different habitat than the one you have selected. If the plant is in bloom, try looking in the "Color Index". Then look up the description and illustration for the plants with flowers that are the correct color. Or, perhaps you can find a description of its general characteristics in the "Plant Family Index". Then look up the Kodiak members of that family.

The "Plant Family Index" may also be used to identify close relatives of a plant you know from outside the Kodiak area. Look up the family name; review its characteristics; then read about the species of that plant that are found in this book. You might find a relative whose properties and uses are very similar. In some cases, species found outside the Kodiak area will also be mentioned with the description of a related plant that is found on our island.

For an overview of the many and varied Alaskan berries, check out the section titled "Berries, Low and High". If you have collected a supply of edible plants and wish a quick summary of the ways in which they can be prepared, read, "Hints on Cooking Wild Edibles". If you wish to learn which plants were traditionally used to treat a certain physical condition or illness, consult the "Medicinal Index". Physical ailments or problems are alphabetical, and under each is a listing of the plants that were used to treat them, along with a one-line description of how the plant was used. If your desire is to dye some yarn or fabric, check the recipes in the section titled "Dyes From Wild Plants".

A plant can have many names. Each individual plant in a habitat is identified first by the common names used in our area, with the name most familiar to us listed first. These are followed by the family name, which may be used to look up the plant family in that index, should you wish information about the family to which the specific plant belongs, or a clue as to other possible habitats of this particular plant. The next name, written in italics, is the Latin botanical name, which is specific to that exact plant. Related plants in other areas will belong to the same genus but will have a different species name. Again, use of the "Plant Family Index" will help you determine if a plant in your area is a close relative, perhaps with similar uses. (Please note: My definitive authority on Latin nomenclature for both editions of this book has been Eric Hulten's *Flora of Alaska and Neighboring Territories,* copyright 1968. His book has also provided information as to whether a plant grows in Alaska or in our area.)

Some of the plants may include a listing of an Aleut name and/or a Russian name. Although this list is not complete for all plants in the book, it contains all the names that we learned from the elders and local plant foragers whom we interviewed from our area in the course of our research. Sometimes both Russian and Aleut names are listed; sometimes one or the other. It is interesting to note that, among the elders we interviewed over the years in which we gathered information for this book, more often they knew the Russian name, but the Aleut name was already lost. Such is the plight of arriving on the scene to do research a bit too late.

RUSSIAN AND ALEUT PLANT NAMES

As you can see, some of the foraging done to complete the original book was for information rather than for local flora. Before typing the final copy of the first manuscript, I searched out the phonetic English spelling of the plant names we had learned.

At that time, Marion Brown and Nina Gilbreath in Kodiak supplied me with their spellings of the name. Marian Johnson of the Kodiak Historical Society also furnished me with valuable information she had gathered. My next step was to consult Father Gerasim, who then resided at the New Valaam Russian Orthodox Monastery on Spruce Island, as he was fluent in the Russian language.

While comparing notes with our language advisors, we learned some interesting things. First, much old herbal knowledge was handed down verbally rather than in writing. As a result, both Russian and Aleut words varied a little from village to village. To confuse matters further, we found a few plant names that appeared to be a Russian word and an Aleut word mixed together. The word as we present it in this book is the one most commonly agreed upon among the sources we consulted.

Both Nina Gilbreath and Father Gerasim looked up the Russian spelling of the plant names first. Often they would find the Russian root word that was closest to the pronunciation we knew, and from these they supplied us with a noun form and an English spelling. Many times these roots would have a meaning that described some characteristic of the plant. For example, "zholti golovnik", or goldenrod, translates as "yellow-headed". Yarrow, or "poleznaya trava", means "the healing herb" in the Russian language.

It is much more difficult to provide proper spellings for Aleut plant names since few people know written Aleut. Whenever possible, we used spellings found in Jeff Leer's *A Conversational Dictionary of Kodiak Alutiiq* to assist us in determining the appropriate spelling.

COLLECTING PLANTS

Two cautions about collecting wild plants: First, *never* use a plant for food or medicine unless you are sure you have properly identified the plant. And, secondly, when gathering wild plants, *never* take all the plants in the area. Leave some there to repopulate the species, so that you and others may have the pleasure of using the plant again.

In his *Root, Stem and Leaf,* Glen Ray lists nine techniques to use when gathering plants. These techniques are designed to help preserve the natural environment while still using the resources available. They are part of a system called "traditional conservation". We feel these techniques are important for Alaskan foragers to follow, so have repeated them here:

1) Learn the habitat and conditions under which each plant flourishes.
2) Know the area in which you live well enough to know where each plant can be found in abundance.
3) Take time to ask Native elders if the locale where you would like to harvest a plant is not already a harvesting spot for a group of people.
4) Find a place to harvest not already harvested.
5) If the plant seems not to be abundant in the area where it is found, it would be best not to harvest until it can be found growing abundantly. If one feels that some harvesting is possible, then take only a few plants or only some portion of several plants.
6) Leave the roots of perennials intact along with a portion of the leaves so the plant can regenerate.
7) Take only a part of a plant so the plant can flower and reproduce.
8) Take only what can be processed and used.
9) Take time to enjoy the process and appreciate the surroundings.

PLANTS AS FOOD

Where applicable, we have included a note about the nutritional value of each plant. Scientists have not tested wild edibles as thoroughly as they have domestic crops, so nutritional information is not always available. However, the testing that has been done has shown that edible wild plants are consistently higher in nutritional value than their domestic cousins. Seeking out these free foods and adding them to our diet can only improve our bodily well-being.

Wild food foragers should keep in mind that fresh edibles of any kind begin to lose their nutritional value as soon as they are harvested. Therefore, eat wild foods as soon as possible after they are gathered to gain the fullest nutritional benefit they can provide.

This book gives complete instructions for preparing each edible plant. In many cases, specific recipes are listed for the plant under discussion. "Plants Class" tried many of these recipes at monthly potlucks or in and out of class. Some were written by class members. They are offered with the hope that you, the reader, will discover for yourself how very tasty these wild dishes can be. Feel free to experiment with these recipes and modify them to suit your own taste, if necessary.

PLANTS AS MEDICINE

As "Plants Class" learned ways to prepare wild plants for the dinner table, we also learned ways they were used for medicine. As one Russian-Aleut grandmother told us, "There's medicine growing all over out there in the woods." She said that in the days when her mother and grandmother were young, there were no doctors like we have today. Instead, there were Aleut doctors who had learned of the medicinal uses of the plants around them, and had gathered and stored them in case they were needed in the winter months. When a person was sick, the Native doctor treated the patient. He mixed the herbs according to his knowledge of their uses. The patient was usually cured, according to the grandmother, though sometimes the process took longer than it does these days. There were no wonder drugs or pills for everything, but people did get well.

One reason people got well was probably due to the high nutritive value of many of the wild plants used. Often a disease was contracted because of a vitamin deficiency that allowed the sickness to gain a hold. It is quite possible the herbs prescribed often contained the right vitamin content to fill the body's need and eventually restore it to health. An obvious example was the use of wild greens high in vitamin C by early seagoing peoples to counteract the effects of scurvy. Though other curative properties existed in the herbs as well, the high vitamin content in many of them certainly contributed to their usefulness.

Due to the increased interest today in preventative methods as well as natural remedies for treating the physical body, I have supplied additional information in this edition as to how these plants have been used medicinally, from ancient times to the present. Uses by Native Alaskan groups have been highlighted in this presentation. The "Medicinal Index" is a new addition to the book, and is designed to give you a quick overview of specific plants and how they were used for a variety of physical conditions.

As previously noted, modern medical treatment was often not available to early Alaskan residents, so their only choice was to use the remedies they might find available in nature. Some interesting conclusions might be drawn about the health problems of the early residents of the area, both Native and non-Native, from this medicinal listing, incomplete as it certainly is. If one looks at the variety of plants used for certain conditions, one sees some interesting patterns. For example, it is easy to see that the common cold was just as common to early Alaskans as it is today. Many remedies are listed for colds and sore throats. As might be expected, remedies for sores, wounds and cuts, or methods to staunch bleeding are also numerous. Bruises or skin conditions contain a long list of plants. Toothache or sore gums generated a hefty list of favorite remedies as well. The absence of a modern "eye doctor" gave rise to a number of plants used for a variety of eye problems. Tuberculosis, which was a common disease among early Alaskans, has a great number of remedies as well, depending on the plant most plentiful in a certain area.

Today we are blessed with the advances of modern medicine. Therefore, the presentation of these remedies is intended only to further your knowledge about the historic uses of a specific plant. We do not advocate using herbs in place of a modern doctor's care, nor do we suggest using these remedies in addition to prescribed medication without first consulting your doctor, as harmful side effects or overdoses might occur.

However, these teas and tonics have their place. For simple ailments, or in a situation where a doctor cannot be consulted, you may find that these mixtures prepared from wild plants can provide relief and aid in recovery. Most important is the delight in discovering the long history of interaction between humans and the wild plants that share their habitat.

SOME NOTES ON HABITAT

As mentioned earlier, plants can often be found in more than one habitat. As an example, consider the bog/alpine plants, or the range of terrain covered from stream banks to moist, sunny hillsides; or the wet, rocky cliffs at the edge of the streambed or ocean. Yet all of these are placed in one grouping. Be sure to read the "habitat" description carefully for a specific plant, as its choice of residence may overlap other areas fringing on the spot where you have found it. For additional information, read the description in the "Plant Family Index".

The decision as to which habitat to choose for the plants in this book was not an easy one. I ended up placing the plant in the setting where I saw it most often. Therefore, my judgment was somewhat subjective, and not set in stone.

In some cases, when there are descriptions for two or more species of the same genus, they have been placed together because of their relationship rather than because of their habitat. For example, this book includes both fireweed (*Epilobium angustifolium*) and dwarf fireweed (*E. latifolium*). These are both described in the section titled "Gravel Bars and Riverbeds or Dry Slopes", because there are fewer plants growing in this habitat and species should therefore be easily recognized. Dwarf fireweed may be found here. However, the taller *E. angustifolium* grows in open meadows or hillsides or along roadbeds.

Two species of Jacob's ladder share the same dilemma. They are placed with fireweed in the "Gravel Bars…" habitat because the smaller *Polemonium pulcherrimum* often grows in such an area. Tall Jacob's ladder (*P. acutiflorum*) prefers to grow in open, moist meadows.

The raspberry, or *Rubus* genus of the rose family, might also be confusing. There are three species of the *Rubus* genus discussed in this book, and all are placed together because of their relationship to each other. Their descriptions may be found in the "Open Woods and Forests" habitat. However, in reality all three grow in separate habitats. American red raspberry (*R. idaeus*) grows in thickets or clearings or is often transplanted to cultivated gardens, at least in our area of Alaska. Cloudberry (*R. chamaemorus*) is found in bogs and moist, open areas. Trailing raspberry (*R. pedatus*) grows in woods and mossy areas.

Therefore, if you find a plant in a certain habitat, yet can't find a plant description that fits in the appropriate section of the book, try checking the "Plant Family Index" for clues as to where it may be located. If you find a habitat that fits, read the family description. Does your plant follow that general description? If so, you may have found a match. Look up the plants listed under "Species Found in This Book" to see if you have solved your mystery.

Poisonous Plants: These dangerous species are mixed in with other plants that share the same habitat. Read carefully: I have placed a label of **POISONOUS!** beneath the names of these plants.

Ferns: The ferns are grouped together at the end of the "Open Woods and Forests" section. They do not appear in the "Plant Family Index".

The bracken fern is not found on Kodiak Island. I have included it because it is known in Southeast Alaska. It has been determined that it may prove harmful to eat this particular fern. If you locate it near you, don't eat it!

And now, my friends, take a walk with "Plants Class" along a Spruce Island trail and meet a most interesting group of the flora of Alaska!

INDEX

Angelica *(Angelica genuflexa; A. lucida)*
Arrow Grass *(Triglochin maritimum; T. palustris)*
   (See under goosetongue)
Beach Lovage *(Ligusticum scoticum)*
Beach Peas *(Lathyrus maritimus)*
Chiming Bells *(Mertensia paniculata)*
   (See under oysterleaf)
Goosetongue *(Plantago macrocarpa; P. maritima)*
Lambsquarter *(Chenopodium album)*
Marsh Marigold *(Caltha palustris)*
Northern Bedstraw *(Galium aparine; G. boreale)*
Oysterleaf *(Mertensia maritima)*
Seabeach Sandwort *(Honckenya peploides)*
Shrubby Cinquefoil *(Potentilla fruticosa)*
   (See under silverweed)
Silverweed *(Potentilla anserina; P. egedii)*

SEASHORE AND BEACH MARSHES

Angelica
Angelica lucida

Angelica
Angelica genuflexa

ANGELICA, Wild Celery
PARSLEY FAMILY
Angelica genuflexa
Angelica lucida

Description: There are two species of *Angelica* in our area. Though similar, they are easily distinguished from one another. *A. lucida* is a stout perennial that grows from a strong taproot. Its height ranges from 1 ½ to 4 feet tall. It has irregularly toothed, hairless, roughly egg-shaped leaves divided two to three times into 3's. The thick, celery-like stem is erect and hollow, with numerous oil tubes. The leaf stalk (petiole) has an inflated base, with sheaths that clasp the stem. Flowers are white, small, and numerous, with 20 to 45 small compact heads (rays) forming one umbel. Fruits are oblong with thin-edged ribs.

A. genuflexa differs from *A. lucida* in a few ways. Its range of size is 3 to 6 feet. Its leaves are the identity giveaway: They are compound, with 3 major divisions of 3. The primary leaf divisions are bent back instead of forward. Moreover, the leaf stalk is also bent downward with each new triplet of leaves. These "kinks" give rise to the species name *genuflexa*, meaning to kneel, or bend the knees. Flowers are white or pink. Fruits have broadly winged ribs; root is chambered.

Habitat: Angelica ranges from moist meadows and ditches to coastal beaches. *A. genuflexa* must enjoy having its feet wet, as one place on Spruce Island where I have found it flourishing is in a very moist, lush meadow near my "sundew" bog. Angelicas are often found in areas close to the sea.

Edible Parts: *A. lucida* got its common name of "wild celery" from the ancient native custom of eating the peeled stems raw, like celery. **CAUTION:** Make sure you have positively identified the plant if you wish to try eating it, as it looks a great deal like poison water hemlock. Also, there is talk in the air from some sources about cross-pollination. (See **CAUTION** section, following.)

Uses in Native and Traditional Folk Medicine

"Angelica" is Latin for "angel" and derives from *"Archangelica"* (The European Latin species name). During the middle ages, an archangel reputedly told a man that *archangelica* was a remedy for cholera and plague. *A. archangelica* was highly touted by ancient healers as a protection against such contagious diseases, and for curing a great many illnesses. A Chinese angelica is known as the herb " *dong quai*", and is used for treating female problems, such as regulating menstruation and expelling afterbirth.

Native Alaskan groups have used angelica externally for a variety of ailments. Tanana Natives have used *A. lucida* root for pain, sores, cuts, blood poisoning, and infections. The root was cut and mashed, then boiled or soaked in hot water, and used as a poultice. Leaves could also be used as a poultice. Eskimos cut the root in half, heated the halves, and placed them over the painful spot. Both Native groups and Europeans used angelica juice to relieve toothache. Athabascan (Dena'ina) use, according to Priscilla Kari, was to place a piece of the raw root in a cavity of a rotten tooth and to leave it there until the tooth broke up and fell out. Eric Hulten (1968) tells us that Siberian Eskimos roasted the angelica roots and inhaled them to remedy seasickness.

Comparison of roots of angelica and water hemlock

Angelica

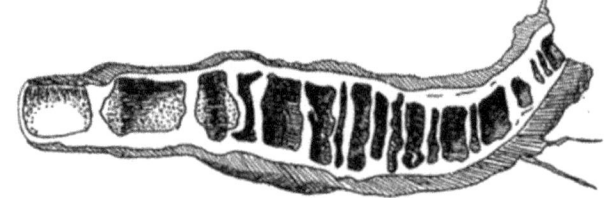
Water hemlock

CAUTION: Be sure you know you have *A. lucida* and not the poison water hemlock species, *Cicuta douglasii*, before attempting to use this plant medicinally! These two plants are not easy to distinguish. *A. genuflexa* is much easier to recognize because of its jointed stems, causing the branches to bow toward the earth. *A. lucida* is a bit trickier. In fact, it took me a number of years to feel confident I could identify the two.

Two of my earliest teachers, Sasha and Jenny, were unable to clarify the difference. I remember one early walk with them, when Sasha poked a patch of *A. lucida* with her ever-present cane and said, "Don't eat that – it's poisonous." Jenny said, "Oh, no, that's not poisonous. I know, because my cows eat it."

Ann Garibaldi in Medicinal Flora of the Alaskan Natives states that angelica root is toxic. To be safe, perhaps one should abstain from gathering roots from any angelica species for internal use. However, using heated roots as a poultice to draw out deep pain is reportedly very effective, and might make it worthwhile to make a positive identification of this plant.

Though early Native groups ate stalks of *A. lucida* as a wild celery, I have found more than one reference stating that this use has been discontinued due to evidence of possible cross-pollination between water hemlock and angelica. A few years ago, I had an experience that might also point to the same conclusion. Some friends from the Bell's Flats area near Kodiak came to me because their goats were sick, and they wanted me to identify the plants near where the goats were eating. We found both species of *Angelica* near the spot. Water hemlock was not found in the immediate area, although my friends said they thought it had been found nearby. We sent roots from plants we had collected to the Cooperative Extension at the University of Alaska for positive identification and were informed they were, indeed, *A. lucida* and *A. genuflexa*. Did these plants cross-pollinate with water hemlock? Or did the goats simply eat some of the angelica roots that were toxic enough to make them sick?

In Discovering Wild Plants, Janice Schofield says that *A. genuflexa* roots are chambered, though not in the same manner as water hemlock. To assist with identification, Barbara Burch has reproduced an excellent drawing from Eleanor G. Vierick's Alaska's Wilderness Medicines that shows the difference between the root chambering of *Angelica* and *Cicuta*.

If one is trying to identify a plant before harvesting, it is a bit inconvenient to dig up each one to insure it is the correct plant. Also, it effectively destroys the whole plant, when perhaps one only wishes to use some of the leaves. Therefore, I will repeat the little rhyme we learned from Janice Schofield's 2004 workshop in Kodiak, as I believe it is the best guide for determining quickly whether one is about to gather *A. lucida* or *C. douglasii*. Look closely at the leaf veins and remember this:

Veins to the tip – plant is hip
Veins to the cut – pain in the gut!

Now you know everything I know about angelica!

Beach Lovage
Ligusticum scoticum

BEACH LOVAGE, Scotch Lovage
PARSLEY FAMILY
Ligusticum scoticum
Petrushki (Russian)

Description: The leaves of petrushki, as it is known in the Kodiak area, are divided into 3 groups of 3 leaflets. This combination of 3's makes this plant readily distinguishable from all other umbels in the area. These leaves are shiny and roughly toothed. Leafstalk bottoms and sometimes the very edges of the leaves have a reddish or purplish tint. The white or pinkish flowers of this perennial grow in flat-topped, umbrella-like clusters (umbels). The plant may grow up to 3 feet tall.

Habitat: Lovage is found along sandy and gravelly seashores. Sometimes these plants grow in pockets of soil on rocky cliffs.

Edible Parts and Nutritional Value: Leaves and reddish stems are edible and high in vitamins A and C.

Ways to Prepare for Eating: Pick petrushki in early summer before the flowers bloom. There are a variety of ways to cook this plant. The plant can be boiled with fish or placed on baked fish. It can be used as a green vegetable. It makes a good cooked celery substitute. Petrushki can be added to salads, soup stocks and stews, and can be used as a seasoning. Use any way you would use fresh parsley.

Older plants might be bitter. Bring these to a boil, drain, and then boil again.

Uses in Native and Traditional Folk Medicine

People in the Kodiak area prepared an infusion from this plant for kidney problems. The tea was used as a digestive aid.

Deviled Eggs with Petrushki
Georgia Smith

Every Ouzinkie community gathering included a feast, and deviled eggs were a favorite dish. These were especially good when made with fresh eggs from Jenny Chernikoff's chickens.

6 hard-boiled eggs
2 tablespoons mayonnaise
Dash vinegar
Salt and pepper
Petrushki
Sweet pickle
Paprika

Peel eggs, cut in half. Remove and mash yolks. Add mixture of mayonnaise, vinegar, salt and pepper. Chop petrushki and sweet pickle in equal amounts, sufficient to double the volume of the yolk mixture. Refill the egg whites, sprinkle with paprika, and serve.

To Complete the Meal:

Fish Chowder with Petrushki

Sasha Smith

Late in the summer Sasha would say, "Bring me some black humpys (salmon) from the creek." Then she would make fish chowder.

> 2 to 3 pounds halibut or salmon, cubed
> 2 potatoes, diced
> 1 onion, diced
> ½ cup rice
> ½ cup chopped fresh petrushki
> Salt and pepper

Put halibut or salmon, potatoes, onion and rice in saucepan. Cover with water and bring to a boil. Cook 10 minutes and add petrushki; season with salt and pepper. Boil 10 minutes longer.

Variations: Halibut or salmon heads can be used in this recipe.

Octopus Salad

Jim Tsacrios

Octopus was a special treat to some local people; however, it was not really easy to prepare, as you can see from the following recipe:

Kill octopus. Turn inside out and remove innards. Beat carcass about 75 to 80 times, *hard*, on rocks at water's edge. After every 10 smacks, rub carcass on a rough rock until it foams; then rinse in sea water. Repeat process until carcass stops foaming.

Cut into pieces small enough to fit in a pot, and cover with water. Boil for 20 to 30 minutes. Slice into thin pieces; very thin if octopus is fairly large. Put in marinade of:

> 1 part vinegar
> 2 parts oil
> 2 or 3 onions, sliced in small moons

Marinate and chill for at least 24 hours, then serve.

BEACH PEAS
PEA FAMILY
Lathyrus maritimus

Description: The beach pea grows in large clumps. Its leaves are thick and fleshy, with 6 to 12 oblong leaflets. The flowers, with a reddish banner and bluish violet wings and keel, resemble those of cultivated peas. Curling tendrils reach out at the stem ends. Smooth pods containing small seeds (peas) replace the flowers after pollination.

CAUTION: Do not confuse with wild sweet pea (*Hedysarum mackenzii*) or with lupine (*Lupinus nootkatensis*). These plants are reportedly poisonous.

Habitat: Beach peas may be found along beaches or in marshy areas nearby.

Edible Parts: The peas are good to eat. Also, the young unopened blossoms may be gathered in the early spring. They make a great addition to salads and fritters.

Ways to Prepare for Eating: Eat the peas raw or cooked. Add them to salads, or cook until just tender when pierced with a fork.

Try stuffing a salmon with a mixture of rice, onion, soy sauce, and beach peas, wrapping well with foil, and cooking on a grill over an open fire on the beach.

Beach peas may be canned. A local friend tells of a camping trip where the beach peas were especially prolific. He said they gathered enough to can 3 pints of beach peas.

Gather the new green unopened blossoms. They are excellent in salad or with your favorite wild green mix for fritters.

CAUTION: It is wise to eat <u>all</u> peas – even domesticated ones – in moderation, due to chemicals that become harmful in large quantities.

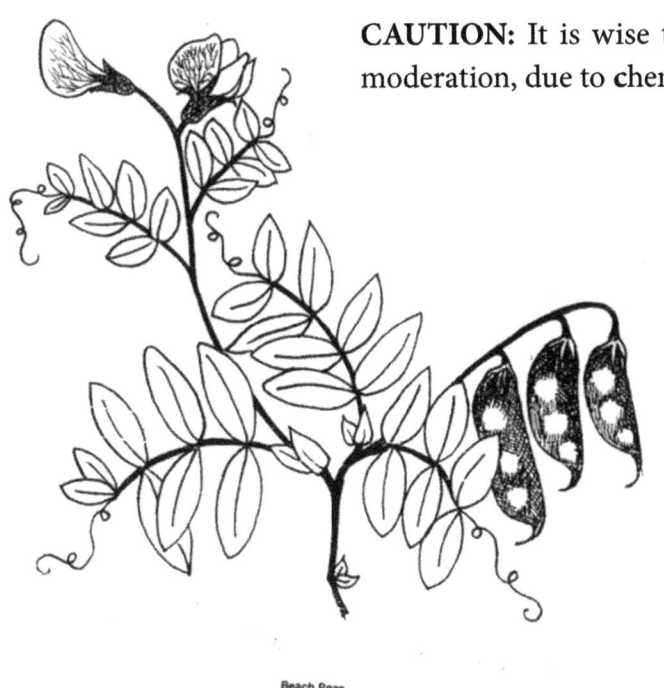

Beach Peas
Lathyrus maritimus

THE PLANTS, BY HABITAT | 37

Seasonal Herbcakes
(From Janice Schofield's Kodiak workshop materials.)

2 cups of herbs of choice
2 cups flour
½ teaspoon baking soda ¼ teaspoon salt
Enough milk to make a smooth batter Oil for frying

Mix dry ingredients. Add enough milk to make a smooth batter. Chop herbs and mix together with the batter for a pancake-like consistency. Place spoonfuls on greased griddle. Cook until brown on one side, then flip over and cook other side. Serve with butter or syrup or other topping of choice.

Suggested spring plants to use in fritters: dandelion flowers (with green bits removed), devil's club shoots, twisted stalk shoots, (watermelon berry) fiddleheads, elder flowers, beach pea (new growth of blossom), goosetongue, beach greens, chickweed, petrushki (lovage, or wild parsley).

To Complete the Meal:

Codfish Bacon Bake
Rosemary Squartsoff

Rosemary's husband, known in the village as Freddy the Bear, would bring her lots of codfish from his fishing boat.

> Clean and fillet fish; lay out meat side up in baking pan. Sprinkle all over with soy sauce, then dill pickle liquid. Marinate 4 hours. Cover fish with bacon and pan with foil. Heat oven to 450 degrees; bake 20 to 25 minutes depending on thickness of fish. Take off foil and cook 5 to 10 minutes longer, until bacon browns.

On a fishing boat, one of the crew members was designated as cook. Many original recipes resulted from these arbitrary appointments. Following are three examples:

Nell's Favorite Scallop Recipe
Nell Tsacrios

Open shell. Remove meat. Dip in lemon juice and soy sauce. Eat.

Scallop Broth
Ozzie Walters

Here is a tasty, invigorating drink for a fisherman on a cold night.

Take a handful of fresh-shucked scallops and poach them in 1 can of beer for 6 to 8 minutes. Throw the scallops away and drink the broth. (If you want to keep the scallops, chill them and serve them cold in a salad.)

Poached Halibut
Ozzie Walters

(At the time of the writing of this new edition, Ozzie is still cooking on fishing boats. He must be doing something right!)

> Water
> Soy sauce
> White wine

In a wide pan, make a poaching liquid of any combination of the above ingredients. Have the following ingredients ready:

> Onions
> Halibut fillets
> Paprika or cayenne

Chop or ring onions and add to poaching liquid; cook 3 minutes. Place skinned fillets of halibut in the poaching liquid so they are not too crowded. Poach 10 minutes per inch of thickness of fillets. Garnish with paprika or cayenne.

Sauce: Tart berry jam or sauce goes well with the halibut. Try a sweet and sour sauce composed of salmonberry jam, a little sugar, and a little vinegar.

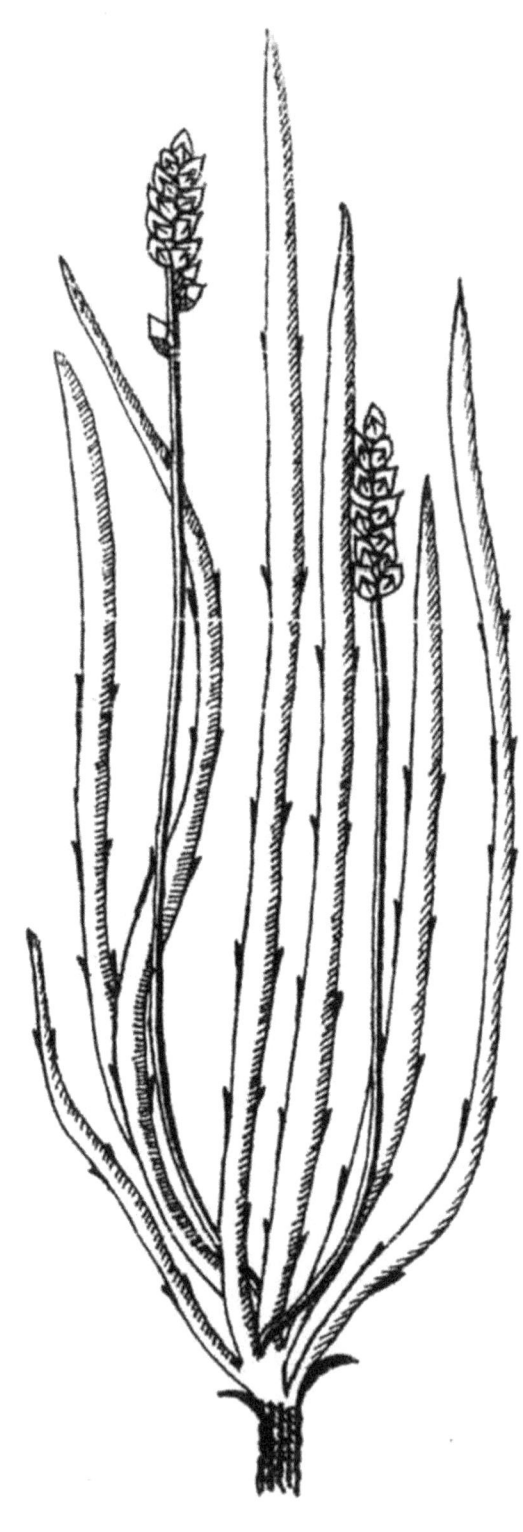

Goosetongue
Plantago maritima

40 | THE PLANTS, BY HABITAT

GOOSETONGUE, Seashore Plantain
PLANTAIN FAMILY
Plantago macrocarpa, Plantago maritima

Description: Goosetongue, a perennial, has many long, narrow leaves rising from the plant base. Look for a few shallow teeth along the edges of the leaves. The central stalk has a dense, blunt spike of flowers on the end. These flowers are very small, greenish or white, with 4 petals.

Habitat: Goosetongue is found along the seashore, sometimes back some distance from the tide line. The plant can also be found growing from tiny pockets of soil on rocky cliffs near the water's edge.

Edible Parts and Nutritional Value: The leaves are edible. They contain vitamins C and A, and some minerals. Goosetongue is a preferred spring food of Kodiak and Alaska Peninsula brown bears. They couldn't be wrong!

CAUTION: Goosetongue has a look-alike companion plant that might be growing in the same area. (I have found them growing side by side on the Kodiak beach that I have nicknamed "Grocery Store Beach".) The genus *Triglochin* has two Alaskan species: *Triglochin maritimum* or *Triglochin palustris*. The leaves of these species contain hydrocyanic acid.

Triglochin, whose common name is "arrow grass", has leaves very similar in shape to goosetongue. However, arrow grass leaves spring from a grass-like sheath, while goosetongue leaves are arranged in a cluster at the base of the plant. Arrow grass leaves are flat on one side and rounded on the other, while goosetongue has occasional small "teeth" spaced along its leaf edges. The flowers of both plants grow on a long stalk, the most notable difference being that the arrow grass flowers grow spaced along a good part of the stalk, while goosetongue flowers cluster along the upper part of the stem.

Arrowgrass
Triglochin species

Though arrow grass leaves are toxic, the seeds from this plant furnish an acceptable coffee substitute, when roasted and ground. Several Western Native groups used the raw ground seeds at one time as a flour substitute.

Ways to Prepare for Eating: Goosetongue is excellent when prepared as a cooked green. Cut into small, bite-sized pieces and boil or steam until tender. Add a little butter and seasoning and serve. Joyce Smith (Ouzinkie) told us her favorite method for preparing goosetongue: Boil potatoes. During the last few minutes, place leaves on potatoes and steam until tender. Angeline Anderson says this green makes a tasty addition to perok (salmon pie). Georgia Smith says to add chopped, steamed goosetongue to fried bacon and onion and sauté 3 to 4 minutes. This dish is reminiscent of green beans.

For a tea, use ½ handful leaves to 1 cup boiling water. Steep ½ hour.

Wildwood Fritters

Ouzinkie Botanical Society

Other greens may be substituted in this recipe, if available.

1 cup goosetongue leaves
2 cups lambsquarter leaves
1 cup sourdock leaves
2 eggs, beaten
2 tablespoons cottage cheese or yogurt
1 small onion, chopped fine
½ teaspoon blended salad herbs Salt and pepper
⅔ cup flour

Steam leaves until tender and chop into small pieces. Add eggs, cottage cheese or yogurt, onion, seasonings, and flour. Drop by spoonfuls on hot, oiled griddle and brown on both sides.

For a number of years, our Plants Class went on a plant-discovery outing once a week. On one such occasion, 16 of us (a large percentage in a village of 250) went on a trek to Big Lagoon, across the island. Sasha Smith was our leader, as she was the only one in the group who remembered the trail. She led us to a huge tide flat filled with goosetongue, which we gathered in garbage bags. We then took it home and canned it or froze it for the winter ahead.

To Complete the Meal:

Ooeduck (Baidarka or Gumboot) Soup

Angeline Anderson

Boil cut-up cabbage, potatoes, carrots, celery and rice in water.

In another pot, boil water; put in gumboots for 1 minute. Remove gumboots from water; clean and take out milk (yellow and white part). Chop into small pieces. Fry in butter with onions. Add some petrushki, if available, for seasoning.

Stir flour into vegetables to make gravy, or make a white sauce and pour it into vegetables. Add gumboots and onions to thickened vegetables. Heat through and serve.

Sasha could be relating this story…

It is nearly time for the evening meal. After gathering a good pile of beach driftwood, the menfolk build a fire. Some of the youngsters find ooeducks stuck to the rocks at the low tide line and gather a large bucket of the sea creatures. The mothers prepare a pot of ooeduck soup, saving some of the baidarka (another local name for ooeducks) to roast on the fire; then they can chew the meat from the shells. A couple of women gather a quantity of goosetongue; these are then cooked with the soup for an added vegetable dish. A basket of wild salmonberries is served for dessert, and the beach provides a natural feast for all.

Lambsquarter
Chenopodium album

44 | THE PLANTS, BY HABITAT

LAMBSQUARTER, Pigweed, Goosefoot
GOOSEFOOT FAMILY
Chenopodium album

Description: One of the tastiest and best-known wild edibles, lambsquarter is an annual plant that grows from 1 to 4 feet tall. One of its common names, "goosefoot", comes from the fact that the leaves of many varieties resemble a goose's foot. These leaves are alternate, and have a mealy texture and a whitish film that can be rubbed off. The leaves are resistant to water. Small grayish-green flowers form in the joints between branch and stalk near the top of the plant, and in a cluster at the very top. These later turn into many small, black seeds.

Orach (*Atriplex* species) is another member of the goosefoot family that is also a tasty, spinach-type wild vegetable. It is similar to lambsquarter in appearance. It grows from 6 to 24 inches high, and has small, greenish inconspicuous flowers growing at the junction of leaf and stem. Orach leaf shapes are variable with the species, and lighter in color on the underside. This plant can be used as an edible in the same way as lambsquarter.

Habitat: Since pigweed, as it is sometimes called near Kodiak, or lambsquarter is an introduced plant, it is found where people have been. In our area it often grows along the beaches, in the comparatively loose soil at the high tide mark. Lambsquarter also seeks out old garden areas and roadsides. Once I baffled a friend in Seattle when I asked if I could pick the weeds growing in his garden. I was delighted to go home with a garbage sack full of lambsquarter: fresh green vegetables for a week!

Edible Parts and Nutritional Value: The leaves, flower buds, flowers, and seeds are edible. This beet and spinach relative is one of the tastiest wild greens. Lambsquarter contains high amounts of calcium, vitamins A and C, and protein, and significant amounts of thiamine, riboflavin, and niacin. It is more nutritious than spinach or cabbage.

Ways to Prepare for Eating: Lambsquarter leaves can be used in salads or substituted in any spinach recipe, raw or cooked. These leaves are especially good wilted with vinegar and bacon.

Steam the leaves for a short time. Lambsquarter does not require a long cooking period, as leaves are tender and not at all bitter. They also make a flavorful creamed soup or puree.

Cook flowers and buds until tender and serve as a vegetable.

Seeds can be gathered in autumn, dried, and ground into flour. For baking, mix half-and-half with regular flour. The whole seeds can be sprinkled over a salad or baked in bread, or boiled until they are soft and served as a cereal.

This plant can be blanched and frozen.

Uses in Native and Traditional Folk Medicine
This plant was used as a dietary aid in diseases caused by deficiencies of calcium or vitamin A and vitamin C.

Orach
Atriplex species

THE PLANTS, BY HABITAT

Pigweed Pie

Jim Tsacrios

3 eggs
½ pound feta cheese
    (more to taste)
⅓ ounce cream cheese
1 cup (packed) chopped, cooked
    pigweed (lambsquarter)
Freshly ground pepper
Dash salt
Pastry for double-crust, 12-inch
    deep-dish pie
Butter

Beat eggs, crumble feta cheese, cut cream cheese into small cubes and mix together. Stir in pigweed. Add pepper and salt. Pour into partially baked pie shell. Dot with butter and add top crust. Bake at 375 degrees until top crust is brown.

Variation: Nettles may replace pigweed.

Wild Green Soufflé

A simple way to create a tasty, wild dish – Keeping it simple, as caretaker Greg would remind us…

1 quart leaves
    (lambsquarter or mixed
    greens)
2 eggs, beaten
1 cup thick white sauce
½ cup grated cheddar cheese

Cook leaves in 1 cup water until just tender. Leave in water until cool. Drain. Add beaten eggs and white sauce. Put in casserole and cover with grated cheese. Bake at 325 degrees until cheese is browned – check after 15 minutes.

To Complete the Meal:

Elk Mulligan

Rosemary Squartsoff

Ouzinkie was still a subsistence village to some degree while I lived there. An elk from the herd of Roosevelt elk that had been "imported" to nearby Afognak Island years ago was a great boon to the winter larder.

1 pound elk meat
2 large potatoes
2 carrots
1 stalk celery
1 rutabaga
1 medium onion
¼ pound butter (optional)
½ cup rice
½ cup petrushki
Salt and pepper

Cut elk meat into 2-inch cubes. Place in pot, cover with water, and boil until almost done (about 1 ½ hours). Cut vegetables into fairly small pieces and add with rice and butter during the last half-hour. Chop carrot leaves and petrushki and add during last 20 minutes or so of cooking time. Season with salt and pepper.

MARSH MARIGOLD, Cowslip
CROWFOOT FAMILY
Caltha palustris, ssp. asarifolia

Description: A perennial plant with stout, hollow stems from 1 to 2 feet tall, marsh marigold has only a few leaves. These are large, rounded, and somewhat kidney-shaped, from 2 to 7 inches wide, with scalloped edges. The flowers, either single or in clusters, are bright yellow. A cluster of pods with many seeds follows the flowers.

CAUTION: Marsh marigold leaves contain a poison that is destroyed by cooking. Buttercup, baneberry, columbine, larkspur, monkshood and anemone are interesting relatives, and all contain a toxin to some degree. These toxins are not destroyed by cooking.

Habitat: Marsh marigolds are found in marshes and along creek beds. They usually grow in abundance rather than in ones or twos.

Edible Parts: When gathered in spring before flowers appear, the leaves are tasty. The marsh marigold contains a poison, helleborin, which is destroyed when the plant is cooked. Always boil and drain twice.

Ways to Prepare for Eating: Drop leaves into boiling water. As soon as the water starts to boil a second time, drain off the liquid. Pour more boiling water over the leaves and drain again as soon as the liquid begins to simmer. *This procedure is important; without it the plant is poisonous.*

Add a little more water and steam or simmer leaves until just tender. Cut them into small pieces; add a little salt and a good quantity of butter. A little vinegar can also be added, if desired. Leaves are tasty seasoned with vinegar and bacon.

To cream the leaves, boil them as described above, season with salt, then drain well and chop fine. Make a white sauce in a frying pan with 1 tablespoon butter, 1 tablespoon flour, and salt and pepper to taste. Add ½ cup cream or rich milk and the leaves. Stir well and serve.

> My caretaker, Greg, discovered a lovely, abundant patch of marsh marigold behind the lagoon at Eskimo Cove, over the hill from my house. We had never eaten the plant so at lunch one day we tried our "scientific experiment", and carefully prepared our batch of leaves, boiling them twice, and then seasoning with butter and salt. We agreed that the resulting dish was delicious, and worth the careful preparation.

Marsh Marigold
Caltha palustris

NORTHERN BEDSTRAW, Alaskan Baby's Breath, Cleavers
MADDER FAMILY
Galium aparine
Galium boreale

Description: *Galium boreale*, or Alaskan baby's breath, as it is known in our area, is a sweet-smelling plant that grows about 3 feet tall. It has sprays of small white flowers and small, coarse leaves with a long narrow shape. The leaves grow in whorls of 4 under the flower sprays. The plant looks dainty and has a sweet fragrance.

Another species of this plant that grows in our area is *Galium aparine*. It is known as "cleavers" because it is weak-stemmed. It compensates for its stem with hooked bristles on the underside of its leaves that stick to one another for support. This bristly little plant also sticks, or cleaves to everything else it contacts, and spreads its seeds in this way. The leaves of this species grow in whorls of 6 to 8.

Habitat: *Galium* is found in meadows, along roads and trails, and in gravelly areas. *G. aparine* grows along the sandy shores of our beaches. We found bedstraw (*G. boreale*) on our "Plants Class" hikes in a wet meadow that bordered both sides of a section of a popular trail.

Uses in Native and Traditional Folk Medicine

Herbalists tell us to warm the *Galium* plants in hot water and place externally on wounds, to help coagulate (clot) the blood.

They also say to prepare as above and use as a hot pack for sore muscles. Or, the herbalist would brew a tea or squeeze out the juice of the fresh plant for a wash for skin problems such as psoriasis, rashes, cuts, insect bites, infections, and blood poisoning. The juice or tea would be applied daily as a wash. Then the cloth with which it was applied would be destroyed. Herbalists also make a salve for the skin by mixing the fresh juice with butter. It is suggested to reapply this salve every 3 hours.

Bedstraw tea was taken internally for painful urination due to bladder infection or kidney stones. The following method was recommended: Steep 1 tablespoon dried bedstraw in ½ cup water. Drink 1 cup a day, made fresh each time.

G. aparine has been used for lymphatic cancer, tumors, cysts, cystitis, and for gravel in the urinary tract. Shelf life of this herb is poor;

Cleavers
Galium aparine

Northern Bedstraw
Galium boreale

so the fresh herb is gathered from the beach to brew a tea. A suggested method of use is to drink the tea before every meal, or for more serious conditions, to take a sip or two every 20 minutes.

Galium is also a traditional ingredient in reducing diets since it is said to help regulate fluid balance and body weight. For a dietary drink, it is used in a tea combined with *Stellaria media* (chickweed) and *Fucus* (bladderwrack, a seaweed).

> Since *Galium* is from the same family as the coffee tree, it has been used as a caffeine-free coffee substitute. If taken frequently, it should be mixed with a demulcent herb, such as *Fucus* (bladderwrack), to avoid irritation to the mouth. Proponents drink this brew in place of morning coffee to eliminate caffeine and to lose weight as an added benefit!

Other Uses: With an alum mordant, the leaves produce a yellow dye. A pink to purple dye can be made from the roots.

Edible Parts and Ways to Prepare for Eating: The young plants (above ground) can be eaten as a cooked green. Bring to a boil, drain, and boil again to eliminate any bitterness.

To Complete the Meal:

Fish Head Soup
Rosemary Squartsoff

In the true subsistence lifestyle, the Native way was to use the entire animal. Remnants of this custom still prevail, as in this popular village recipe:

Fish heads
1 onion, chopped
2 potatoes, chopped
1/3 cup rice
Petrushki
Salt
Pepper

Boil fish heads, onion, potatoes, and rice for 20 minutes. When done, add some petrushki, season with salt and pepper, and boil 10 minutes longer. Serve.

OYSTERLEAF
FOREST-ME-NOT OR BORAGE FAMILY
Mertensia maritima

Description: Oysterleaf is a low-growing plant that forms into large mats, similar to beach greens, though not so prolific. It has alternate, fleshy, lance- or egg-shaped leaves. These leaves are smooth and a bluish-green color. They turn up at the ends and surround the flowers. Flowers may be blue or a pink shade that fades to blue with age. These blossoms have 5 petals that unite in a basal tube. The fruits are 4 flattened nutlets clustered together. These may be smooth or slightly wrinkled.

Another Alaskan member of the *Mertensia* family is known as chiming bells (*Mertensia paniculata*). Though this plant does not grow in the Kodiak area, it is found on the Alaskan mainland. Chiming bells can grow from 18 to 30 inches high. Chiming bells' blossoms fall downward on short stalks off a single stem, their bell-like flowers suggesting their name. These funnel-shaped blossoms are pink when they first bud, later turning blue. Chiming bells' basal leaves have long stalks and are egg-shaped or heart-shaped. One or both surfaces of the leaf are hairy. Leaves on the stem are alternate and numerous, with little or no stalk; broad at the base and tapering to a long point.

Both these plants are edible, though oysterleaf, with the smooth, almost succulent texture of its leaves, is a more enjoyable wild vegetable.

The Latin name, *Mertensia*, is taken from the name of a German botanist, F. C. Mertens (1764 to 1831).

Habitat: Oysterleaf may be found on sandy beaches and gravel shores. The chiming bells plant prefers moist woods and meadows or riverbanks, dry slopes and burned-over areas.

Edible Parts: The leaves of oysterleaf may be eaten and have a flavor reminiscent of oysters.

Ways to Prepare for Eating: Oysterleaf is an excellent addition to salads. Its name comes from the oyster-like flavor of the leaves. When I gather, I pick the desired quantity of leaves from the plant, leaving the rest of the mat of leaves and flowers undisturbed. As oysterleaf is usually less abundant than the prolific beach greens, I tend to be rather protective of it, being careful not to over-harvest.

Try the leaves in chowders, casseroles, or other vegetable dishes, such as quiche. Oysterleaf blends especially well with eggs.

Though chiming bells is also edible, due to the hairy texture of the leaves it is not as desirable as a salad green. Try this wild herb in soups. The blossoms are also edible, and make an attractive garnish to a wild salad creation.

To Complete the Meal:

Nellie's Halibut Supreme
Nell Tsacrios

Over a meal including a gourmet dish such as this one, we'd say gleefully, "Wonder what the rich folks are eating tonight?"

About ½ stick butter
1 large clove garlic, pressed
Halibut, cut in 2 by 3-inch pieces
White flour
½ cup half-and-half
½ cup Chablis
1 tablespoon chopped petrushki (or parsley)
Salt
Sliced almonds

In a 12-inch skillet, sauté garlic in butter. Add enough fish to nearly fill skillet. Remove fish when browned. Add more butter, if necessary, to make at least 2 tablespoons in pan. Add flour to make sauce. Thin with half-and-half and Chablis. Simmer until thick; add chopped petrushki and salt to taste. Put fish back in pan; cover with sauce. Simmer on as low heat as possible until fish is cooked through (approximately 5 to 7 minutes). Sprinkle with sliced almonds before serving.

Oysterleaf
Mertensia maritima

SEABEACH SANDWORT, Beach Greens, Sea Purslane, Sea-Chickweed, Scurvy Grass
PINK FAMILY
Honckenya peploides

Description: Seabeach sandwort is a perennial plant and a big brother of chickweed. It has smooth, sturdy stems with many branches that trail over the sandy beaches. It puts down roots at the stem joints as it spreads, forming dense mats of bright green along the shoreline. Its fleshy, succulent leaves are paired opposite each other. They are bright yellow-green and longer than they are broad. Small, five-petaled greenish-white flowers grow either at the ends of the leaf clusters or scattered among the upper leaves.

Habitat: Beach greens are found on sandy beaches, starting just above the high tide point.

Edible Parts and Nutritional Value: The leaves are the edible part. They are high in vitamins C and A.

Ways to Prepare for Eating: Before the flowers appear, the young, juicy, sweet-tasting leaves can be eaten raw in salads. Or, mix them with other greens, such as mountain sorrel or sourdock, and make into a kraut.

The Eskimos made a dessert by chopping the greens, cooking them in water, then allowing them to sour. The soured leaves were then mixed with reindeer fat and berries. The soured leaves were also eaten with dried fish.

Glen Ray, in his *Root, Stem and Leaf,* suggests cooking beach greens with sausage. This dish has become one of my favorites for breakfast, or as a nutritious, quick supper dish. Cook ground sausage until nearly done. Drain excess fat, leaving enough to oil the pan well. Add a large portion of chopped beach greens and cook until greens are quite soft. Then enjoy!

Uses in Native and Traditional Folk Medicine

Because of its ready availability to seagoing people and its high vitamin C content, this plant was gathered and eaten as a cure for scurvy (a disease caused by lack of vitamin C). Arctic explorers gathered beach greens to combat this disease among their crews.

Seabeach Sandwort
Honckenya peploides

Franny's Favorite Spruce Island Weed Salad
Fran Kelso

At home and at our monthly "Plants Class" potlucks, this recipe was a Spruce Island standard, used all spring and summer. Ingredients would vary depending upon availability.

Mix together equal portions of any combination of the following young plants, chopped in small pieces:

Seabeach sandwort leaves
Sourdock leaves
Fireweed
Wild cucumber
Add the following if available:
½ portion saxifrage leaves
½ portion spring beauty leaves
1 tomato, finely chopped
Minced onion (optional)
Minced garlic (optional)
Season with these:
Salt and pepper
2 or 3 dried crushed mint leaves
Blended salad herbs
Creamy dressing

Toss the salad. If desired, garnish with salmonberry blossoms and/or wild violet blossoms.

To Complete the Meal:

Salmon Perok
Sasha Smith

My young Ouzinkie friend and frequent visitor, Teddy Panamarioff, would say, "It's a (choose one: community feast, wedding, repast) – there will be perok!" This dish is a recipe learned from the Russians that remains a universal village favorite, and one of mine as well!

> Pastry for 2 double-crust pies
> 2 cups rice, cooked with
> 2 tablespoons butter
> 1 small head cabbage, chopped and boiled for 8 minutes.
> Salt and pepper
> 1 salmon, filleted and skinned
> 1 large onion, chopped

Use half of pastry to line a 9 by 13-inch pan. Place half the cooked rice over the pastry. Then spread half the cabbage over the rice. Sprinkle lightly with salt and pepper. Add a layer of salmon. Add more salt and pepper; place onion on salmon. Top with the rest of the cabbage and another layer of rice. Season again with salt and pepper. Fold top crust under edge of bottom crust to seal. Make slits in top crust for steam to escape. Bake at 400 degrees for 1 hour or until brown on top.

> Everyone made perok a little differently. Every cook tweaked the recipe to fit her style of cooking, and pretty soon her perok took on a life of its own. Though I have never eaten a perok I didn't like, I must admit that all peroks are not created equal. I can understand why certain women were revered for the way they made the dish.

Sasha's Old House (taken 2002)   Photo by: Timothy Smith

SILVERWEED, Wild Sweet Potato, Silver Cinquefoil, Crampweed
ROSE FAMILY
Potentilla egedii
Potentilla fruticosa

Silverweed
Potentilla egedii

Description: Silverweed is a perennial with basal leaves that have saw-toothed edges and many leaflets. These leaves are bright green and smooth on top and silvery and woolly underneath. The plant produces reddish, strawberry-like runners above the ground. It has single, large yellow flowers with 5 petals. (Cinquefoil, a common name for many of the *Potentilla* species, may be translated as "5 petals".) The root is long and narrow.

Habitat: This plant grows along seashores, lakesides and streams.

Edible Parts and Nutritional Value: The edible root is a source of carbohydrate.

Ways to Prepare for Eating: Collect the silverweed roots in late autumn or early spring. Eat the roots raw or, preferably, boiled or roasted like potatoes. They taste a little like sweet potatoes. (Perhaps we should say, "They taste like LITTLE sweet potatoes.") Roots are small; however, they could be valuable survival fare.

Uses in Native and Traditional Folk Medicine

The "*Potentilla*" genus name for this plant translates as "potent". In view of this definition, it is not surprising that traditional healers have used this plant for a number of physical conditions. Here are some of the suggested uses: Make a tea with fresh green leaves by steeping 1 teaspoon chopped herbs in 1 cup boiling water. Allow to cool. Drink 1 to 2 cups a day to relieve diarrhea. Drink hot as a tonic. To help gain relief from menstrual cramps, add 1 scant teaspoon silverweed leaves to 1 cup milk and scald. Drink warm. This remedy has also been used to relieve colic and aid digestion, to break a fever, and to help treat asthma and whooping cough.

To soothe toothache or sore gums, or to help tighten loose teeth, traditional healers mix 1 ounce dried and crushed silverweed and 1 teaspoon alum with 1 pint white vinegar. This mixture is boiled 5 minutes, or until the liquid is ½ to ¾ the original amount. This blend is used as a gargle for sore throat relief, or put on freckles, skin blemishes, or sunburn.

The entire plant may be dried, chopped, and stored in airtight containers for later use. It may also be prepared as a tincture. Its proponents say that its astringent quality helps in reducing inflammation and tightening tissues.

Another *Potentilla* known by the common name of "shrubby cinquefoil" or "tundra rose" (*P. fruticosa*) does not grow in the Kodiak area. It tends to be an inland plant, growing in wet or dry ground, from lowlands to mountain slopes. It is mentioned here because it was widely used by Native groups as a medicinal. Alutiiq people made an infusion or decoction of this plant for colds and flu, pneumonia, sore throat, stomach ulcers or inflammations, or for tuberculosis. Several other Alaska Native groups commonly used it in the same way, especially for tuberculosis. The tea was consumed regularly until the condition was relieved. Drinking the tea is also said to lessen fevers and diarrhea.

Of the numerous species of *Potentilla* shown in Alaska, Eric Hulten (1968) indicates 5 that grow in the Kodiak area. One of these cinquefoils, *Potentilla villosa*, is commonly found growing in the rocks on our beaches. Its 5-petaled yellow flower is a bright contrast to its 3-lobed leaves, dark green to grey-green at the edges. It appears extremely hardy, growing as it does in minimal soil.

Shrubby Cinquefoil
Potentilla fruticosa

Other Uses: A reddish dye can be made from silverweed roots.

Silverweed Cakes
Bradford Angier,
Feasting Free on Wild Edibles

If you have found a beach crowded with silverweed plants, you might enjoy this recipe:

> 1 pound silverweed roots, scrubbed and boiled
> Salt and pepper
> Butter
> Breadcrumbs

Mash the silverweed roots and add salt, pepper and butter. Form into cakes, roll in breadcrumbs, and sauté in oil until browned.

To Complete the Meal:

Deer Roast
Georgia Smith

Spruce Island's small herd of deer still provides an important winter source of protein. It has been harvested carefully, and enjoyed for many years.

> 3 to 4-pound deer roast
> Cooking oil
> 1 package dry onion soup mix
> 1 can cream of mushroom soup
> 2 tablespoons Worcestershire sauce

Brown roast on each side in oil in electric skillet. Combine soups and Worcestershire sauce. Pour over roast; cover and reduce heat. Simmer 2 ½ to three hours. Thin with water if sauce thickens.

INDEX

Bog Rosemary *(Andromeda polifolia)*
    See under Labrador tea

Blueberry

Bog Blueberry *(Vaccinium uliginosum* ssp. *microphyllum)*

Alpine Blueberry *(Vaccinium uliginosum)*

Early Blueberry *(Vaccinium ovalifolium)*

Bunchberry *(Cornus canadensis)*

Cranberry

    Lingonberry *(Vaccinium vitis-idaea)*

    Lowbush Cranberry *(Oxycoccus microcarpus)*

Crowberry *(Empetrum nigrum)*

False Hellebore *(Veratrum viride)*

Labrador Tea *(Ledum palustre* ssp. *decumbens)*

Marsh Fivefinger *(Potentilla palustris)*

Monkey Flower *(Mimulus guttatus)*

Pond Lily *(Nuphar polysepalum)*

Sundew *(Drosera anglica; D. rotundifolia)*

Sweet Gale *(Myrica gale)*

58 | THE PLANTS, BY HABITAT

BOGS, POND EDGES, DAMP TERRAIN, OR ALPINE SLOPES

BLUEBERRY
HEATH FAMILY
Cuawak (Aleut)

Chernika (Russian)

Blueberry: Nature's #1 Antioxidant

Recent research has established the blueberry as one of the world's healthiest foods. In a recent study from Tufts University, 60 fruits and vegetables were analyzed, and blueberries were ranked as the #1 antioxidant. This small nutritional giant is packed with antioxidant phytonutrients whose function is to neutralize free radical damage to cells and tissue.

Of the seven closely related species or subspecies of blueberry growing in Alaska, three can be found in the Kodiak area. The berries can be used interchangeably in recipes. Any of the blueberry species can also be used to make a dye. The plant produces a lavender to purple hue when boiled with alum, but the color tends to fade when exposed to sun.

1) **BOG BLUEBERRY,** Bilberry
   Vaccinium uliginosum, ssp. microphylum

Description: The bog blueberry, or bilberry, is a shrub with erect, branching stems. It is a small plant, growing to 2 feet tall. Its leaves are small, alternate, and rather thick, with smooth edges. Tiny, bell-shaped, light pink flowers grow from buds that form right on the old wood of last year's branches. The berry is blue-black.

Habitat: This shrub can be found in bogs and marshy areas, and in the high country.

Edible Parts and Nutritional Value:
The berries are high in vitamin C, with a juicy, sweet flavor, yet low in calories. Fruits are high in iron and mineral salts.

Ways to Prepare for Eating: The berries can be eaten raw, frozen, canned, or cooked in various blueberry desserts, pies, puddings, pancakes, and muffins. These berries can also be used in jams, jellies, or sauces.

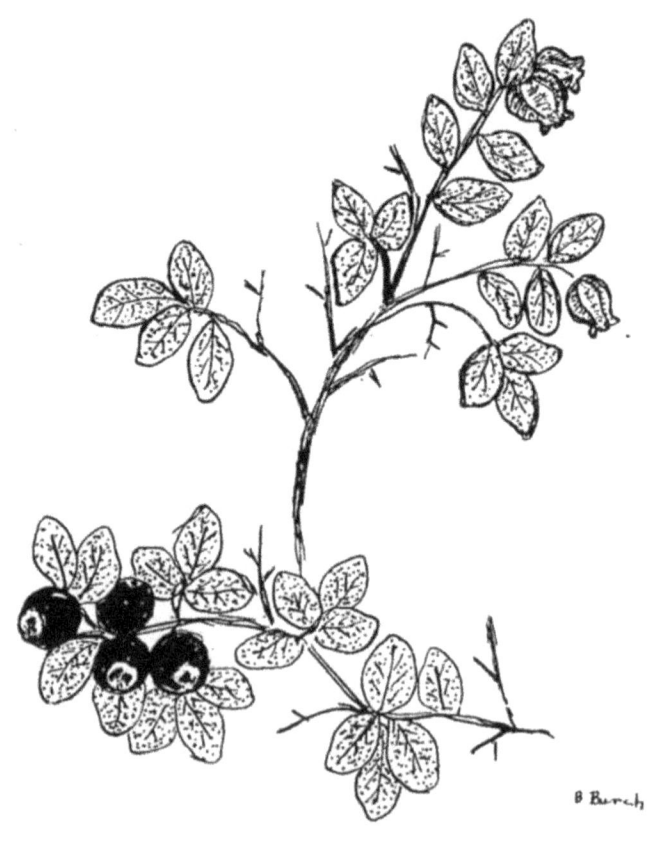

Bog Blueberry
*Vaccinium uliginosum,
Ssp. microphylum*

THE PLANTS, BY HABITAT

These fruits can be picked from early summer through winter if you can find them then. In our area, bog blueberries are sometimes wormy. However, if they are picked after the first heavy frost the worms will be gone. Or, if harvested earlier in the season, the berries can be soaked for 30 minutes in a saltwater solution. The worms will float to the top of the bowl and can then be removed.

Uses in Native and Traditional Folk Medicine

Blueberry's value as an antioxidant is purported to impact the health in a number of ways. Such antioxidant-rich foods are said to protect the heart from damage. Pterostilbene, a compound found in blueberries, is known to fight cancer and may help lower cholesterol. The juicy berry has been shown to improve night vision and to restore normal vision after exposure to glare. Studies report that eating three or more servings per day protects against vision loss among older adults. Also, we are told that diets rich in blueberries can protect against Alzheimer's disease or dementia, and may significantly lessen brain damage from strokes.

Blueberry Jelly

Blueberries (enough to make 4 cups juice)
2 tablespoons lemon juice
7 ½ cups sugar
1 bottle liquid pectin

Crush fully ripe berries. Place in jelly cloth and squeeze out juice. Measure 4 cups juice into *very large* saucepan. Add lemon juice and sugar and mix well. Place over high heat and bring to a boil, stirring constantly. At once, stir in liquid pectin. Then bring to a full rolling boil and boil hard for one minute, stirring constantly. Remove from heat, skim off foam with metal spoon, and pour quickly into hot, sterilized glasses or jars. Seal with paraffin and lids. Makes 5 ½ pounds.

---

2) ALPINE BLUEBERRY
Vaccinium uliginosum

This subspecies has generally the same description, habitat, and uses as the bog blueberry or bilberry. Its habitat, as its common name suggests, is chiefly in alpine areas.

Blueberry Pie

Cooperative Extension Service,
Wild Berry Recipes

Our earliest forays of the season into the blueberry patches, ostensibly to check the year's crop, often resulted in the creation of one of these delicious pies.

> Pastry for 9-inch double-crust pie
> 2 cups blueberries
> 3 tablespoons flour or quick-cooking tapioca
> 1 ½ cups sugar
> ⅛ teaspoon salt
> 1 tablespoon butter

Mix all ingredients except butter and arrange in lower crust of pie. Dot with butter. Cover with the second crust and bake at 450 degrees for 10 minutes. Lower the temperature to 350 degrees and continue baking for 20 or 30 minutes or until juice bubbles up and the crust is browned.

---

3) EARLY BLUEBERRY
Forest Blueberry
Vaccinium ovalifolium

Description: This blueberry is a tall shrub, quite similar to other members of its genus. Its branches are stout and reddish colored, and it has little, bell-shaped pink-white flowers. The fruit is round and blue.

Habitat: It likes open woods, thickets, and slopes where there is peaty soil.

Edible Parts and Nutritional Value: Berries are edible and supply vitamin C. This low-calorie fruit is teeming with antioxidants. These berries are also high in iron and mineral salts.

Ways to Prepare for Eating: Prepare in the same way as you would use other blueberries. Remember, if you harvest after the first frost, the berries are sweeter and any worms are gone.

Uses in Native and Traditional Folk Medicine

See discussion under bog blueberry.

Early Blueberry
Vaccinium ovalifolium

Blueberry Jam

4 ½ cups blueberries
7 cups sugar
2 tablespoons lemon juice
1 bottle liquid pectin

Crush fruit and measure 4 cups into a very large saucepan. Add sugar and lemon juice. Mix well. Place over high heat and bring to a full rolling boil. Boil hard for 1 minute, stirring constantly. Remove from heat; at once stir in liquid pectin. Skim off foam with metal spoon. Stir and skim for 5 minutes to cool slightly (at high temperatures, fruit will float). Ladle into hot, sterilized glasses or jars and seal with paraffin and lids. Makes 6 pounds.

Our Ouzinkie "Plants Class" blueberry-picking treks were our most enjoyable. Even Georgia, who didn't like blueberries, would join us, and pick for her family. We would look for the bushes with the biggest berries, of course. Sometimes the wild berries got to be dime-sized; very occasionally we discovered some penny-size ones, which we greeted with chortles of delight. Often, though, the berries were much smaller, but they made up for lack of size by the profusion with which they grew. We never used berry rakes when we went picking. We hand-picked: no breaking of branches and twigs; pick clean with fingers only; leave behind every part of the plant one did not intend to use; prolong the experience of the group outing by doing the picking the old-fashioned, labor-intensive way. We got all the berries we needed in this way. We got much more than just the berries – our spirits rejoiced in the experience!

Bunchberry
Cornus canadensis

BUNCHBERRY, Canadian Dwarf Cornel
DOGWOOD FAMILY
Cornus canadensis

Description: Usually, many of these low-to-the-ground plants will be found growing together. The large leaves are oval with veins running their length, much like common plantain. These leaves are bright green and rather shiny. The flower grows from a single short stalk at the plant's top just above the leaves. It has four white bracts, which are modified leaves, not petals, and a greenish center. When the bright red, round berries form, they grow in tight clusters, several to a plant.

Habitat: Bunchberries like spruce forests, birch forests, and alpine areas.

Edible Parts: The berries are edible, though of doubtful value, as they are tasteless. They are said to cause vomiting and headaches if too many are eaten. However, as this berry is high in pectin, it can be mixed with other berries for making jelly.

Uses in Native and Traditional Folk Medicine

Dogwood family plants contain cornine, which can be used as a substitute for quinine. A tea from the bark of larger dogwood shrubs was a favorite fever and colic remedy of several Indian tribes.

The liquid from an infusion of this bark was also given as a painkiller. It was an Alutiiq remedy to apply a poultice of the leaves for cuts and scrapes. According to Yakutat Tlingit women, the heated leaves of bunchberry could be placed on eyes with cataracts and left overnight. The cataracts could be removed in the morning.

> One of the things I love best about my favorite Ouzinkie people is their sense of humor. Both Sasha and Jenny had their share of that commodity. Both of them believed laughter to be a great medicine. There was some of that humor at work in the conversation between us that I included in its entirety in the first edition of this book. For example, shortly after I had transcribed our talk from the tape, I gave the draft of our conversation to Sasha to read. I glanced over at her a few minutes later and saw her shoulders shaking in silent laughter. I went over to her. "What are you laughing at, Sasha?" I asked. "This," she replied, pointing to the place in the script. Jenny had been looking at the picture of Canadian dwarf cornel, or bunchberry. Locally it is called "airberry" because its fruit seems filled with air when eaten. "That's a pirdunia," Jenny had said. "That's called 'pirdunia' in Russian," Sasha had agreed.
>
> Sasha explained to me that the Russian word they had used referred to the gentle art of passing gas.

Lingonberry
Vaccinium vitis-idaea

66 | THE PLANTS, BY HABITAT

CRANBERRY
HEATH FAMILY
Kenegtaq (Aleut)
Brusnika (Russian)

There is a very interesting article about cranberries online at www.cranberryinstitute.org. The article discusses new research into foods such as cranberries that contain resveratrol, an anti-cancer compound. A research team headed by Dr. Bharat Aggareval from the University of Texas found that this compound had the ability to suppress proliferation of a wide variety of tumor cells. The list of types of cancer cells that can be suppressed is very impressive: Lymphoid and myeloid cancers; cancers of the breast, colon, pancreas, stomach, prostate, head and neck, ovary, liver, lung, cervix; also melanoma. The researchers conclude that there is great potential in cancer therapy and prevention from the resveratrol compound.

It has long been known that drinking cranberry juice helps prevent urinary tract infections. Cranberries have an anti-adhesion property that prevents bacteria from binding to the cell surface, thus thwarting the development of urinary tract infections. Dosage recommended is 8 ounces of pure unsweetened cranberry juice 3 times a day. However, it is said that even a single glass of juice can be helpful as a preventative. Moreover, no harmful side effects result from drinking cranberry juice.

Due to their high antioxidant content, cranberries, like wild blueberries, strawberries, or raspberries, are said to help prevent age-related memory loss. Eating cranberries may decrease the brain's sensitivity to oxidation and inflammation. A diet high in cranberries may help ward off Alzheimer's.

The two types of "cranberry" (*Vaccinium vitis-idaea* and *Oxycoccus microcarpus*) can be used interchangeably medicinally or in recipes.

1) **LINGONBERRY,** Lowbush Cranberry, Bog Cranberry
   Vaccinium vitis-idaea

Description: This plant is a miniature, creeping evergreen shrub with slender, woody stems and tiny, shiny, dark green oval leaves with curled under margins. The stems can grow up to 6 inches high. The pink, bell-shaped flowers grow either alone or in clusters and form at the stem ends. The berries are bright red and quite sour.

Habitat: Grows in rocky places, in bogs, and on mountain slopes.

Edible Parts and Nutritional Value: The berries are edible and contain vitamin C. Cranberries are high in antioxidants.

Ways to Prepare for Eating: Preferably, pick after the first frost. These berries can be picked all winter if they are available. They have excellent flavor, and can be prepared in any way that commercial cranberries are used. They contain a considerable amount of benzoic acid that will keep them from spoiling without sealing, whether they are raw or cooked.

These berries also can be made into an excellent cordial.

Uses in Native and Traditional Folk Medicine

These cranberries, which grow all over Alaska, have been a Native remedy for headaches, swelling, and sore throats. They can be heated, wrapped in a cloth, and placed as a hot pack on the sore area, or raw berries can be chewed for sore throat. They may be eaten as an effective antioxidant, which destroys free radicals in the system.

Other Uses: Boiling lingonberry leaves and stems with alum produces a red dye.

Cranberry Jelly
Georgia Smith

We cook the wind and the zing of the fresh air right into the jelly!

Wash cranberries, removing stems. Place in 3 ½ quart saucepan. Add water and bring to a boil. Reduce heat. Simmer, covered, 20 minutes. Strain through cheesecloth. Bring cranberry puree to a boil. Boil uncovered for 3 minutes. Add sugar and boil 3 minutes longer. Pour into hot, sterilized jars and seal with paraffin and lids. Makes 2 ¾ cups.

Lowbush Cranberry
Oxycoccus microcarpus

Lingonberry Relish
Fran Kelso

Excellent! Try as a garnish with any white meats or with fish.

1 quart lingonberries
2 medium-sized tart apples
½ cup raisins
⅔ cup vinegar
1 cup brown sugar
¼ teaspoon cloves
½ teaspoon cinnamon
¼ teaspoon salt
½ cup well-chopped walnuts

Clean and wash berries. Peel and dice apples. Combine all but walnuts and simmer 1 hour, until thick. (Mash mixture with potato masher when cooked enough to soften.) Stir in nuts and seal in hot jars. Makes about 5 half-pints.

---

2) LOWBUSH CRANBERRY, Bog Cranberry, Swamp Cranberry
Oxycoccus microcarpus

Description: These cranberries grow on a tiny evergreen vine with slender, creeping stems. The vine grows in the moss, putting down roots through its stem joints. The small, shiny green leaves are thick and leathery. The leaf edges roll under. Pink and yellow flowers at the top of erect stems look like miniature shooting stars. The berries are white at one end, where they attach to the stem. Some of our Plants Class members call them "pinkheads" because of their predominantly pink color. (They are maroon when ripe.)

Our references tell us that in Alaska these relatives of the commercial cranberry are not as plentiful as the lingonberry. In fact, they're downright scarce. On Spruce Island, however, both varieties seem to flourish, and we have found good patches of *Oxycoccus* in our favorite gathering areas. These small lowbush cranberries are very good and can be mixed with lingonberries.

Habitat: These delicate plants prefer boggy or peaty soil. They like to grow on top of sphagnum moss. I recently explored a newly discovered bog near my house and found hummocks of brown sphagnum moss so thick with "pinkheads" they seemed like tiny fields, planted there for me to harvest.

At first glance, it appeared that someone had thrown a large handful of these berries on the top of the sphagnum hump. When I looked closer, I noticed the berries were attached to a tiny vine that blended in with the moss underneath.

Edible Parts and Nutritional Value: The berries of this plant are excellent fruits and contain vitamin C. Some Alaskans also eat the blossoms. The berries are very high in antioxidants and share the important role of lingonberries in reportedly providing suppression of cancer cells, preventing urinary tract infections, and keeping brain cells healthy (See cranberry introduction).

Ways to Prepare for Eating: These wild berries can be used in the same ways as commercial cranberries.

Cranberry Muffins
Georgia Smith

⅔ cup unbleached white flour
⅔ cup soy flour
⅔ cup whole wheat flour
½ teaspoon salt
2 teaspoons baking powder
1 egg, beaten
2 tablespoons melted butter
1 cup cranberries

Combine dry ingredients. In a separate bowl, mix egg, honey, milk, and melted butter. Blend with dry ingredients just until moistened. Stir in cranberries. Fill greased muffin tins two-thirds full and bake at 400 degrees for 20 minutes.

> Small monarchs of the berry kingdom! You draw us to our knees to do you homage as we search for you on mossy hillock or high alpine slope. Close to the earth you grow, seeking or giving protection for the ground below. Your ripe fruits are enjoyed by many creatures, from very small to very large. To each you grant equal pleasure in the enjoyment of your excellence...."

Village Holiday Celebrations

The villagers celebrated two sets of holidays every year, Russian and American. At the end of the year American Christmas was celebrated, with its set of traditions. About two weeks later came Russian Christmas. (Russian holidays are set in the village by the Julian calendar, which is still the calendar of the Russian Orthodox Church.) For this Russian holiday, the custom of starring was celebrated. This custom comes originally from the Ukraine, and has found its way into the Alaskan villages. A brightly decorated star attached to a handle in such a way as to allow it to be spun was carried from house to house, and Russian carols were sung.

As part of the Russian New Year's celebration, villagers often participated in a custom known as "masking". Villagers might go masking at any time between Orthodox Christmas and Russian New Year. Revelers dressed in outlandish costumes, with masks or headdresses that were sometimes much taller than the wearers, to make them harder to identify. The costumed

Ouzinkie Easter, Georgia and kulich
Photo by: Timothy Smith

participants traveled from house to house, where they were served refreshments. Maskers could blow whistles or make strange noises, but were not supposed to speak. Those visited were required to guess the maskers' identities. It was considered bad luck to allow a masker to leave without learning his/her identity.

In the days before Russian Easter, village cooks dug out their metal coffee cans or shortening cans saved for the occasion and baked kulich. This round Russian sweet bread was often frosted and decorated with candy sprinkles; chopped, dried fruit was included in the dough. If the baker were lucky enough to find a priest in the village, she would have her kulich blessed. Guests during the season were served this wonderful treat with tea and butter or homemade jelly. Here is a kulich recipe as made by Angeline Campfield:

Russian Easter Kulich

(Bake this bread at 350 degrees for 30 minutes. The recipe as written below makes 5 tall loaves, using 1-pound coffee cans. For a 3-pound shortening can, increase baking time to 45 minutes.)

¾ cup milk
¾ cup sugar
1 ½ teaspoon salt
1 cup butter or margarine
3 envelopes active dry yeast
¾ cup very warm water
6 eggs, beaten
8 ¼ cups sifted all-purpose flour
¾ cup raisins
½ cup chopped blanched almonds
¾ teaspoon lemon flavoring
¾ to 1 cup chopped mixed candied fruit
Confectioners' Sugar Icing

Combine milk, sugar, salt and butter or margarine in saucepan. Heat just until butter is melted; cool to lukewarm.

Sprinkle yeast into very warm water in a large mixing bowl. ("Very warm" water should feel comfortably warm when dropped on wrist.) Add lukewarm milk mixture, eggs and 4 cups of the flour; beat until smooth. Stir in raisins, almonds, vanilla and fruit. Add just enough of the remaining flour to make a soft dough.

Turn out onto lightly floured board; knead until smooth and elastic, using only as much flour as needed to keep dough from sticking.

Place dough in greased bowl; turn to bring greased side up. Cover; let rise in warm place 1 to 1 ½ hours, or until double in bulk.

Punch down dough; knead a few times. Let rest 5 minutes.

Divide dough into 5 even portions; shape each into a bun shape. Place in 5 well-greased 1 pound tall coffee cans.

Cover; let rise 30 minutes, or until top of dough is slightly above cans.

Bake in moderate oven (350 degrees for 30 minutes), or until tops are brown and loaves give a hollow sound when tapped. Cover with a piece of foil if tops are browning too fast. Cool slightly in cans on wire racks; remove from cans. Cool completely before frosting with Confectioners' Sugar Icing.

Confectioners' Sugar Icing

Blend 2 ½ cups sifted powdered sugar with 3 tablespoons milk. Icing should have a somewhat runny consistency. Spread over tops of loaves, allowing icing to run down the sides.

American Easter in Ouzinkie

American Easter was celebrated by a sunrise service and community breakfast at the big, white 3-story house, Baker Cottage, built by the Baptist ministry, and known in Ouzinkie as "the mission". In the ground floor chapel, Reverend Norman Smith conducted the service and his wife, Joyce, played a small organ.

On American Easter morning, a large part of the village would arrive for Norman's service. Afterward, all would go upstairs, where every bit of available space on the first floor was set with tables and chairs so all could eat. The traditional baked treat for this feast was Joyce's hot cross buns. Tim Smith told me that his mother just made an extra-big batch of kulich dough, and used part of it for hot cross buns, as the dough recipes are quite similar. Angeline Campfield tells us she uses the "Hot Cross Buns" recipe from Betty Crocker.

Hot Cross Buns from Kulich Dough

To use the kulich dough recipe, modify it as follows: Grease 12 (or more, if needed) large muffin cups. Once the dough has doubled in size, stir it down, then spoon into muffin cups, filling them half full. Let rise in warm place until the dough reaches the tops of the muffin cups, 20 or 30 minutes. Heat oven to 400 degrees. Bake 15 to 20 minutes, or until brown. Make a cross on each bun with the confectioners' sugar icing.

CROWBERRY, Blackberry
CROWBERRY FAMILY
Empetrum nigrum
Shiksha – crowberry (Russian)
Shikshonik – crowberry bush (Russian)

Description: Crowberries grow on a low, sprawling evergreen shrub with small, narrow leaves that look like spruce needles. The blossoms, small and purplish, grow singly or in clusters. The berries are juicy and black.

Habitat: Crowberries grow in bogs and tundra.

Edible Parts: The berries can be eaten, and are better cooked than raw. Gather in late summer or early fall. They are best after the first frost. The fruits sweeten due to the cold. These berries, along with their companions, cranberries and lingonberries, often winter over and may be gathered after the snows melt.

Ways to Prepare for Eating: Crowberries are usually picked in the autumn, but are good all winter and into the next spring if they remain on the plant. By themselves they don't have much flavor, but are tasty mixed with other berries. They are a "watery" berry, lacking natural pectin, so they mix especially well with blueberries. They are good in jelly and pies.

Uses in Native and Traditional Folk Medicine

Traditional folk remedies include the following: For relief from diarrhea, boil crowberry leaves and stems and drink the tea. The cooked berries can be eaten for the same purpose. The berry juice, prepared as a drink, is said to relieve kidney troubles. An infusion of twigs and stems may be used in the same way. Use also for colds or tuberculosis.

For sore eyes, herbalists made a remedy from crowberry roots. They would clean roots thoroughly, boil them in water to make a tea, cool the liquid, and wash the eyes with it. Some Native people have been known to use the bark of crowberry stems to remove cataracts.

Crowberry
Empetrum nigrum

Crowberry Pie

Cooperative Extension Service,
Wild Berry Recipes

I have Ouzinkie friends who claim crowberry pie as their favorite. Try this recipe for yourself and see what you think!

One 9-inch pie shell, baked
4 cups crowberries
1 cup sugar
1 tablespoon lemon juice
3 tablespoons cornstarch
¼ teaspoon salt
¼ cup water
1 tablespoon butter

Line the cooked pie shell with 2 cups of the berries. Cook the remaining berries with the sugar, lemon juice, cornstarch, salt and water until medium thick. Remove from heat, add butter, and cool. Pour over berries in the shell. Chill. Serve with whipped cream.

FALSE HELLEBORE, Corn Lily
LILY FAMILY
Veratrum viride

POISONOUS!

Description: A perennial plant, false hellebore has a stout stem, 3 to 8 feet tall, growing from a thick root. Leaves are alternate, 6 to 15 inches long, and broad. They are roundly oval in shape, with a pointed tip, and they enclose the stem. These leaves are folded lengthwise like the pleats in a skirt. The flowers are small and greenish with 3 petals. They gather in large, spike-like clusters at the top of the stem.

Habitat: False hellebore grows in bogs, meadows, and creek bottoms. I have also found it growing on open, sunny hillsides, in the company of spreading wood ferns.

Poisonous Parts and Conditions of Poisoning:
The whole plant is poisonous. It can cause salivating, vomiting, diarrhea and abdominal pain, weakness, general paralysis, and spasms that sometimes become convulsions. The alkaloids in the plant can slow heart rate and lower blood pressure. In fact, the plant has been used medicinally for these purposes, and for some other purposes as well. However, it is best to avoid this plant because it can be dangerous if used incorrectly.

Some people have become poisoned by false hellebore by mistaking it for skunk cabbage – an edible wild plant that false hellebore resembles when it is young. Skunk cabbage, by the way, does not grow in the Ouzinkie vicinity, although it has been found on Kodiak Island near the village of Karluk. Our monks once mistook the early false hellebore shoots for wild cucumber. Fortunately, they checked with caretaker Greg before they made the mistake of eating it.

CAUTION: Just because this plant has been used medicinally by those trained in its use does not make it a good idea to experiment on your own. It might be the last mistake you ever make!

False Hellebore
Veratrum viride

LABRADOR TEA, Hudson Bay Tea
HEATH FAMILY
Ledum palustre, ssp. decumbens
Mogulnik (Russian)

Description: This subspecies is a small relative of a shrub also called Labrador tea. It has long, narrow, needlelike leaves that stay olive green on the upper surface the whole year. These leaves are very aromatic when crushed. Leaf undersides are reddish brown and woolly. Little white flowers with 5 petals and 5 stamens form at the stem top in clusters. The plant has a very pleasant aroma.

CAUTION: An effective laxative in large doses. At first, drink tea brewed from this plant in small amounts.

Habitat: Labrador tea sometimes grows in woods; however, it especially likes bogs and swamps. Our class has found that it favors bog cranberries and crowberries as companion plants.

Edible Parts and Nutritional Value: The leaves and branches are brewed in "chai" (tea) and are high in vitamin C.

Ways to Prepare for Eating: Labrador tea can be gathered year-round. It can be dried for winter, or dug up from under the snow.

Boil the leaves and branches until the water is the color of regular tea. Or, add 1 tablespoon dried herb to 1 cup boiling water. Steep 5 minutes and sweeten to taste. Makes a good hot drink, but use sparingly to avoid a laxative effect. It can be mixed with other teas for a blend.

Native Alaskans made a meat spice and a marinade from this plant for game with a strong wild taste. The meat would be soaked in tea made from the boiled plant, or the meat, stems, and leaves would be boiled together.

Uses in Native and Traditional Folk Medicine

Native Alaskans taught me to prepare a tea by boiling fresh or dried leaves and branches until the water turns dark. It must not be brewed too long as the plant contains ledol and can cause a toxic reaction. I was informed that I could drink this tea for anemia, colds and tuberculosis. The tea has also been used for arthritis, dizziness, stomach problems, heartburn and hangover. Labrador tea, known on Spruce Island by its Russian name, "mogulnik", has been used locally as a remedy for chest ailments and tuberculosis.

Labrador Tea
Ledum palustre

CAUTION: The poisonous bog rosemary (*Andromeda polifolia*), which is quite similar in appearance to Labrador tea, shares the same habitat. The leaves are similar in shape; however, bog rosemary leaves are smooth and light-colored underneath, while the underside of the leaves of Labrador tea are wooly and rust-colored. The blossoms of the two are different. The flowers of Labrador tea are white with 5 petals, while bog rosemary has pale pink, bell-like flowers, similar to those of the blueberry.

Bog rosemary contains a toxin called andromedotoxin. It causes low blood pressure, diarrhea, and vomiting, and should not be consumed.

> **Jenny:** …"And then that mogulnik (Labrador tea)…That is so good for chest and so forth. There was a priest's wife… she had TB…we used to pick mogulnik (for her) by the sacks… It's pitchy, you know. It's pitchy, and she took it, and there was nothing wrong with her when she died…"

Bog Rosemary
Andromeda polifolia

How to Cook A Seal
Katie Ellanak

There is a strong "gamey" or "fishy" taste to some of the wild game used by villagers to enhance their diet. Labrador tea is an effective seasoning to use in recipes such as these.

> Seal meat contains a great deal of blood; so first genus that isn't yellow boil it alone in lots of water. As it boils, keep taking off the scum that forms on top – just pour off the top part of the juice. Continue this process until the juice is clear. Cook at least 1 hour from the time the juice begins to boil. After the juice is clear, add vegetables if you wish.

MARSH FIVEFINGER
ROSE FAMILY
Potentilla palustris

Description: This plant grows to 18 inches tall, often in a low, sprawling form. Its stems branch in "V's". The leaves, palm-shaped with 4 to 5 long and slender leaflets, form near these stem junctions. Brownish-purple flowers form at the top of the stalk. The flower petals are pointed. Marsh fivefinger is the only member of the *Potentilla* genus that does not have yellow blossoms.

Habitat: Marsh fivefinger grows along rivers and sloughs and at the edges of ponds. As its name implies, it likes wet, marshy places.

Edible Parts: The leaves are said to be dried for tea by the Eskimos. Plants Class has found them to be a satisfactory ingredient to use in tea blends. Use dried leaves.

CAUTION: Use in blends in moderation, as the plants contain tannic acid (as does black tea), and in large amounts can act as a gastrointestinal irritant and a toxin to the kidneys.

Marsh Fivefinger
Potentilla palustris

MONKEY FLOWER
FIGWORT OR SNAPDRAGON FAMILY
Mimulus guttatus

Description: Monkey flower is a leafy plant that can range in size from 3 inches to 3 feet. Sometimes it is small and spindly and sometimes large and bushy. Its size seems to be dependent on soil conditions. Its opposite leaves grow in pairs, from round to oblong shape, with toothed edges. The leaf stalks and stems are often tinged with red. The large, yellow flowers, two-lipped, are trumpet-shaped; the flower throat is hairy and often has red spots at the base. The two lobes of the upper lip of the flower are bent upward, and the three lobes of the lower lip are bent downward.

Habitat: Monkey flowers like to grow in moist spots, particularly near rocky areas where water seeps to the surface. They are fond of stream banks. The first ones I found were in Kodiak, growing near a stream. Some of the plants were standing in the water!

Edible Parts: The stems, leaves and flowers of this plant are all edible.

Ways to Prepare for Eating: Monkey flower leaves can be added to soups, casseroles, or other vegetable dishes. Try a few leaves in your favorite green salad. Add the blossoms to a salad for a splash of color.

Uses in Native and Traditional Folk Medicine

Native people in parts of Alaska used an infusion of monkey flower for constipation. They also taught that leaves and stems could be mashed and applied as a poultice for minor skin irritations and insect bites.

Other Uses: For a lovely addition to your flower garden, gather seeds or cuttings and transplant to a moist area.

Monkey Flower
Mimulus guttatus

To Complete the Meal:

Danny's Spicy Steamed Mussels
Danny Konigsberg

In the years when there were no "red tide" warnings, my neighbor, Danny, and I often ate the delicately flavored mussels from our island beaches. (A "red tide" refers to waters in which there are very high quantities of a certain algae that contains a toxin harmful to humans. Shellfish contaminated by this algae can cause PSP, or Paralytic Shellfish Poisoning, a serious illness that can result in death.)

If you can find mussels harvested from a safe area, try this recipe:

4 dozen large mussels in shells
1 crushed bay leaf
1 small onion, chopped
3 tablespoons chopped petrushki
1 stalk poochki, peeled and minced
1 tablespoon wine vinegar
4 ounces butter
⅛ teaspoon cayenne
¼ teaspoon Worcestershire sauce
Salt

Scrub mussels; pull off any sea animals. Soak in seawater for 3 days, changing water daily, to clean.

Place mussels in large saucepan over medium heat; add bay leaf, onion, petrushki and poochki. Cover tightly and steam for 3 minutes, or until shells begin to open. Drain broth from saucepan and save. Cover mussels to keep hot.

Strain broth into a smaller pan and add wine vinegar, butter, cayenne, Worcestershire sauce, and a little salt. Heat over medium flame to boiling point, but do not boil. Meanwhile, open mussels and remove top shell; take out dark, hairy beard. Serve mussels on half shells with seasoned butter sauce on the side. Dip each mussel in sauce and eat.

Variation: Use 1 teaspoon lemon juice in place of vinegar in butter sauce.

POND LILY, Yellow Pond Lily, Spatterdock
WATER LILY FAMILY
Nuphar polysepalum

Description: A perennial, the pond lily grows in water. It has a large, fat, spongy root that spreads along the lake bottom. The leaves, large and nearly heart-shaped, float on top of the water. The flowers, often with many petals, are large and yellow, with touches of red. Only one flower grows on each thick, spongy stalk. Urn-shaped pods, an inch or two long, replace the flowers. Inside each pod are several glossy, yellow or brown seeds.

Habitat: As their name implies, these lilies are found in ponds or at the edge of shallow lakes. Often the roots, a favorite food of beavers, are found on top of beaver lodges.

Edible Parts and Nutritional Value: Roots and seeds can be eaten as a source of carbohydrates.

Ways to Prepare for Eating: Gather the roots from autumn to early spring. Boil them twice or roast, peel, and eat as a vegetable.

The seedpods are ready to be gathered in the autumn. Take the seeds from the pods, put on a cookie sheet, and roast in the oven at a low heat until they crack and the kernels can be removed. Then cook the kernels in the same way as popcorn. They will swell, and can be eaten as they are with salt and butter. They can also be ground into flour, or boiled and eaten as cereal.

Uses in Native and Traditional Folk Medicine

According to Pojar and Mackinnon in *Plants of the Pacific Northwest Coast*, Native Alaskans used yellow pond lily for a variety of medicinal uses. The Tsimshian drank an infusion made from scrapings of the toasted rootstock. They ate the boiled rootstock heart for bleeding of the lungs and as a contraceptive. The Haidas used the boiled root for numerous illnesses: colds, tuberculosis, ulcers, chest pain, rheumatism, heart conditions, and cancer. Though quite bitter, rhizomes were roasted and eaten for tuberculosis. Rhizomes were also used by the Nuxalk for tuberculosis, as well as for rheumatism, heart disease, and gonorrhea. The Kwakwaka'waku drank an extract of the rhizomes for asthma. Leaves were heated and applied to the chest for chest sores. The Quinault heated roots and applied to painful areas, especially for rheumatism.

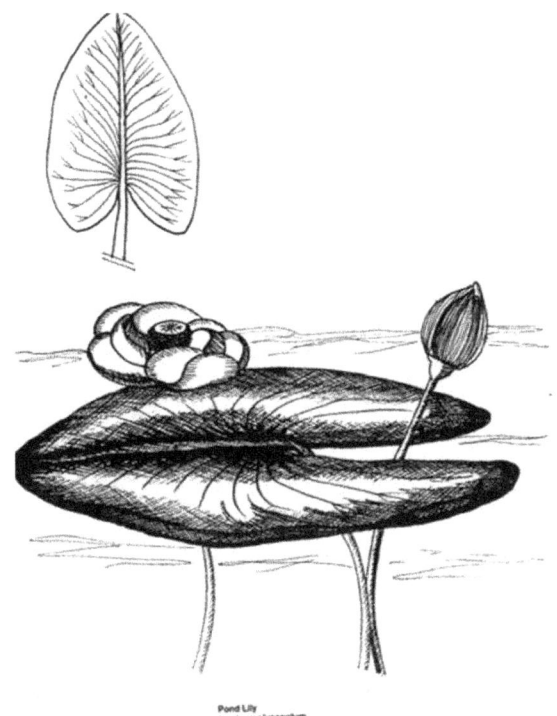

Pond Lily
Nuphar polysepalum

SUNDEW
SUNDEW FAMILY
Drosera anglica
Drosera rotundifolia

Description: Sundew is an insect-eating perennial. Often this plant is quite small, but it can grow to 10 inches tall. It has fibrous roots. The dewy leaves are sticky and designed to trap unsuspecting insects, such as mosquitoes, midges, and gnats, which are sundew's favorite foods. Sundew grows in a basal rosette; leaves are 1 to 5 inches in length. The blades are round or egg-shaped, with long, reddish, glandular hairs, or tentacles. The flowers are white with small petals, and are fully open only in strong sunlight. Fruits are many-sided partitioned capsules.

Habitat: Sundews like sphagnum bogs and wet meadows at low to middle elevations. The tiny plants can be found growing atop the sphagnum humps.

Edible Parts: The sundew is not edible. However, the fresh leaves were once used in Europe in the preparation of cheeses and junkets, as the juice was known to curdle milk. It has also been combined with brandy, raisins and sugar and fermented into a cordial called *Rossalis*.

Uses in Native and Traditional Folk Medicine

Some Northwest Native groups used the sticky leaves for removing corns, warts, and bunions. I would guess the leaves were applied as a poultice, though I have found no specific instructions for its use.

Until we looked in Janice Schofield's book, we regarded sundew simply as a highly unusual little plant. Through Janice, we made some important discoveries. The round-leafed sundew (*D. rotundifolia*) is said to relieve spasms and promote mucus discharge. It has been used to treat tuberculosis, whooping cough, asthma, bronchitis, and severe coughs. It is prepared as a tincture to relieve such conditions (see tincture recipe). Sundew tincture is always taken in small doses.

Various sources mention sundew as a plant that contains an antibiotic substance that is reputed to be effective against several bacteria. In pure form, it is said to be effective against streptococcus, staphylococcus, and pneumococcus.

Sundew is not always easy to find. Be sure you find a habitat where it grows in profusion before you harvest it for making a tincture.

CAUTION: Use sundew in small doses. This herb contains substances that are corrosive and irritating to the human system. Medical supervision is advised for internal use, as overdoses could endanger human health.

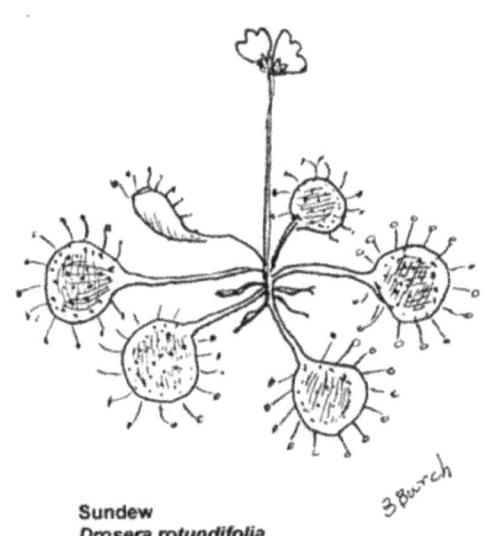

Sundew
Drosera rotundifolia

> There is a hidden little bog on Spruce Island where colonies of the elusive sundew make their homes atop the sphagnum humps. Once, when my knees were younger, I squatted for long minutes, watching a small winged insect flying back and forth, low, across the top of one such little settlement. He seemed unable to break his flight pattern; he flew as if under a compelling spell. He drew closer and closer to the tops of the waiting plants. At last he drew too near, and touched one of the hungry leaves, and he stuck there, held fast by the sticky surface. No more would he fly free – and the sundew colony had fresh meat for supper!

Basic Tincture Recipe
(Janice Schofield: "Discovering Wild Plants")

Place fresh herbs in a glass jar. Cover herbs with 80-proof brandy or vodka*. Keep in a warm dark place for at least 2 weeks, shaking daily. (Traditionalists recommend beginning tinctures on the new moon and straining on the full moon.) After desired time period has elapsed, strain herbs through muslin or double layers of cheesecloth. Squeeze herbs well to extract as much of the fluids as possible. Discard herbs and bottle the tincture. Dosage varies, depending on which herb is used. For sundew, 3 to 6 drops in a cup of water is maximum dosage.

*NOTE: Cider vinegar can be used in place of brandy. Use vinegar tinctures for babies, alcoholics, and any person with a liver problem. Vinegar tinctures, however, have a shorter shelf life. They maintain potency for 1 to 2 years as opposed to 30 to 40 years for an alcohol tincture.

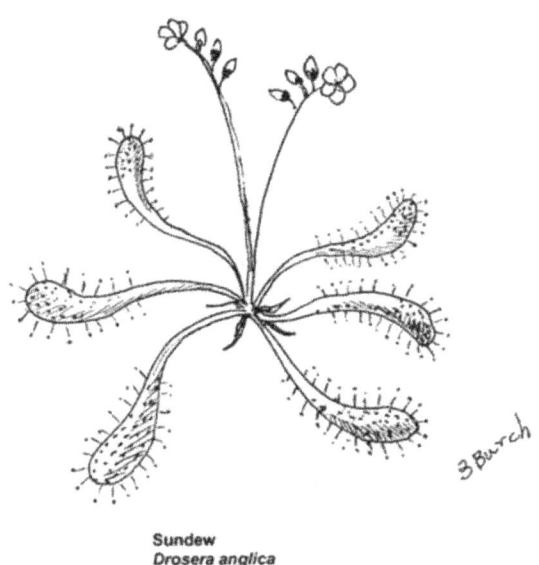

Sundew
Drosera anglica

THE PLANTS, BY HABITAT | 83

SWEET GALE, Bog Myrtle
WAX MYRTLE FAMILY
Myrica gale

Description: Sweet gale is a shrub with leaves that fall off in winter. Its reddish branches grow almost vertically to 3 feet tall. The alternate, gray-green, oblong leaves have a few small teeth toward the end. This leaf is dotted with bright yellow wax glands that show whitish underneath.

Crumple a leaf in your hand and smell the fragrant, pungent odor that remains on your skin. This odor, reminiscent of its bayberry relative, accounts for the "sweet" part of its name.

Sweet gale flowers form in greenish-yellow waxy catkins. Male and female flowers are borne on separate plants. Male catkins grow to twice the size of their female counterparts, which can be as long as 1 cm. These catkins appear before the leaves.

The fruits are tiny, greenish, winged nutlets that form in brown, cone-like spikes. They are about 3 mm long and may have wax glands. They stay on the plant all winter.

Habitat: Sweet gale is commonly found in bogs.

Edible Parts: Leaves and berries can be dried and used in small amounts as seasoning. Fresh leaves also make a tea that blends well with other herbal ingredients.

Ways to Prepare for Eating: A small amount of dried leaves or berries can be used as seasoning in meat dishes. Janice Schofield reports that Ed Berg of Homer, AK, suggests drying a supply of sweet gale leaves and using them in place of bay leaves. Another method of use is to dry and grind the leaves and use with wild game as a sage substitute. It seems to me that it would be the perfect pungent accompaniment for red meat dishes.

Sweet gale was popular at one time in northern Europe as a flavoring for beer.

To Complete the Meal:

Sea Lion Pot Roast
Rosemary Squartsoff

Over the years when we had regular "Plant Class" potlucks, Rosemary sometimes contributed this dish when it was her turn to bring the main course. It's a good, rich meal – I would employ the word "robust". Sweet gale is a good choice for seasoning such wild meats.

1 sea lion roast
Water
Salt
2 bay leaves (or 2 or 3 sweet gale leaves)
½ onion, chopped
2 cloves garlic
¼ pound bacon
Mustard

Cut meat into bite-size pieces and place in mixing bowl. Cover meat with water, salt, and bay leaves. Let soak about 16 hours, then drain and change water until it stays clear. Place meat in pot and cover with cold water. Bring to boil and remove blood as it forms. When blood stops coming to top, drain and reserve water and set meat aside. Saute onion, garlic, and bacon over medium heat, stirring often, until tender. Add ½ to 1 cup reserved water to pan; add meat. Simmer, stirring often, from ½ to 1 hour, until done. Serve hot with mustard.

Uses in Native and Traditional Folk Medicine

The leaves were boiled into a tea and given by some Native Alaskans to aid tuberculosis sufferers. The tea was also reported to be good as a wash for boils and pimples. At one time the tea was applied externally to treat scabies.

Other Uses: A sweet gale branch can serve as a steam bath switch.

The dried, crushed leaves can be scattered in an infested area to repel and destroy insects such as fleas. A safe, non-chemical flea collar can be made by sewing a liberal quantity of the crushed leaves into a soft cloth strip and putting this collar on your pet.

The leaves can also be crushed for a sachet, or scattered in the bottom of bureau drawers to give contents a pleasant smell.

Sweet gale berries contain myrtle or myrica wax, which is similar to that contained in the berries of its wax myrtle or bayberry relatives. This wax can be added as scent to homemade candles.

Dye can be made from this plant. The roots and stem bark dye wool yellow; the leaves make a golden yellow, warm yellow-brown, or cool yellow-green dye.

Sweet Gale
Myrica gale

INDEX

Arnica *(Arnica* spp. – four found in Kodiak area)
Cottonwood *(Populus balsamifera)*
Death Camus *(Zygadenus elegans)*
Geum *(Geum macrophyllum – Avens)*
Goldenrod *(Solidago multiradiata; S. lepida)*
Indian Rice *(Fritillaria camschatcensis)*
Iris *(Iris setosa)*
Monkshood *(Aconitum delphinifolium)*
Nagoonberry *(Rubus arcticus)*
Narcissus-Flowered Anemone *(Anemone narcissiflora)*
Nootka Lupine *(Lupinus nootkatensis)*
Wild Chives *(Allium schoenoprasum)*
Wild Geranium *(Geranium erianthum)*
Yarrow *(Achillea borealis)*

GRASSY MEADOWS AND FOREST CLEARINGS

Arnica
Arnica **species**

ARNICA, Leopard's Bane
COMPOSITE FAMILY
Arnica spp.
(Four in Kodiak area)

Description: Arnica is a yellow composite flower with <u>opposite</u> leaves. Three of the species found in the Kodiak area, *A. frigida*, *A. lessingii*, and *A. alpina*, start from a flat rosette, out of which rises a stalk. *A. amplexicaulis* does not start from a rosette. *Arnica* species can be from 6 inches to about 2 ½ feet high; all have yellow ray flowers (similar to a daisy).

Our common *A. lessingii* blooms late and nods slightly. *A. alpina*, which has the same properties as *A. montana*, referred to in so many herb books, has narrower, sometimes hairy leaves.

According to Eric Hulten (1968), *A. lessengii* is the arnica most abundant on Kodiak Island. Second place goes to *A. amplexicaulis*. *A. frigida* is the most common species over most of Alaska, while *A. alpina* is found in the more Northern areas.

Habitat: Arnica is commonly found in sunny meadows. However, on Kodiak Island our favorite field of arnica grows in the gentler light of a stand of cottonwood trees. Arnica's habitat ranges from moist sunny meadows to stony slopes.

Uses in Native and Traditional Folk Medicine

Herbal sources tell us that any arnica species found in your area can be gathered for use, though *A. montana* is the species they mention most often. In North America, the arnica flower is the part of the plant that is most commonly used.

CAUTION: Use for <u>external</u> treatment only! This herb is recommended by traditional healers as a remedy for bruising, sprains, and overworked or pulled muscles. However, it should be applied to unbroken skin only. Arnica contains several substances that can alter cardiovascular activity. These irritants can cause severe reactions that can result in death. The FDA lists the plant as unsafe, and bans the herb for human consumption. DO NOT USE INTERNALLY!

The arnica-iris oil recipe included here has been used as an aid in reducing swelling and discoloration from bruising. However, do not use this oil on or near cuts or open wounds. Also, do not use if you have a tendency for allergic skin reactions.

Other Uses: Arnica flower decoctions can be added to a footbath to relieve swelling or sore, achy feet. Arnica flowers may be blended with other herbs in shampoos and rinses, as the plant is said to promote hair growth.

Arnica-Iris Oil

To make infused or scented oil, one follows a process similar to making a tincture. The basic instructions for this oil can be used for other herbal or floral combinations that you may wish to try.

> You will need:
> Equal quantities of dried iris flowers and dried arnica flowers
> Oil (such as almond oil, or use your favorite kind)
> Clear glass jar and cheesecloth
> Liquid vitamin E

Crush dried flowers well, using a mortar and pestle. Fill the clear glass jar with equal portions of these crushed dried iris and arnica flowers. Pour in oil until flowers are completely covered. Close the jar; shake vigorously. Place the jar in a warm and sunny location (opposite from making a tincture) and shake well, morning and evening, for 2 to 6 weeks. Strain the herbs through cheesecloth and squeeze out all the oil. Add a few drops of vitamin E, as it will help preserve the infusion. Pour the infused arnica-iris oil into dark glass bottles, label, store, and enjoy!

Herbalists use this oil to relieve discomfort from bruising, sprains, arthritis and muscle pain. They claim it is also useful for skin irritations, so long as there is no open sore.

CAUTION: If you are prone to allergic reactions do not try this oil.

COTTONWOOD, Balsam Poplar
WILLOW FAMILY
Populus balsamifera
Ciquq (Aleut)

Description: The cottonwood, or balsam poplar, is a medium-sized tree, growing from 60 to 80 feet in height, with a trunk diameter of 1 to 3 feet. This tree grows rapidly, spreads extensively from the roots, and often occurs with others of its species as companions. It is easily transplanted and can be propagated from cuttings.

Young and old species are at times mistaken for distinct species due to the difference in their appearance. In youth, this tree, up to 40 or 50 feet tall, has a symmetrical form, with stout branches pointing upward. With age and full growth, cottonwood's limbs become very thick, irregular, and crooked, and turn to point downward. The top flattens as the higher limbs break.

Young trees have smooth, green bark. Furrows increase with age. The bark of mature trees has dark gray ridges with deep furrows.

Cottonwood leaves are alternate, deciduous and roughly oval, with a rounded to heart-shaped base and sharply pointed tip. The leaf margin is finely round-toothed. Leaves are yellowish-green on top and much lighter underneath.

In winter or early spring, brown, very resinous and fragrant buds form on the ends of branches. In spring, male and female catkins grow on separate trees. In summer the capsules containing seeds split and burst open in a cottony mass. Bits of this cotton float through the air, seeking new places to grow. This fluffy, white cotton-like material, which is actually made up of a dense mass of white silky hairs, gives cottonwood its name.

Habitat: Cottonwoods like to grow in open meadow areas and moist soils.

Edible Parts: Various Native groups scraped off the sweet inner bark in the spring, dipped it in grease, and ate it. This cambium layer may also be boiled, or dried and ground for a flour substitute.

Uses in Native and Traditional Folk Medicine

Native healers crushed the leaves to apply as an antiseptic. For a sore throat, they boiled the bark and gargled the liquid. The bark was also ground into a drying powder for sores.

Janice Schofield tells us to collect the cottonwood buds from winter to spring to make Balm of Gilead, reputed to be an excellent skin salve (see recipe). These buds are best gathered when the temperature is around freezing, as they are less sticky. She says that the buds can also be boiled into a decoction for colds and flu, headaches, hangovers, and stomachache.

Cottonwood
Populus balsamifera

Cottonwood, like willow, its cousin, contains the "natural aspirin" glycosides salicin and populin, which are helpful in reducing pain and inflammation. A powerful tincture can be made from the inner bark from the cottonwood tree. This tincture has been used for colds and flu, headache, or hangover.

Other Uses: Because cottonwood is a relatively soft, porous wood, it is excellent to burn for smoking fish. It often gives off more smoke than fire. Because it likes wet places, it is a good indicator that water is nearby. Talented carvers in our area carve the thick outer bark into masks or other artwork. In other areas of the country, cottonwood is being farmed for paper production.

Balm of Gilead

From Janice Schofield's book comes this recipe for the well-known "Balm of Gilead". Janice says that this salve can be used for piles, burns, cuts, diaper rash, and assorted skin irritations. Place a dab inside the nose for nasal congestion, or boil 1 tablespoon in water and inhale the vapors. Use the salve on horse saddle sores and animal wounds.

1 cup balsam poplar (cottonwood) buds
1 ½ cups lard (Oil and beeswax may be substituted for the lard)
1 dropper liquid vitamin E

Boil buds and lard in top of double boiler. Heat (covered) over boiling water for 2 hours, then strain and squeeze through a muslin cloth. Return strained oil to pan; add vitamin E; stir well. Pour into containers, cool, and cap.

DEATH CAMAS
LILY FAMILY
Zygadenus elegans

POISONOUS!

Description: This lily family member is a perennial growing from an onion-like bulb. Its long, grass-like leaves clasp the stem. The stem itself is smooth and grows from 1 to 2 feet tall. The greenish white flowers grow in a long cluster at the top of the stem. Each flower has 3 petals. This plant does not have a distinctive odor. (Note the way in which the flowers of this plant differ from the similar wild chives, whose blossom is a rose-purple head, or umbel.)

Habitat: Death camas likes open, dry areas such as meadows, roadsides, and forest edges.

This plant has not been found in the Kodiak area, but, because it is poisonous, is included for the benefit of other Alaskans who may be using this book.

Poisonous Parts and Conditions of Poisoning: All parts of the plant contain a poison similar to that contained in false hellebore (see also). The poison affects the nervous system. Symptoms are salivating and nausea, vomiting, lowered body temperature, abdominal pain and diarrhea, difficulty in breathing, and coma.

When not in bloom, death camas might be mistaken for wild onion. Smell it first – if it doesn't smell like an onion, don't pick it!

Death Camas
Zygadenus elegans

THE PLANTS, BY HABITAT

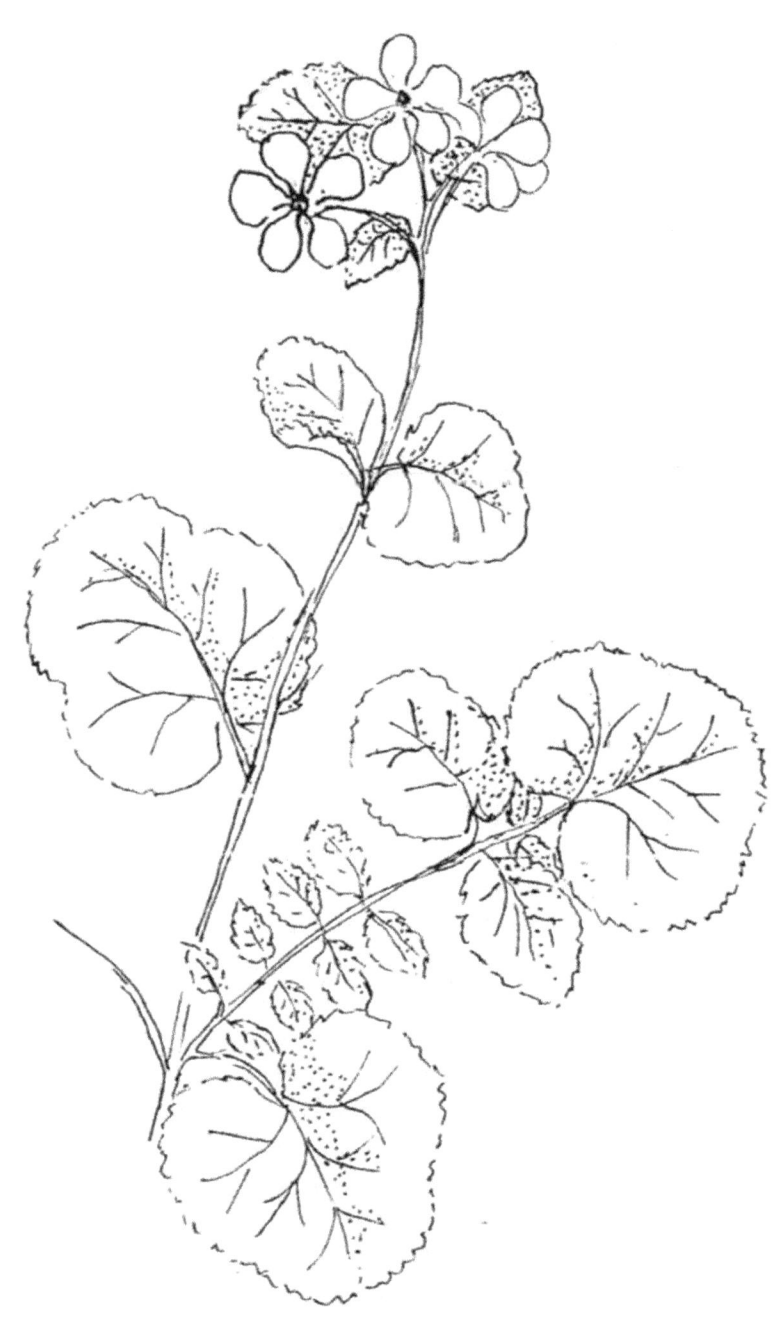

Geum
Geum macrophyllum

GEUM
ROSE FAMILY
Geum macrophyllum (Avens)

Description: *Geum* is a perennial herb with a stout, thick root. The first part of the plant to appear in spring is a rosette of many-leaved stems. Closest to the ground, small, opposite leaves grow on the stems of the rosette. A series of opposite leaves, each pair a bit larger than those below, grow along the stem. A large leaf with 3 lobes (curved or rounded parts) grows at the upper end. The leaves are fuzzy and the stems are hairy. As summer progresses, a stem, or stems with several branches, grow upward from the center of the plant. These have fewer leaves. Small, deep-yellow flowers appear at the stem ends. Round green seed balls that turn a brownish color with age later replace these flowers.

The botanical name, *Geum,* comes from a Greek word meaning, "to produce an agreeable scent." This refers to the aromatic roots. The dried rhizome (underground stem) of *Geum* was once used as a clove substitute.

Habitat: This plant grows in meadows, thickets, and wooded areas where the soil is moist and rich in nitrogen.

Uses in Native and Traditional Folk Medicine

The dried rhizome, fresh flowering plant, or the leaves alone have been used medicinally. Herbalists have brewed the plant into a bitter tonic used to increase the appetite after an illness or to help stop diarrhea. The tonic was also used as a gargle to soothe sore gums or to get rid of bad breath. This tonic was made by boiling one ounce of the fresh plant in a pint of water. Suggested dosage was to drink this tea cold, a small glassful daily.

People in the villages in our area have used *Geum* leaves as a pack for aches and sprains and pulled muscles. A local friend remembers using *Geum* for such a purpose. She says to put the fresh leaves in hot water, and then put them on the sore spot. They can be wrapped in a thin layer of cheesecloth first, if desired. Then wet a rag with very hot water and wring it out hard. Put it around the leaves. The moisture and heat will soak the beneficial substances out of the leaves and into the sore area.

Goldenrod
Solidago multiradiata

GOLDENROD, Woundwort
COMPOSITE FAMILY
Solidago multiradiata
Solidago lepida
Zholti golovnik (Russian)

Description: Goldenrod is a perennial that can grow up to 3 feet tall. Its stem has only a few branches close to the main stalk, or, sometimes, only a single stem. Goldenrod leaves are alternate, and smaller toward the top of the plant. Golden-yellow flowers cluster on the top section of the stem.

Habitat: This plant grows in dry, open areas, such as treeless hillsides.

Edible Parts: Dried leaves and flowers, either alone or blended with other ingredients, make an aromatic tea. Goldenrod can be mixed with other medicinal herbs to help improve their flavor.

Uses in Native and Traditional Folk Medicine

Leaves and flowers can be steeped in a tea that is said to act as a stimulant and helps get rid of gas (drink cold). Herbalists give goldenrod the distinction of being the number one herb for kidney problems, as it is said to help with the passing of stones. They recommend taking it as a tea in daily doses for a kidney cleanse. As it acts as an astringent, it is said to be useful for controlling internal hemorrhaging or diarrhea. For this purpose, healers recommend infusing 1 ounce flowering tops in ½ cup water, steeping for 5 minutes, and then drinking 1 cup daily, made fresh each time.

Fresh leaves and flowering tops can be crushed and placed on cuts, sores, or insect bites.

Other Uses: Stems and flowers can be picked for a steam bath switch. They may also be used as a hair rinse for blond hair. The flowers can be boiled to make a yellow-gold dye.

> During the crusades, goldenrod was frequently carried into battle as a wound-healing herb, giving rise to its common name of "woundwort". The botanical name, *Solidago,* means, "to make whole".

Spruce Island Goldenrod Tea

Combine 1 heaping teaspoon each of dried rose petals and dried spearmint or peppermint. Add 2 teaspoons dried goldenrod leaves and flowers. Steep in 4 cups boiling water for 5 minutes and serve. Add honey if desired.

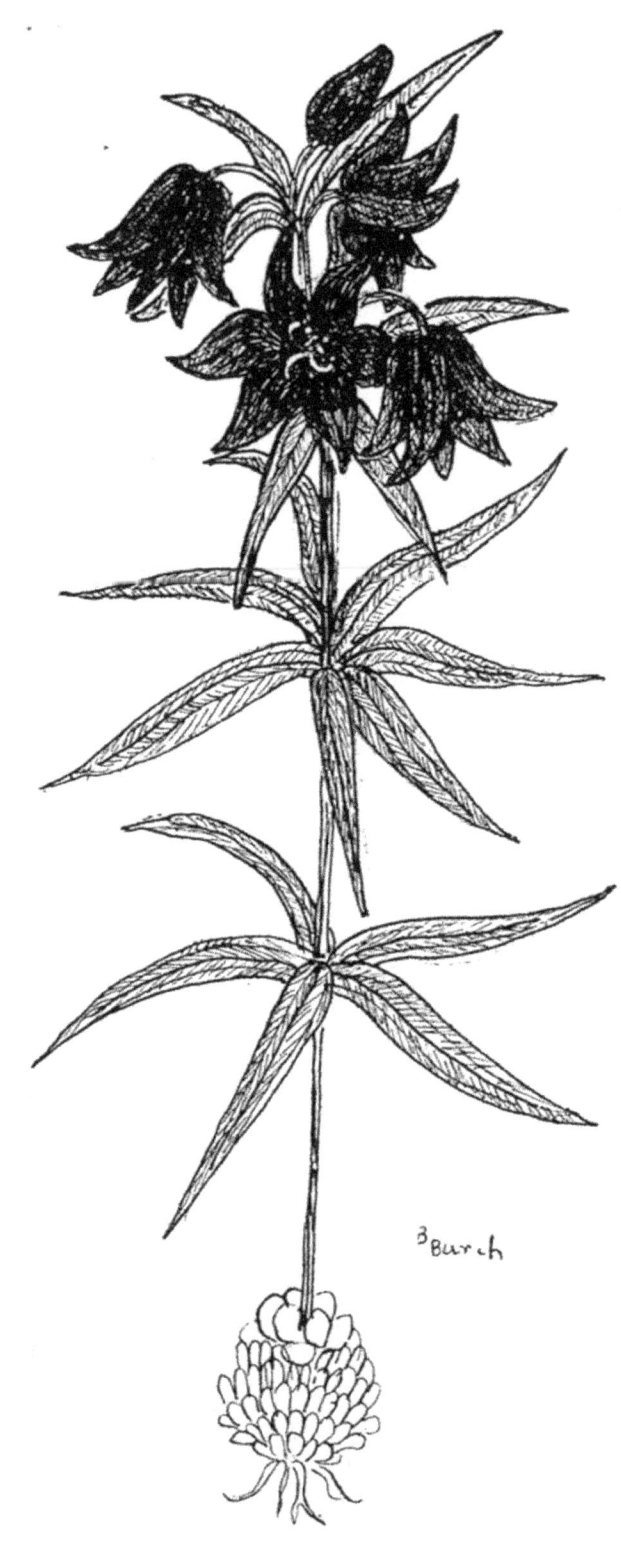

Chocolate Lily
Fritillaria camschatcensis

INDIAN RICE, Chocolate Lily, Kamchatka Lily, Riceroot
LILY FAMILY
Fritillaria camschatcensis
Laaqaq (Aleut)
Sarana (Russian)

Description: Indian rice is a perennial that grows from a bulb with many ricelike bulblets attached to it. Its single stem reaches 1 to 2 feet tall. The leaves circle around the stem (grow in whorls) in 2 or 3 places. These leaves have parallel veins. There may be 1 to 6 large, nodding, bell-like flowers. The flowers are dark purple-brown to nearly black.

If you smell this flower you won't forget it, because it has a very disagreeable odor. Some of our class members have nicknamed it the "toe-jam flower". Some of its common names describe the odor.

Habitat: The chocolate lily is found in open coastal meadows.

Edible Parts and Nutritional Value: The bulblets can be eaten as a carbohydrate.

Ways to Prepare for Eating: Dig Indian rice in the autumn. It is said to have better flavor later in the season. Break up the bulbs and soak bulblets in water overnight to help rid them of any bitter taste. They can be eaten raw with fish eggs.

If you wish to harvest this plant, survey the area where it is found well ahead of the fall harvest. Sometimes you can find the plant in the fall by finding the stalk with its seedpods. Sometimes the plant will be indistinguishable at the time of harvest. I have considered tying a colored string to the stalk in late summer so I could find it later.

To cook, boil the soaked bulblets like rice until they are soft. A little lemon juice added to the water helps remove bitterness. Try them in stir-fry dishes or in casseroles as a rice substitute. Mix them with oil and add to soup or stew, or steam and top with garlic butter or spaghetti sauce. The cooked bulblets are also good seasoned with tart berries such as raspberries.

For winter use, dry the bulblets and cook them in fish or meat stew later on, or pound them into flour.

Uses in Native and Traditional Folk Medicine

Jenny Chernikoff was taught that Indian rice was good for stomach problems. She said you ate it to aid digestion.

> **Jenny:** Here's the chocolate lily. You can eat them; cook the bottoms. They're most delicious! Make sure you have that middle part.
> **Sasha:** She means that little wild rice that's on the bottom.
> **Jenny:** And then, don't take off the little ones, and cook it.
> **Sasha:** You cook them like potatoes.
> **Jenny:** You can season it any way you want to…best when you put berries with it…ahh, wild raspberries…oh, that's delicious…

Indian Rice a la Russ

Russ Mohney

(from *Root, Stem and Leaf* by Glen Ray)

> 3 cups Indian rice
> 3 tablespoons butter
> ½ cup chopped onion
> ½ cup chopped celery Mushrooms (optional)
> 1 cup leftover cooked pork, finely chopped
> 2 teaspoons soy sauce

Boil the Indian rice until it just begins to soften. Drain and set aside. In a large skillet, sauté the onion and celery in butter until transparent (the addition of a few sliced mushrooms at this stage doesn't hurt a bit). Stir in the cooked Indian rice and pork. Keep turning the mixture as you would fried rice until the Indian rice begins to brown in the butter. Add the soy sauce, stir well, cover, and lower the heat. Turn the Indian rice mixture occasionally until quite soft. Serves 6.

To Complete the Meal:

Duck Soup

Sasha Smith

Try some wild rice bulblets in this Spruce Island favorite, a popular dish among Native duck hunters.

> 2 medium ducks, cut up
> 2 potatoes, diced
> 3 carrots, diced
> ½ cup rice
> Salt
> Pepper

Cover the duck pieces with water and simmer for 2 hours on slow heat. Add potatoes, carrots and rice; cook for 40 minutes longer. Season with salt and pepper.

IRIS, Wild Flag
IRIS FAMILY
Iris setosa

POISONOUS!

Description: The iris, or wild flag, is a perennial that grows to 30 inches tall. The plant has long, wide-bladed, grass-like leaves. It has a roundish, stout stem. Large flowers at the top of the stems are blue or purple, shading to white centers. Sometimes white blossoms are found, though these are rare. Iris flower parts are in groups of 3: Three petal-like, drooping sepals, 3 small and upright petals and 3 stamens. The seeds are carried in capsules.

Habitat: Iris grows in meadows and bogs and along streams.

Poisonous Parts and Conditions of Poisoning: The whole plant is poisonous and causes vomiting if eaten. There are various known medicinal uses, but these are dangerous to try unless you are an expert.

Uses in Native and Traditional Folk Medicine

Herbalists have used the rhizome from the root of the iris for centuries as a medicinal. One species, given the common name of "orris root", was widely prescribed by herbal healers. These rootstalks were boiled in water, mashed between two rocks and used as a poultice. It was reported to be very effective in reducing swelling and color in bruises. It was also used to treat staph infections.

The wild flag rhizome is also used to make a tincture, taken in <u>extremely</u> small doses for lymphatic swelling. Overdoses can cause diarrhea and vomiting.

CAUTION: Wild iris contains *iridin*, which is an oleoresin. This substance has a strong impact on liver and digestive organs. If you wish to try the rhizome as a tincture, see a Naturopath! Don't self-medicate internally with iris!

If you tend toward allergies, don't try iris at all, as it can cause strong allergic reactions, such as severe rashes.

Other Uses: As the toxicity in the plants is inconsistent, it is safer to enjoy this plant for its beautiful flowers and refrain from other uses. Perhaps the most notable exception is its use by traditional healers in combination

Iris
Iris setosa

THE PLANTS, BY HABITAT

with arnica as an herbal oil to relieve bruises. Use 2 cups dry iris flowers and 2 cups dry arnica (see arnica for recipe.)

Iris flowers produce a violet blue dye when used with a chrome mordant. Rhizomes may be used to produce black hues when used with ferrous sulfate as a mordant.

The iris transplants well, and makes a lovely addition to your wildflower garden. Transplant in spring before flowers appear.

These flowers were considered weather omens in local folklore. Sasha Smith remembers being told when she was little that it would rain if she picked wild iris flowers. This admonishment was probably intended to keep young children from picking all the beautiful flowers, and may have had nothing to do with rain!

MONKSHOOD
CROWFOOT FAMILY
Aconitum delphinifolium

<u>POISONOUS!</u>

Description: Monkshood is a perennial. It has a straight, thin stem that grows to 40 inches tall. Its few alternate leaves, separated into five toothed "fingers", look a little like delphinium leaves. A few dark blue flowers grow at the top of a branching stem. The flower blossoms have a rounded hood. Occasionally one can find monkshood with white blossoms. This is a very beautiful flowering plant. It makes a great addition to your flowerbed, so long as you are aware that it is deadly poisonous.

Habitat: Monkshood grows in meadows, thickets, and along creeks.

I have found monkshood growing wild once on Spruce Island. It was growing near a meadow, but just at the edge of the forest, shaded by a large spruce tree.

Poisonous Parts and Conditions of Poisoning: The whole plant, including roots, is *extremely poisonous*. (Roots are the most dangerous part!) Monkshood contains an alkaloid, aconitine. This alkaloid paralyzes the nerves and lowers the body temperature and blood pressure. As few as 3 grains of the root are sufficient to kill an adult. For treatment, induce vomiting and immediately seek medical attention. Keep the patient lying down and covered.

Eskimos used to put poison obtained from this plant on the tips of their spears for killing whales. Though the poison affects the nervous system, it does not invade the meat.

Monkshood
Aconitum delphinifolium

Nagoonberry
Rubus arcticus

NAGOONBERRY, Wild Raspberry, Wineberry
ROSE FAMILY
Rubus arcticus
Puyurniq (Aleut)

Description: Locally known as wild raspberry, the nagoonberry is a low perennial plant.

Its erect stems are less than 6 inches tall. Its leaves resemble those of the strawberry: they are divided into 3 leaflets with coarsely toothed edges. The flowers, dark rose to red, are followed by berries made up of numerous small, juicy ovals. These berries look like raspberries.

Habitat: Nagoonberries grow in damp, wet, open woods or hillsides.

Edible Parts and Nutritional Value: Young peeled sprouts and, of course, the berries can be eaten. The fresh fruit, an extremely rich source of vitamin C, retains its high vitamin content if frozen immediately after picking.

Ways to Prepare for Eating: Gather these berries in late summer. When found in sufficient quantity, the berries make an excellent jelly. They are also good in wines and cordials. Make a nonalcoholic beverage by letting the ripe fruit stand in vinegar for 1 month, then straining out the juice. Dilute with water and ice, sweeten to taste, and serve on a hot day.

Uses in Native and Traditional Folk Medicine

This berry is another of those purported to be high in antioxidants, and thus effective in destroying dangerous free radicals in the body.

Nagoonberry Jelly
Cooperative Extension Service,
Wild Berry Recipes

If you gather enough of these small, tasty berries for a batch of jelly, you might find yourself a very popular person at afternoon teatime. Be sure to serve homemade bread with some of your nagoonberry jelly!

> 5 ¾ cups nagoonberry juice
> ¼ cup lemon juice
> 6 cups sugar
> ½ bottle liquid pectin

Bring nagoonberry juice, lemon juice, and sugar to a boil (if some green berries are used, increase the sugar by 1 cup). Add liquid pectin. Bring to a full rolling boil and cook for 1 minute. Pour into hot, sterilized jars and seal with paraffin and lids.

NARCISSUS-FLOWERED ANEMONE, My Darlings
CROWFOOT FAMILY
Anemone narcissiora

POISONOUS!

Description: This plant is a perennial with silky, hairy stems that grow up to 2 feet tall. The leaves, attached with long stalks, sprout mostly from the stem base. A few leaves grow higher on the stem, just below the flower clusters, and completely surround the stem. The silky, hairy leaves are 1 to 5 inches long with many divisions. Flower clusters have white petals, often with a blue tint on the back.

Jenny Chernikoff told me that their name for this plant when she was growing up was "my darlings".

Habitat: Anemones are found in open meadows and on hillsides.

Poisonous Parts and Conditions of Poisoning: It is said that people in the Aleutian Islands sometimes ate the early spring growth at the top of the root of this plant. However, we do not recommend eating it. This is a highly poisonous plant containing anemonin. The plant often causes sickness in animals that feed on it. The poison in the plant does not break down with cooking.

I have transplanted the anemone to a moss bed in my yard successfully. It is attractive as an early bloom and an interesting green plant later in the season, but not recommended for the dinner table.

Narcissus-flowered Anemone
Anemone narcissiflora

NOOTKA LUPINE
PEA FAMILY
Lupinus nootkatensis
Kakoriki (Russian)

POISONOUS!

Description: The lupine is a perennial. It has a long taproot and stems up to 3 ½ feet tall, with many branches. The leaves are alternate, each having 6 to 8 leaflets that radiate out from a center. The leaflets are blunt-tipped, silky, and hairy. Flowers form at the plant top in dense clusters up to 10 inches long. They have up to 5 petals. Usually blue, flowers are often shaded pink or white and are occasionally all white. The fruit is a black, hairy pod, 1 to 1 ½ inches long.

Habitat: Lupines like hillsides, open areas, and gravel bars.

This showy plant may also be found in disturbed soil. One summer I witnessed an incredible sight: A thick bed of lupine about 5 feet tall and all in full bloom, growing in a wide strip in the gravelly soil along both sides of the length of a deserted runway near Chiniak, on Kodiak Island.

Poisonous Parts and Conditions of Poisoning: The pea family absorbs selenium from the soil, making the plant poisonous, though no one seems sure how much selenium is in Alaskan soil. However, the seeds in the pea-pod fruits are the most poisonous part of the plant, so must not be eaten. Cows and sheep have been poisoned by consuming large amounts of these pods and seeds. If the animal consumes only a small amount, its system can flush out the toxins, as the poisoning is not cumulative. However, the lupine, like its relative, locoweed, can cause serious problems for the cow or sheep that overgrazes on the pea-like pods.

Our references disagree on the poisonous properties of this plant, as selenium levels in the soil remain questionable. It is said that the Aleuts used to gather the roots in the fall, scrape off the skin, and eat the inner portion. However, as lupines can contain alkaloids that cause fatal inflammation of the stomach and intestines, it is better not to try eating these plants at all.

Nootka Lupine
Lupinus nootkatensis

Other Uses: Lupine is a plant with showy racemes of flower blossoms. Thus the plant makes an extremely attractive addition to the garden. Be aware, however, that this plant is fussy about being transplanted. I have tried to move full-grown plants unsuccessfully. To transplant lupines, gather seeds in the fall or plant from root divisions.

Lupines are among the first plants to appear after glaciers recede. These herbs are good for the soil, being nitrogen-fixers. They help to prepare the ground for the plants that follow.

Wild Chives
Allium schoenoprasum

WILD CHIVES, Wild Onions
LILY FAMILY
Allium schoenoprasum

Description: This plant is smaller than the domestic onion, but it looks, smells, and tastes like onion. Its leaves are round and hollow, much like those of the domestic onion. The plant forms a rose-purple cluster, or head, of flowers in the latter part of summer. **NOTE:** Flowers of wild chive or wild onion form into heads, or umbels, while death camas flowers grow in upright clusters or racemes.

CAUTION: Don't eat any plant looking like wild onion unless it smells like onion. You might have an extremely poisonous plant by mistake (see death camas). The smell test is probably the easiest identity test. The wild chive or wild onion (both *Allium* species) smell strongly of onion when leaves are bruised. Death camas (*Zygadenus*) lacks a distinctive scent.

Habitat: These wild edibles are found in low meadows and pastures.

Edible Parts: Leaves and bulbs can be eaten.

Ways to Prepare for Eating: Cut up leaves as seasoning. Try in salads, stews, or casseroles. Start collecting leaves in early spring. Try snipping the leaves and adding to sour cream or cream cheese mixes for a zesty flavor. Be an original thinker here, and replace onions, raw or cooked, in your favorite recipes, with this wild cousin.

Bulbs can be harvested in late summer or early autumn. They have a strong flavor, so use only a small amount in place of domestic onions.

To store: Chop leaves. In a container put a layer of salt and a layer of greens, alternating until the container is full. Cover and store in a cool place. Or, chop the leaves fine with scissors, dry thoroughly, and store in spice bottles.

Clam Chowder
Sasha Smith

4 cups fresh clams, minced
2 whole potatoes, diced
1 onion, diced, and/or generous snippings from wild chives
3 slices bacon, diced and fried
Salt
1 cup milk

Combine all ingredients except milk in a saucepan. Cover with water and bring to a boil. Boil 20 minutes and add milk; do not boil after adding milk. Heat well and serve.

Wild Geranium
Geranium erianthum

WILD GERANIUM, American Cranebill
GERANIUM FAMILY
Geranium erianthum
Igoria (Russian)

Description: Wild geranium is a perennial with palmate leaves, deeply divided into 3 to 5 irregularly toothed and lobed sections. It grows up to 30 inches tall. It has a 5-petaled rose purple flower. It has a seedpod that resembles a crane's bill before it pops open and scatters its seeds.

Habitat: Wild geranium is found along roads and trails, in the forests, and in high meadows.

Edible Parts: The leaves can be boiled for a tea. According to Janice Schofield, the flowers are also edible, and can serve as a garnish for salad. The young leaves can be used as a filler, mixed with other plants, but these leaves are not choice.

CAUTION: Make sure the leaves are from geranium and not monkshood, which is deadly poisonous and has a similar leaf. For use as food, gather when flowering.

Uses in Native and Traditional Folk Medicine

Native and local Alaskans prepared the leaves and the roots in the following ways:

Leaves: Used as tea to soothe stomach troubles, to give relief to tuberculosis sufferers, and to wash sore eyes. Wild geranium contains tannic acid, a good astringent.

Roots: Boil or soak roots in hot water. For sore throat, ulcers, or diarrhea, the recommended treatment was either to gargle with the tea or to drink it. It was also used as an aid to people with heart trouble.

This tea was sometimes given to new mothers and their babies as a tonic. The baby was given only a small amount.

For mouth sores or toothache, Native people would chew the raw root.

> Sometimes the knowledgeable old-timers can have a difference of opinion, as in this exchange between Sasha and Jenny:
>
> **Jenny:** Wild geranium is good for sore throat. You use the root. You wash them real good and use the root.
> **Sasha:** They say you scrape the brown part away from there a little bit.
> **Jenny:** Well, they claim that's the best part of it.
> **Sasha:** I suppose, as long as you wash them real good.
> **Jenny:** No, that's not poisonous. That's good for sore throat and chest cold and so forth.

YARROW, Milfoil
COMPOSITE FAMILY
Achillea borealis
Qangananguaq (Aleut)
Poleznaya trava (Russian)

Description: Yarrow is a hardy perennial with alternate, very feathery, slightly hairy grayish green leaves. Because of the many small parts of its leaves, yarrow is often known as milfoil, or thousand-leaves. One of the species names for yarrow, *millefolium,* also has the same meaning. The flowers, atop branched stems, are a flattened mass of tiny flowerets, either white or pale lilac.

Yarrow gets its generic name, *Achillea,* from the legend that soldiers in the army of the Greek hero, Achilles, used the plant to heal their wounds during the Trojan War.

Habitat: Yarrow can be found growing in almost any kind of soil.

Parts Used: Every part of the plant that grows above the ground can be used. Cut the whole plant when its flowers are in full bloom and dry it rapidly, at 90 to 100 degrees.

Uses in Native and Traditional Folk Medicine

Like dandelion, healers consider yarrow to be a good general tonic and a mild laxative. It is also recommended to help stimulate the flow of bile. The plant can be either boiled or steeped in hot water.

For a remedy for severe colds, I was taught to use yarrow in the following way: Make an infusion of 1 ounce dried yarrow to 1 pint boiling water. Steep 5 minutes. To a wineglass of this tea, add 1 teaspoon honey and 3 drops hot pepper sauce. Drink this dose 3 times a day. Stay covered after drinking the tea, as it will open the pores and cause heavy sweating.

The same tea is suggested for soothing menstrual cramps and slowing down extra-heavy menstrual flow. For stuffed up sinuses, boil the plant in water and breathe the steam.

Yarrow has long been used to help increase appetite, relieve stomach cramps and gas, and soothe gallbladder and liver problems. Kodiak people took it to combat asthma. It has also been taken to help stop internal hemorrhaging, especially in the lungs. Locally, the tea has been found to give relief from a hangover.

Yarrow
Achillea borealis

Water in which yarrow has been boiled is considered a good wash for sore eyes, skin irritations, chapped hands, and all kinds of wounds and sores. A hot pack of the cooked or raw wet leaves can be put on an ache or open sore as it is said to help healing and stop infection. A recommendation for easing a toothache is to chew the fresh leaves, or dip leaves in hot water, wrap in a cloth, and apply to the sore spot on the jaw.

Other Uses: A yarrow infusion can be applied as a hair rinse that is said to prevent baldness. The fresh plant can be rubbed on skin and clothes for a mosquito repellent.

Legend has it that Achilles' mother bathed him in a yarrow bath when he was an infant. The bath would supposedly protect him from any future injuries. However, she held on to his heel. A wound in his heel finally resulted in his death.

> My own experience is that yarrow is an excellent blood coagulant. I had a good chance to prove its efficacy on a camping trip with my son. We were camped at the very back of Big Lagoon, on the north side of Spruce Island. David cut his thumb and couldn't stop the bleeding. I picked some nearby yarrow leaves; dipped them in a pan of hot water that was cooling on our camp stove; wrapped the leaves around the cut. The bleeding stopped immediately.

INDEX

Alder *(Alnus crispa)*
Baneberry *(Actaea rubra)*
Burnet *(Sanguisorba stipulata)*
Buttercup *(Ranunculus* spp. – 9 species in Kodiak area)
Highbush Cranberry *(Viburnum edule)*
Mountain Sorrel *(Oxyria digyna)*
Poison Water Hemlock *(Cicuta douglasii; C. mackenzieana)*
Poque *(Boschniakia rossica)*
Roseroot *(Sedum rosea)*
Salmonberry *(Rubus spectabilis)*
Saxifrage *(Saxifraga punctata)*
    (6 species in Kodiak area)

Wild Alum *(Heuchera glabra)*
Wild Cucumber *(Streptopus amplexifolius)*
Wild Rose *(Rosa nutkana)*
Wild Violet *(Viola* spp.)
    (5 species in Kodiak area)
Willow *(Salix* spp.)
    (14 species in Kodiak area)

STREAM BANKS; MOIST, SUNNY HILLSIDES AND ROCKY PLACES

Alder
Alnus crispa

ALDER, Sitka Alder
BIRCH FAMILY
Alnus crispa, A. sinuata
Wainiik (Aleut) – Parts of bush or tree used in banya (steam bath)
Veyniki (Russian)

Description: The alder is usually not a big tree. In size it can range from a coarse shrub to a small tree, with a height ranging from 3 to 16 feet. Alder branches may be stout and long, but often they turn and twist every way but straight up. These low-lying branches form into thickets that are nearly impenetrable.

Alder leaves are alternate. The base of the leaf is rounded and the tip is pointed. The leaf edges are serrated. Touch the leaf underneath and you will find it is sticky. *A. crispa* ssp. *crispa* has oval leaves that are only occasionally lobed, while ssp. *sinuata* has leaves that are larger and broader, and more or less lobed. *A. crispa* ssp. *crispa* has grayish bark with dark spots, while ssp. *sinuata* bark is yellowish-brown and scaly. It is often a home for lichens.

Male and female parts of the alder grow on the same tree, and are easily recognizable. The male part is the drooping "catkin", which produces pollen. The female flower clusters, which look like small pinecones, are green and upright, and grow above the male catkins. These small cones turn brown late in the year. The clusters are oblong and less than 1 inch in length.

Habitat: Alder can be found in a variety of locations. It likes to take over an open hillside. It can often be found on the edges of the forest, with the spruce trees beginning just beyond its protective wall. It also grows in wet places, or close to standing or running water at low to middle elevations.

Edible Parts: The cambium, or inner layer of the bark, is edible.

Uses in Native and Traditional Folk Medicine

Native and traditional healers have used the inner bark for several purposes. They tell us to boil it in water and drink the tea to reduce high fever or to get rid of gas. This tea has also been taken as a gargle for sore throat or laryngitis. This same inner bark, boiled in vinegar, is said to be effective as a wash to kill lice or for other skin problems. Dried alder bark acts as an astringent.

Another local use for the female flower clusters, or cones, is to boil them into a tea and take in small quantities for relief from diarrhea. The new, green cones are used for this purpose in the spring.

Alder branches are cut for steam bath switches. Aleuts claim they give relief for arthritis and sore muscles.

It interests me how modern research finally catches up to ancient knowledge. In 1640, the herbalist Parkinson stated, "Leaves and bark of alder are cooling and drying. Fresh leaves laid on tumors will dissolve them." In 1973, the National Cancer Institute did a study of red alder (*A. oregona*) and found it contains two compounds, lupeol and betulin, that suppress tumor activity. (Red alder is not found in the Kodiak area, but in Southeast Alaska).

Other Uses: Alder wood is good for smoking fish or as a hot-burning firewood. When smoking fish, peel the outer bark from alder before burning the wood – this bark can cause an unpleasant aftertaste in the smoked fish.

Alder bark can be made into a brown dye. With mordant, ice green, orange, and gray-brown dye colors are possible. If red alder is accessible (in areas of Alaska other than Kodiak), a reddish dye can be made from the bark.

Alder is the first tree to grow back on a logged or burned area. It was the first tree to grow in Alaska after the glaciers retreated. It serves an important purpose in future plant development because it adds nitrogen to the soil.

> **Jenny C:** "You take the top of the bark of the ordinary alder and scrape it off. Take the inside of the bark (cambium layer) and scrape that until you get enough. Then you brew it. When you have sore throat or tonsillitis you gargle with it, and it will help you, lots. If you want to sweeten it a little bit, that's fine…"

BANEBERRY
CROWFOOT FAMILY
Actaea rubra

POISONOUS!

Description: Baneberry is a perennial with a thick root and stems that are smooth and somewhat hairy. These stems grow from 2 to 3 ½ feet tall. The leaves are large and their edges have several divisions and coarse teeth. Small white flowers cluster in a spike at the top of the stem. There are 4 to 10 small white petals on each flower. The berry is rounded and usually shiny red; rarely white. Inside are many seeds. These berries, about the size of a pea, are attached to the stem by a short, thick stalk. Each berry has a dark spot, giving rise to a common name of "doll's eyes". The berries are strikingly attractive to little children because they resemble small cherries.

Habitat: Baneberry grows in the woods and along the edges of moist streams.

Poisonous Parts and Conditions of Poisoning: This berry is the only deadly poisonous berry that is native to Alaska. Both the roots and the berries contain poison. It can cause increased pulse rate, dizziness, vomiting, bloody diarrhea, gas pains, burning in the stomach, and trouble breathing. Death can occur by cardiac arrest or respiratory paralysis. For treatment, induce vomiting and seek immediate medical attention.

Other Uses: Baneberry is a very attractive plant and may be used as an ornamental. Just don't eat it!

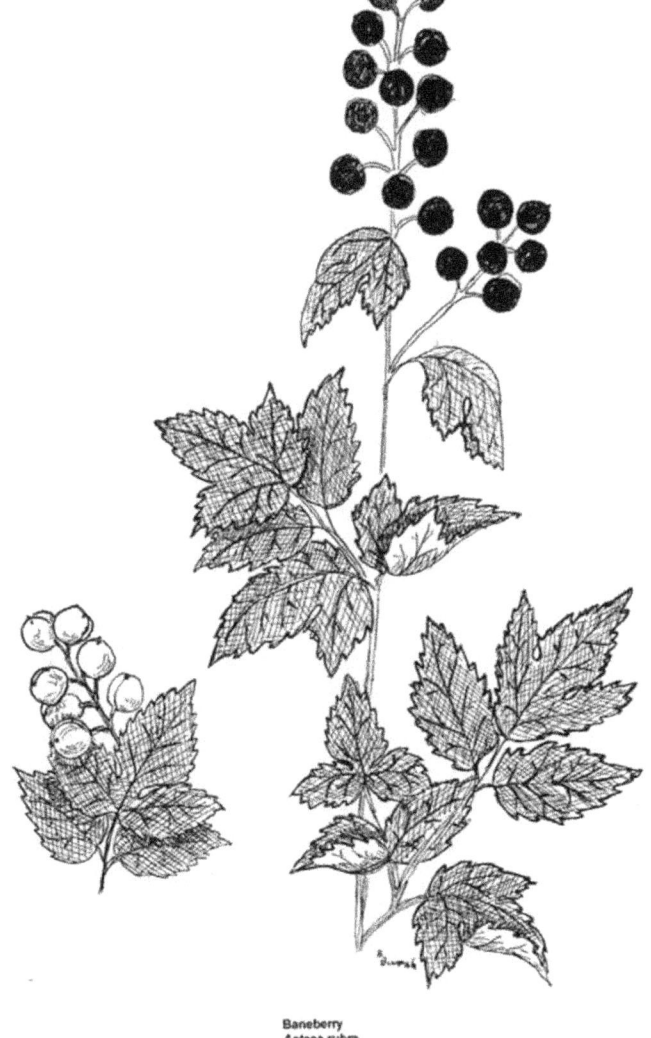

Baneberry
Actaea rubra

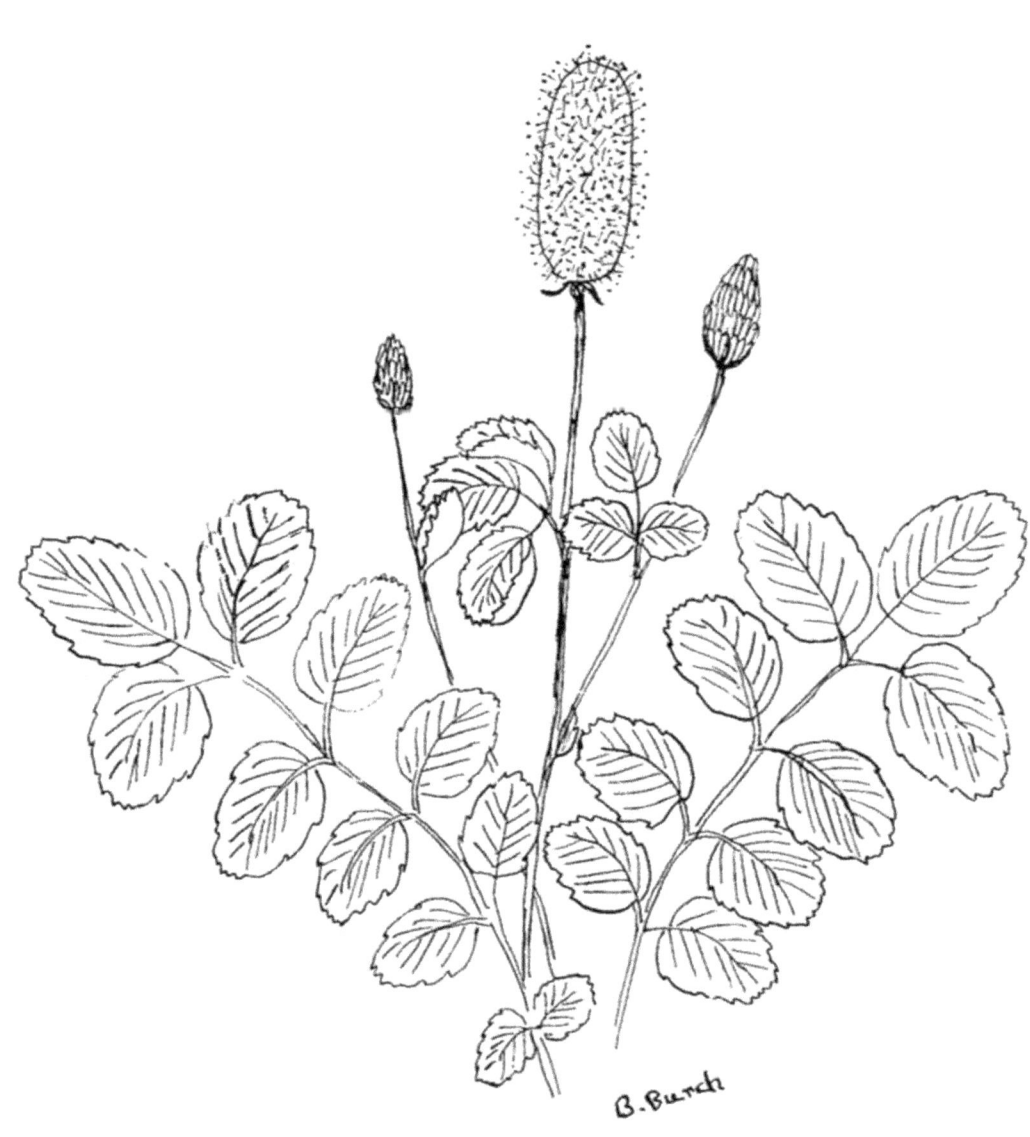

Burnet
Sanguisorba stipulata

BURNET
ROSE FAMILY
Sanguisorba stipulata

Description: Burnet is a perennial plant. Leaves, which are heavily serrated on the edges, are folded and fanlike when they first appear. Basal leaves are opposite and compound with 7 to 15 leaflets. The leaf stalk tends to have a slight downward curve at the top, as if the weight of the leaves causes it to bend slightly. These leaf stalks are the first part of the plant to appear. Later, the tall stem with its few leaves outgrows these basal leafy stems, and a greenish-white or yellowish-white spike of flowers appears at the top. (Some *Sanguisorba* species have reddish flower spikes.) The flower spike produces numerous small flowers with 5 greenish-white sepals, no petals, and many long stamens. To me, these fuzzy flowers resemble a bottlebrush. True to its rose family tradition, burnet has a very fragrant flower.

Habitat: Burnet likes wet places, and may be found in bogs, swamps, and stream banks. I have also found it in the rich soil at the edge of the forest, close to a roadway or path. For example, when one walks from Ouzinkie to Eskimo Cove on the way to my house, one finds it growing along the sunny roadside, close to the forest edge.

Edible Parts and Nutritional Value: In the spring, burnet leaves may be eaten, perhaps in a soup or casserole, or chopped and blended with other herbs as a seasoning. As an edible, this plant is not choice, but it can make a good flavor addition. Try using it in an herbal vinegar mix. Dried flowers and leaves may also be used in tea blends.

Uses in Native and Traditional Folk Medicine

Burnet's Latin name points to an important medicinal use. "Sanguis" means "blood", and "sorbeo" means "to staunch". Since ancient times, its roots, which are very astringent, have been used as a decoction to stop internal and external bleeding. This decoction can also serve as a mouthwash to heal the gums. Another traditional use is to dry and powder the root to sprinkle on cuts.

Burnet root decoctions have also been used for relief from dysentery or for genital discharges. The leaves, when made into tea, either alone or combined with other favorite herbs, are reported to be an effective spring tonic.

Other Uses: Because of its sweet scent, burnet is a welcome addition to the wild garden. It may be propagated by seed or by root division. Try adding the dried flowers to a potpourri.

Buttercup
Ranunculus species

BUTTERCUP
CROWFOOT FAMILY
Ranunculus spp.
(9 species found in Kodiak area)

POISONOUS!

Description: A perennial that grows from 6 inches to 2 feet tall, the buttercup is the first yellow flowering plant in the spring. The plant often has fine hairs. Leaves sprout at the plant's base and (sometimes sparsely) along the stem. The leaves have deep indentations or are made up of more than one part. They are often very dark green. The yellow flowers at the end of the stalk have five *shiny* petals.

Habitat: Buttercup grows in moist or wet soils in a variety of regions. The Latin name comes from a word meaning "frog," probably because many of these plants grow in standing water.

Though it likes wet soils, its habitat can vary. It is often found near people, or along road edges. In the late spring, the open hillside along the Ouzinkie boardwalk is a field of yellow buttercups.

Poisonous Parts and Conditions of Poisoning: All *Ranunculus* species contain a poison that will cause severe digestive problems. It is said that in some species cooking destroys the poison, but it is safer not to try eating them. (Marsh marigold is one exception, but be sure to follow cooking instructions carefully.)

Highbush Cranberry
Viburnum edule

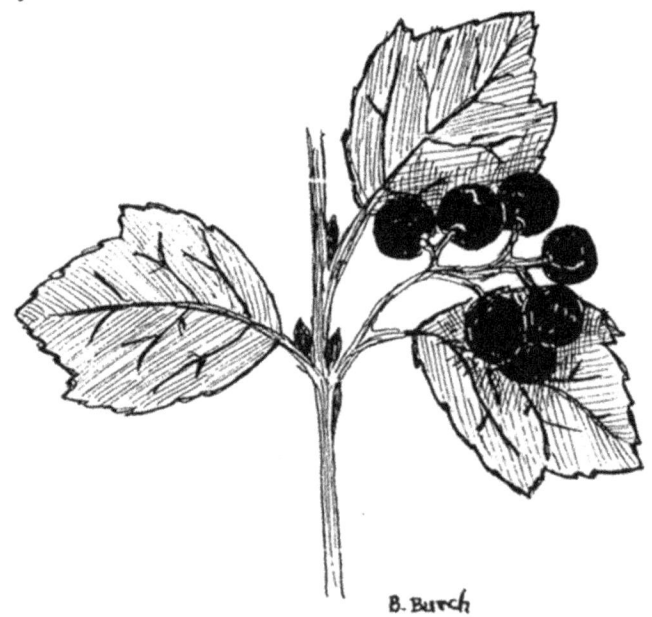

Highbush Cranberry
Viburnum edule

HIGHBUSH CRANBERRY, Crampbark
HONEYSUCKLE FAMILY
Viburnum edule
Amaryaq (Aleut)
Kalina (Russian)

Description: This tall shrub cousin of the elderberry, known as kalina in the Kodiak area, is easy to identify because of the plant's noticeable musty order – even jelly made from the berries has the scent. Often at berry-picking time, one can smell the highbush cranberry shrub before seeing it.

Kalina branches are slender, and can be 8 feet long. The leaves are opposite, have three shallow lobes, and are coarsely toothed and hairy underneath. The bark of this shrub is smooth and often reddish. Small white flowers cluster on short branches.

The red or orange berries grow in juicy clusters of two to five berries that are easily gathered. Each berry contains a single flat stone.

Habitat: This shrub grows from swamps to foothills. It is often found in meadows, open woods, and along stream banks.

Edible Parts and Nutritional Value: Kalina berries are edible and are very high in vitamin C.

Ways to Prepare for Eating: Though one of our class members claims, "it smells like dirty socks," kalina jelly is still a tasty treat. Besides the berries, the only other ingredients needed for jelly are sugar and water, as the fruit contains its own thickening agent.

These berries remain on the plant well into winter and can be harvested whenever found.

However, flavor is best if they are picked before the first heavy frost.

Uses in Native and Traditional Folk Medicine

Viburnum is known by herbalists as "crampbark", because of its purported usefulness for relief from menstrual or stomach cramps, or from asthma.

Traditional healers use the bark, pulp, and berries medicinally in the following ways:

Bark: The inner bark is boiled for a tea for stomach trouble. In the Kodiak area and elsewhere in Alaska the inner bark has been brewed into a gargle for colds, sore throat, and laryngitis. This is also taken for menstrual cramps and asthma.

Pulp: After boiling berries to get juice for jelly making, store the pulp in jars in a cool place to use for colds, sore throat, or laryngitis. Then take 2 large tablespoons in 1 cup of very hot water to help break up the cold. Thelma Anderson treated me in this way in Ouzinkie one winter night when I was ill. Not only is this kalina concoction a healthy vitamin C drink, but it is also a tasty one.

Berries: The berries were eaten uncooked for the same purposes. Raw or cooked, the berries have also been known as a remedy for tapeworms.

Tincture: A popular use is to prepare the inner bark alone or in combination with willow bark as a tincture for relief from cramps or to combat asthma.

Highbush Cranberry Jelly
Georgia Smith

One of Georgia's sons is to blame for claiming that kalinas smell like dirty socks. However, I have witnessed him eating a generous portion of this jelly!

4 cups ripe highbush cranberries
1 cup water
Sugar

Boil highbush cranberries and water for 3 to 5 minutes. When cool, strain through cheesecloth. Use ⅔ to ¾ cup sugar for each cup of juice. Boil approximately 10 minutes. Pour into hot, sterilized jars and seal with paraffin and lids.

MOUNTAIN SORREL, Sourgrass
BUCKWHEAT FAMILY
Oxyria digyna

Description: Mountain sorrel, a perennial, grows from a fleshy taproot. Its erect stems reach from 4 inches to 2 feet tall. There are 1 to 2 kidney-shaped leaves on each stem. Later in the season, these turn reddish-colored. The numerous small flowers that cluster at the top of the stalk are greenish to crimson. These develop on an elongated stem. The plant has a stout rootstock.

Habitat: Mountain sorrel is found at sea level. It likes moist, rocky, gravelly spots, such as sheltered gulches.

Edible Parts and Nutritional Value: The leaves (but not the roots) can be eaten raw or used as a potherb – prepared like spinach.

This plant is a good source of vitamin C. However, because the mild sour taste comes from oxalic acid present in the plant, mountain sorrel should not be eaten often or in great quantities (see additional information under sourdock).

Ways to Prepare for Eating: One of the tastiest wild greens, mountain sorrel leaves make a good lettuce substitute in sandwiches. They can also be included in salads and soups. Try them wilted with vinegar and bacon, or steam the tender leaves briefly, but don't overcook them. They make tasty creamed soup or puree. The Eskimos ferment the leaves into a kind of sauerkraut.

Mountain Sorrel
Oxyria digyna

Mountain Sorrel and Fish Soup
Bradford Angier,
Feasting Free on Wild Edibles

Make a fish stock of heads, tails, bones and fins (try making with salmon and white fish both). Cover with cold water and bring to a boil. Simmer for 1 hour or longer with 1 onion (chopped) and 1 clove garlic.

Just before eating, for each diner, heat 1 cup strained fish stock, ¼ teaspoon salt, and black pepper to taste. Stir in 1 cup mountain sorrel (or sourdock) puree* and simmer 5 minutes. Serve hot with a pat of butter on top.

*See puree recipe in "Hints on Cooking Wild Edibles"

Poison Water Hemlock
Cicuta douglasii

POISON WATER HEMLOCK
PARSLEY FAMILY
Cicuta douglasii
Cicuta mackenzieana

POISONOUS!

Description: Poison water hemlock is a perennial with a stem 2 to 7 feet tall. This stem is stout, jointed, and hollow between the joints. *Cicuta mackenzieana* leaves are alternate, divided into narrow leaflets up to 4 inches long. The edges are toothed and the leaf veins end near the tooth notches. The leaf stalks sheath the stem. The *C. douglasii* leaves are wider than *C. mackenzieana* and the leaf margins are deeply toothed. Both species grow small, white flowers in umbrella-like clusters at the top of the stem.

The plant root is short, ringed on the outer surface, and often has many fibrous rootlets attached. When the root is cut lengthwise, many chambers can be seen inside it. (See illustration under angelica.)

Habitat: These plants grow in wet meadows and bogs and at the edges of streams.

One year when we visited Afognak Island, a large island near Spruce Island, we found a nice sample of water hemlock in open woods, standing in shallow water near the edge of a pool.

Poisonous Parts and Conditions of Poisoning: Water hemlock is one of the most poisonous plants in the Northwest. The whole plant is poisonous, but the root is most deadly. Both the cut stem and the root contain a yellow, oily liquid that has a strong smell. This liquid is especially poisonous.

Symptoms of poisoning include stomach pains, nausea, vomiting, weak and rapid pulse, and violent convulsions. There is some chance of survival by humans if free vomiting can be induced, followed by a laxative. Otherwise, the person will die in a few hours.

This plant is easily confused with other plants that have a similar appearance, especially the angelicas. Janice Schofield taught us a little rhyme that she learned that can be very helpful in making a positive identification. It refers to the placement of the veins on the leaf. Remember these lines:

Veins to the tip – plant is hip

Veins to the cut – pain in the gut

If you are at all unsure as to whether a plant you have found is water hemlock, don't even *touch* it!

POQUE, Northern Ground Cone
BROOMRAPE FAMILY
Boschniakia rossica

Description: Poque, or broomrape, is a parasitic herb that grows from the roots of the alder tree (*Alnus crispa*). It is also called northern ground cone because of its resemblance to a large pinecone growing out of the ground. Poque grows from 8 to 12 inches tall. The scales of the "cone" are actually two-lipped, brownish-red flowers. These have a hairy-fringed bract underneath. Though a flowering plant, it has no chlorophyll.

It is interesting that this genus was named after a Russian amateur botanist by the name of A. K. Boschniak.

Habitat: Poque grows in moist areas, from sea level to timberline, wherever alder may be found.

Edible Parts: Grizzly bears have been known to eat large quantities of poque. In past days, Native people have followed the bears' example, eating the whole plant, especially the thick, underground rhizome, cooked or raw. However, this plant is not one I have added to my list of wild edibles. As it is not poisonous, you are welcome to experiment with eating it if you wish.

Ways to Prepare for Eating: The underground rhizome may be eaten, either raw or roasted. Schofield reminds us not to over-harvest, as these plants usually don't grow in great abundance. She also says to be sure to gather the ground cones located farthest from the alder tree host, so that the plant's source of nourishment is not disrupted.

Uses in Native and Traditional Folk Medicine

Tlingits reputedly used this plant to heal cuts, scrapes, and sores. However, the way it was used is unknown.

Janice Schofield reports using *Boschniakia* as an ingredient in tonic drinks or teas.

Other Uses: Priscilla Kari reports that Dena'inas tied a piece of the plant around the neck of a baby or puppy, as it was said to help them grow. Inland Dena'inas removed the white inner portion from the plant and used the remaining stem as a pipe.

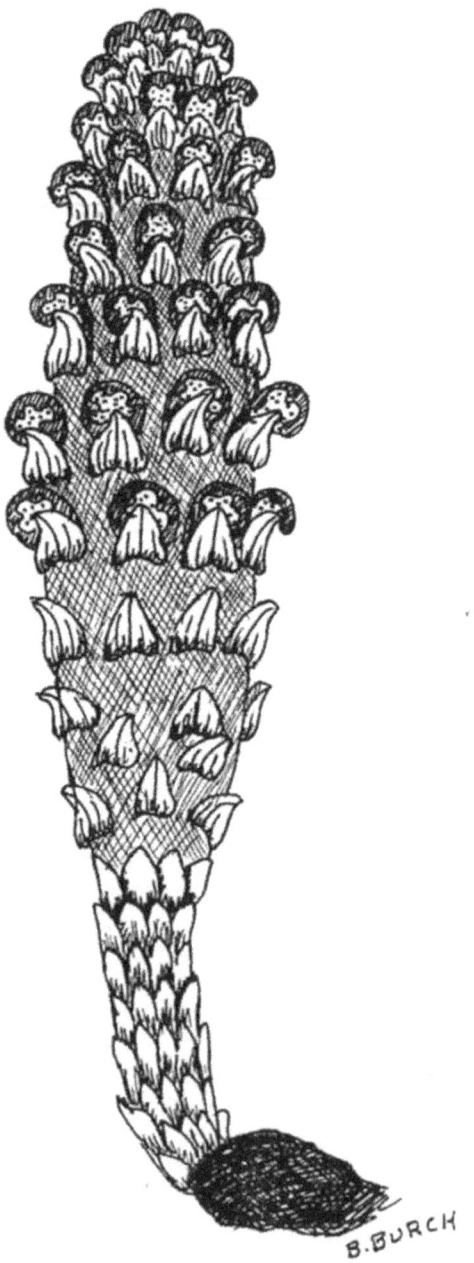

Poque
Boschniakia rossica

ROSEROOT, King's Crown, Scurvy Grass
STONECROP FAMILY
Sedum rosea
Skripka (Russian)

Description: This is a perennial plant named for its thick, fleshy root – it is rose-scented when bruised. Roseroot has numerous leafy, succulent stems, 4 to 12 inches tall. Its leaves are alternate, oblong or oval, with smooth or toothed margins. These fleshy, succulent leaves are pale green. The maroon, four-petaled flowers form in dense heads at the ends of the stems. The fruit is a tiny capsule.

Habitat: Grows in rocky places and high meadows.

Edible Parts and Nutritional Value: Leaves, stems, and roots are edible. This plant is a good source of vitamin C. Roseroot is one of several plants that have been called scurvy grass because of the vitamin C they provided to early travelers and settlers.

Ways to Prepare for Eating: Harvest leaves and stems before the plant flowers. They can be mixed, uncooked, in salads or cooked as a green. To add a sweet flavor, try cooking fresh trout with mushrooms and a handful of the leaves. Where the plant is abundant, the roots can be boiled and eaten.

Inupiat people fermented the roots of this plant in water and ate with walrus blubber or other oil. The plant is another that was dug in spring and stored in oil for later use.

Uses in Native and Traditional Folk Medicine

Traditional healers brew the leaves or roots into a tea (1 ounce herb to 1 pint water) and drink it to alleviate a cold or mouth sores. Thry use this tea as a gargle for sore throat. Or, they cool the tea and use as a wash for a cut or apply as eyewash.

The fresh leaves have a cooling quality that soothes burns, bites, bruises, and other irritations. The leaves have also been used as a sponge for the eyes. Another Native use is to chew the raw root and place it on cuts to aid in healing.

Roseroot
Sedum rosea

THE PLANTS, BY HABITAT

Roseroot "Beach Camp" Omelette
Janice Schofield

2 eggs Dash of salt
1 tablespoon milk
3 tablespoons chopped roseroot leaves

Beat eggs well. Add salt and milk. Pour this mixture into a greased skillet, heated on your camp stove or fire. Add chopped roseroot leaves. When omelette is golden brown, fold in half to finish cooking. Serves one.

Jenny: We called roseroot "skripka".
Sasha: You know what "skripka" is in Russian? It's a violin. When you rub the leaves between your fingers, they make a little noise, like a violin. We find roseroot in the high places.

SALMONBERRY
ROSE FAMILY
Rubus spectabilis
Alagnaq (Aleut)
Chughelenuk (Aleut) – Young salmonberry shoots
Malina (Russian)

Description: Salmonberry is a many-branched shrub that can grow to 7 feet tall. Its branches are biennial canes, like raspberries. The salmonberry grows canes the first year and produces berries the second year; then these canes die. The rhizome lives on, constantly producing new shoots.

The stems are woody, with yellowish-brown bark. The bark peels off in thin layers. The leaves have 3 leaflets. Deep pink flowers bloom from April to June. In June or July, yellow to dark red berries appear.

There are three theories explaining how the salmonberry got its name:

1) The flowers are salmon-colored
2) The berries look like salmon eggs
3) The settlers used the bark to cure upset stomach brought about by eating too much salmon.

Salmonberry leaves contain chemicals that, when dissolved in water, kill the seeds of other plants. Therefore, few plants grow under the bushes.

Habitat: These shrubs live in the openings on a wooded mountainside, or in open, sunny areas near the forest.

Edible Parts and Nutritional Value: Berries, blossoms, leaves and shoots are eaten or used in tea. The berries are an important source of vitamin C.

Ways to Prepare for Eating: Salmonberry blossoms make a pretty addition to salads.

The berries are eaten raw or cooked into jams, jellies, and berry desserts. They are also good in wines and cordials.

Young, tender shoots can be peeled and added to casseroles. They can also be coarsely chopped and sautéed in butter. These young stems were once a food source for the Tlingits and the people on the Kodiak archipelago.

Steep the dried leaves for a hot beverage: use 1 teaspoon dried leaves to 1 cup boiling water and steep 5 minutes.

Salmonberry
Rubus spectabilis

Uses in Native and Traditional Folk Medicine

The bark and leaves have an astringent quality that is said to be good for indigestion. They may be steeped into a hot tea for this purpose. Chewing on the young shoots is also said to aid digestion.

Traditional healers use salmonberry leaves on infected areas because of the plant's astringent properties. Local sources say that the undersides of green or dried salmonberry leaves can be placed on an infection to draw it out. They claim that these leaves can also be used on a wound that won't heal. Some people dig out the old, mildewy leaves from under the bushes and place these over the sore or wound. Locals warn that this technique is to be used only with wounds that won't heal. Another local method is to bathe the wound first in a tea made of star of Bethlehem (shy maiden, wintergreen family) and then apply the poultice of salmonberry leaves.

I was told that leaves could also be chewed and placed on burns. The bark was sometimes pounded and laid on an aching tooth or an infected wound. It is said to kill the pain.

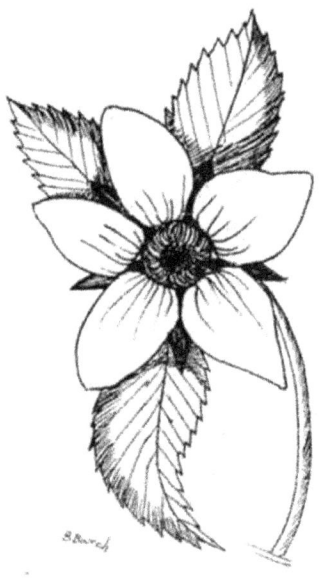

Salmonberry
Rubus spectabilis

Salmonberry Jam

> 4 cups crushed salmonberries
> 7 cups sugar
> ½ bottle liquid pectin

Combine crushed berries and sugar in large saucepan. Place over high heat, bring to a full rolling boil, and boil hard 1 minute, stirring constantly. Remove from heat; at once stir in liquid pectin. Skim off foam with metal spoon. Stir and skim for 5 minutes, until mixture cools slightly (cooling prevents floating fruit). Ladle into hot, sterilized jars or glasses and seal with paraffin and lids.

Cat's Salmonberry Wine
Cathy Klinkert

For a tried, tested, and true recipe for salmonberry wine, follow these directions carefully:

Use a 5-gallon bucket with lid. Open spout and fit an uninflated balloon over the opening.

You will need:

> A couple of gallons of berries
> ½ teaspoon baker's yeast

134 | THE PLANTS, BY HABITAT

Mix together, mashing berries with potato masher.

Boil 1 ½ gallons water; add 1 to 2 cups sugar and stir until sugar dissolves. Cool solution to lukewarm (about 125 degrees). Put everything in the bucket and stir.

Once a week, boil another 1 to 1 ½ gallons water, add sugar, cool, and stir into mixture. (Add yeast only once, when you first add berries.)

Add more sugar-water solution each week until bucket is full.

Keep bucket covered and in a warm place (make sure it doesn't stay sealed or it will explode. The balloon on the spout is your warning system!)

After about a month, strain and enjoy!

> To "pagook" is a Native expression that is popular in our small village. It could be defined as "to borrow with no intention of returning." Pagooking involved harvesting from nature or recycling the castoffs of man; it might be considered a kind of treasure hunt. One notable pagook that I recall involved salmonberries, and was done in complete innocence of spirit. A large group of us – including two nuns – hiked to Sunny Cove to picnic at David's place on Sunny Cove Lagoon. On the last hillside before we reached his house we discovered an open field of salmonberries, with ripe fruit the size of half-dollars. We scattered into the bushes, and the only sounds for a time were occasional exclamations of awe, until we emerged from the far side of the field with red fingers, red tongues, and bags bulging with berries. Later, over lunch, we remarked to David about the prolific crop of berries this year. He agreed and said, "There is a large field of huge berries just above my place here that we have been watching. We plan to pick them this weekend."
>
> We sheepishly confessed our crime, but we did not return the berries. Consequently, our enjoyment of our salmonberry jelly that year was rose-tinted with the knowledge that we had pagooked successfully.

Saxifrage
Saxifraga punctata

SAXIFRAGE, Salad Greens, Lettuce Saxifrage
SAXIFRAGE FAMILY
Saxifraga punctata
(16 saxifrage species found in Kodiak area)

Description: *Saxifraga punctata* is a perennial. Its leaves are low-lying, with scalloped edges. The plant has a central flowering stem that reaches from 4 to 20 inches tall. This hairy stem has no leaves. The flowers at the stem-tops are small, with 5 white petals.

This plant is one member of a large and varied family. In the Northwest area alone, there are dozens of species. Hulten (1968) shows 16 species growing in our area. *S. punctata* is singled out because we have gathered it as an edible. The saxifrage group, though large, does not include poisonous plants.

These varied species have some common characteristics: they are generally found in compact groupings and are not too tall. They have flowers borne on an upright stem from 4 to 20 inches high. They all have 5 petals, 10 stamens, and, usually, paired prominent follicles (some species have 3 follicles).

Habitat: Found in moist, rocky, shady places. Saxifrage means "rock-breaker." Because it sometimes grows in cracks in rocks, it was thought that it could split the stones. However, it doesn't create the cracks; it thrives in them because it is a small plant requiring little water.

Ways to Prepare for Eating: Collect leaves in the spring, before the flowers bloom. Saxifrage can be substituted in any lettuce recipe.

Add leaves to salads, or fix as wilted saxifrage or saxifrage soup. Or, cook with bacon and just a touch of sour cream. Try adding saxifrage to omelettes or casseroles.

Native Alaskans gathered saxifrage leaves and stored them in oil for winter use.

Janice Schofield notes that mist maiden (*Romanzoffia* species) has leaves that are quite similar to some saxifrage, and is also edible. Mist maiden fruits, however, have a single round fruit instead of two follicles. Also, this family member has only 5 stamens. Mist maiden does grow in the Kodiak area.

Wild Alum
Heuchera glabra

WILD ALUM, Alum Root
SAXIFRAGE FAMILY
Heuchera glabra

Description: This very attractive perennial has short, stout rhizomes and one to several flowering stems that can grow to 20 inches high. The leaves are mostly basal, and have long stalks. They are an elongated heart shape. They have 5 lobes and are coarsely sharp-toothed. These leaves are slightly hairy beneath and around the edges. The tiny, white 5-petaled flowers are grouped in threes along the branched stem. Many seeds fill their beaked capsules.

Habitat: Wild alum grows along stream banks or from wet, rocky outcroppings.

Edible Parts: The leaves are reportedly palatable, though not choice. Try adding to soups or to baked vegetable dishes. **CAUTION**: Consume this plant in very small quantities. Its roots are high in tannins, which are gastrointestinal irritants and can cause kidney or liver failure.

Uses in Native and Traditional Folk Medicine

Various Native people and herbalists reportedly used the pounded, dried roots as a poultice. They were applied to cuts and sores to stop bleeding and promote healing.

Michael Moore, in *Medicinal Plants of the Mountain West*, suggests boiling 1 teaspoon of chopped alumroot in water for 20 minutes to treat stomach flu, especially when symptoms include diarrhea and dry vomiting.

The powdered root has been used as an antiseptic to soothe diaper rash. The method of use was to blend one cup arrowroot powder with 3 teaspoons alumroot powder.

Early Tlingits used this plant for testicular inflammation, but the method of use is unknown.

Other Uses: Wild alum's common name refers to its use as a natural mordant, which sets color in yarn or fabric when dyeing.

Mordanting Recipe
Janice Schofield

½ cup scrubbed, chopped alum root
1 gallon water
8 ounces yarn (or fabric)

Place alum root in pot with water and yarn. Bring to boil. Simmer two hours. Remove from heat and let stand overnight. In morning, remove yarn and rinse well. Proceed to dye bath, or dry for storage. This process prepares the yarn for holding the colors of the dye.

Note: Club moss is another natural mordant, and may be substituted for alum in this recipe.

Wild Cucumber
Streptopus amplexifolius

WILD CUCUMBER, Watermelon Berry, Twisted Stalk
LILY FAMILY
Streptopus amplexifolius
Oogoortsi (Russian)

Description: This plant is a perennial. Wild cucumber grows from 1 to 3 feet tall from thick, stringy, horizontal roots. The leaves are alternate, parallel-veined, longer than wide, and broad at the base. The small flowers are bell-shaped and greenish-white. They hang from slender stems underneath the leaves. The berries are yellow-white to orange or red when ripe. They have many seeds. A definite kink in each flower or berry stem near its middle gives the plant the name "twisted stalk".

Upward a short distance from the ground, the stem of the plant is hugged, or encircled by the base of a leaf that fits around the stem like a collar. Thereafter, every time the stem branches, a new collar-like leaf encircles the stem at that spot. This clasping seems more apparent at the branch points, but all of the leaves clasp the stem at the leaf base.

Habitat: Watermelon berry grows in moist woods and along stream banks.

Edible Parts and Nutritional Value: The young shoots and leaves and the berries are edible. The succulent stem, leaves, and berries have a cucumber-like flavor. The juicy berries are high in water content and sweet and refreshing in taste.

These plants contain vitamins C and A.

Ways to Prepare for Eating: The young shoots and leaves of wild cucumber are excellent in salads, creamed soups, and purees. The berries can be eaten alone or mixed with a little orange for a nice jelly combination

Uses in Native and Traditional Folk Medicine

Eaten in quantity, the berries act as a laxative. It is always wise to eat any food new to your system in small quantities until your body becomes accustomed to it. However, if you have need of a laxative, you might try eating a lot of these right away!

CAUTION: Carol Biggs in Volume 1 of her "Wild, Edible, and Medicinal Plants" states that young spring twisted stalk shoots can be confused with deadly false hellebore. Believe it! One spring the monks from Spruce Island's New Valaam Monastery brought some false hellebore shoots to caretaker Greg for identification, as they thought the plants were twisted stalk. It's well they asked!

Wild Cucumber Salad

4 cups (loosely packed) finely shredded wild cucumber leaves and chopped stems
1 large sweet onion
1 cup sugar
¼ cup mild vinegar
Salt and pepper

Put greens in a bowl and cover with thin onion slices. Pour the sugar over the top and allow to stand for a couple of hours in a cool place. Add vinegar, salt and pepper to taste, and serve.

To Complete the Meal:

Baked Deer Spareribs
Georgia Smith

One or two deer harvested for winter use made a nice change from frozen fish. Baked spareribs were a village standby.

2 sides spareribs
1 teaspoon onion salt
½ teaspoon celery salt
½ teaspoon garlic salt
1 teaspoon sage
½ teaspoon marjoram
Salt and pepper
About 1 cup water
4 medium potatoes
10 small carrots
2 medium onions

Cut spareribs into serving size pieces. Mix seasonings; rub into meat. Place spareribs in roasting pan. Add 1 cup water. Cover; bake at 350 degrees for 1 hour. Remove lid for last 15 to 20 minutes if you want them to brown more. Cut potatoes, carrots, and onions in half; arrange around meat. Cover and bake 1 hour longer. Add more water if needed.

> A trickle of water navigated the rocks in the corner of the beach where I gathered wild cucumber. The plants loved the rich, moist banks of that little creek – it must have been a plant version of a chocolate bar. For a salad, I harvested them while they still formed only a single stem. Later, they branched and grew taller, producing blossoms that dropped on a tiny stalk with a kink in the middle; these then became the oval berry called a "watermelon berry". Before they branched, many of the young stalks along that creek were as thick as my little finger, and tasted much like a cucumber. They were a delicious vegetable to chop and add to the salad mix.

WILD ROSE, Prickly Rose
ROSE FAMILY
Rosa nutkana
Roza (Russian) – Rose
Shipoynik (Russian) – Wild rose bush

Description: Wild rose is a shrub with many thorns on the stems. The canes, or shrub branches, can grow to 8 feet tall. The branches have alternate leaves made up of 3 to 9 narrow, oval leaflets. These leaflets are smooth on top, downy underneath and have toothed edges. The fragrant, rose pink flowers grow alone or in clusters of a few and have 5 petals. The yellow stamens are arranged in a circle. The "hips" are behind the flowers. They look something like little apples when they are ripe.

Habitat: Wild rose grows in thickets and on rocky slopes or open hillsides.

Edible Parts and Nutritional Value: Petals, leaves, and hips can be eaten. The hips are so high in vitamin C that foods made from them will retain enough vitamin content for winter use. Three little rose hips contain as much vitamin C as 1 orange. The rose hip seeds contain vitamin E.

Ways to Prepare for Eating: Gather leaves and petals in summer when roses are in full bloom, dry on a screen, and store for use in tea. The leaves are boiled in water for tea – 1 teaspoon of dried, crushed plant per 1 cup of boiling water. The petals are added to 1 cup of regular tea or used in aromatic blends. In the old tradition, Sasha used to keep a pot of tea "concentrate", with rose petals soaking in the bottom, on the back of her wood stove. When she wanted tea, she poured about 1/3 cup of this concentrate into the cup and added hot water.

Fresh petals can be added to salads. Rose petals can be kept frozen for several weeks before using in jelly.

Rose hips are gathered in the autumn or winter when they are red. They should be prepared soon after they are collected. Wash them, remove the "tails" (the leafy part attached to the end), cut them in half, partially cover with water, bring quickly to a boil and then simmer for about 15 minutes. Strain through cheesecloth to remove the juice. Store this juice in a cool place until it is made into syrup or jelly.

Sieve the pulp to remove seeds and skins and put this pulp in jam, marmalade, and ketchup.

Grind the seeds, boil, and use in combination with juice from the hips to utilize the vitamin E contained in the seeds. Or use this fluid in place of water in jelly recipes.

Wild Rose
Rosa nutkana

Rose hip juice is good combined with that of a tart fruit (for example, bog cranberries) when making jelly. The juice can also be fermented to make wine.

Uses in Native and Traditional Folk Medicine

Traditional healers tell us that the petals can be soaked in hot water and used to wash sore eyes. They also recommend boiling a dark tea from broken-up stems and branches and drinking to alleviate colds, fever, stomach troubles, and to start menstrual flow. If it is necessary to cause vomiting, the method used is to peel the bark and soak it in hot water until the tea is very strong. Drinking this liquid is said to produce the desired effect.

People here have used both petals and rose hips to help cure colds, especially when there is a persistent cough. For this remedy, the petals and rose hips are brewed into tea and taken regularly until the cough goes away.

Other Uses: Rose petals can be put in talcum powder, potpourris, rose oil and perfume.

Rose Hip Syrup

4 cups rose hips
2 cups water
2 cups sugar

Remove stems and flower remnants from rose hips. Wash thoroughly. Boil rose hips in water for 20 minutes in a covered saucepan. Strain through a jelly bag to clear the sediment from the mixture. Return the clear juice to the kettle. Add sugar to the juice and boil the mixture for 5 minutes. Store in a refrigerator or jar until you use it. Keeps indefinitely.

> **Jenny C:** There's lots of vitamin C in those rose hips, you know. I knew one person who had a bad cough and he didn't know what to do, what to do. He was coughing, coughing, coughing. And then he comes to my aunt and he said, "Can you help me?" He tried store-bought medicine – everything. And then my old aunt took my dried rose hips and brewed them. She told him, "Keep on, keep on, keep on taking it." Next thing, that person, he thanks her so much, as he is well."

WILD VIOLET
VIOLET FAMILY
Viola spp.
Fialka (Russian)
(5 species in Kodiak area)

Wild Violet
Viola species

Description: Violets are small perennial plants. Their alternate, heart-shaped leaves often stay green all year. The flowers can be bluish or purple, yellow or white. There is usually a single flower with 5 petals. The lower petal is spurred and larger than the others.

Habitat: Violets grow in moist woods or thickets. I've also found these plants in moist, sunny meadows or hillsides.

Edible Parts and Nutritional Value: The leaves and flowers can be eaten. One-half cup of violets has as much vitamin C as four oranges. The plant is also high in vitamin A.

Ways to Prepare for Eating: For a pretty, nutritious mixed salad, add violet leaves and flowers – or use them as a garnish. Also, they may be added to herb omelettes or fritters. Both leaves and flowers can also be used in puddings and desserts. The leaves can be steamed and eaten. Just don't over-harvest! Save some for future forages. Of course, as with any wild plant, eat sparingly at first until your system adjusts to the new food.

Enjoy a tea made of leaves and flowers and sweetened with a little honey, or add a little of this mixture to a cup of regular tea.

Uses in Native and Traditional Folk Medicine

Herbalists say that violet tea is good for colds and sore throats. They recommend heating the leaves briefly in boiling water and placing on bruises to promote healing. They also suggest preparing a violet salve as a remedy for skin inflammation and abrasions.

Violet Jelly
Sandra Coen

3 cups violet flowers
2 cups boiling water
Juice of 1 lemon
1 package liquid pectin
4 cups sugar

Put violets in Mason jar with the boiling water. Let stand a few minutes, then strain. Add lemon juice, liquid pectin, and sugar to the violet water. Bring to rolling boil and boil 1 minute. Skim off foam and pour into hot, sterilized jelly glasses. Seal with paraffin and lids.

Willow
Salix species

Willow
Salix species

146 | THE PLANTS, BY HABITAT

WILLOW
WILLOW FAMILY
Salix spp.
Verba (Russian)
(14 species in Kodiak area)

Description: Several willow species grow in Alaska. Hulten (1968) lists 14 in the Kodiak area; by this time there may be more, as willow hybridizes with ease. The catkins or "pussy willows" from a willow tree are a familiar sight, and may help in identifying the willow to the early spring forager.

Willows can be shrubs or small trees. Though parts of the plant are edible, the bark is characteristically bitter. The leaves may vary in size depending on species, but are generally long and narrow. They are alternate and stalked and have a simple leaf shape. There are many branches. The leaves and bark of *Salix* contain salicylic acid, which is a precursor to aspirin.

Habitat: The willow thrives in moist ground. Look for it along streams and rivers.

Edible Parts and Nutritional Value: All willows have edible parts. The leaves, buds, new sprouts, and inner layer of the bark can be eaten.

Willow is 7 to 10 times richer in vitamin C than the same quantity of orange.

Ways to Prepare for Eating: Young willow leaves can be eaten raw with an oil dressing. For a vitamin C boost, suck the juice from young stems or munch on young leaves or new sprouts that have been peeled of their outer layer.

The Eskimos scrape the inner bark and eat it with sugar and seal oil. It has a somewhat sweet taste so doesn't need much sugar. The inner bark can be cooked in strips like spaghetti or dried and pounded into flour.

Uses in Native and Traditional Folk Medicine

Willow has long been used for relieving pain and inflammation. To combat fever or gain relief from a stomachache or headache, the herbalist might peel off the bark from new willow growth and chew the inner layer, or make a tea from the bark or the leaves. He might suggest gargling a decoction of the bark for relief from a sore throat. Willow bark contains salicin, a close relative to the pain reliever found in aspirin. This natural combatant of pain has no harmful side effects.

Bruised willow leaves, applied to cuts and wounds, are said to help promote healing. They also have an astringent effect (they help reduce discharge or secretions from body tissue).

Healers might recommend a decoction or tincture of willow bark for easing rheumatic or arthritic pains. A strong decoction of willow has been used for internal bleeding and lung hemorrhages. This decoction is made by boiling leaves and bark for several minutes and drinking the tea before eating. For mouth sores, the inner bark has been chewed.

A tincture of willow bark is said to be an effective aspirin substitute. A tincture combining willow bark and "crampbark" (highbush cranberry, or *Viburnum edule*) is said to be a natural remedy for menstrual cramps.

Other Uses: Boil willow leaves and young twigs in water for a hair rinse to remove dandruff. The bark can be made into string. Baskets made of willow bark will hold water without caulking because the wood swells when it is wet. Our neighbors in Ninilchik use willow branches for a steam bath switch.

INDEX

Alaska Spring Beauty *(Claytonia siberica)*
Devil's Club *(Echinopanax horridum)*
Elderberry *(Sambucus racemosa)*
Fir Club Moss *(Lycopodium selago)*
Horsetail *(Equisetum arvense)*
Mountain Ash *(Sorbus sitchensis)*
Raspberry
    American Red Raspberry *(Rubus idaeus)*
    Cloudberry *(Rubus chamaemorus)*
    Trailing Raspberry *(Rubus pedatus)*
Shy Maiden *(Moneses uniflora)*
Spruce *(Picea sitchensis)*

Ferns
Bracken Fern *(Pteridium aquilinum)*
Licorice Fern *(Polypodium vulgare)*
Maidenhair Fern
    (Adiantum pedatum)
Spreading Wood Fern
    (Dryopteris dilitata)

OPEN WOODS AND FORESTS

Spring Beauty
Claytonia siberica

ALASKA SPRING BEAUTY, Siberian Spring Beauty, Alaska Miner's Lettuce, Rain Flower
PURSLANE FAMILY
Claytonia siberica
Lostochki (Russian)

Description: Spring beauty is a small perennial plant with one to several stems. Each stem bears one or more pairs of opposite leaves. Above the leaves sits a many-flowered cluster. The flowers are small with 5 white or rose-colored petals. In the Kodiak area, the blossoms are sometimes pale lavender.

According to Eric Hulten (1968), *Claytonia acutifolia* and *C. tuberosa* do not grow in our area. These two members of the genus have edible roots that the Eskimos use like potatoes.

Habitat: Spring beauty grows along seashores and on moist open hillsides. It can be found in wet places near running water, or on the rainforest floor. Each year I find it growing in a little "plant village" just above the high-tide line of my beach, near the forest's edge.

This lovely little flowering plant can be transplanted quite successfully. My neighbor, Linda, has placed several spring beauty plants along her garden path as ornamentals.

Edible Parts and Nutritional Value: Because the roots of spring beauty are slender, only the leaves are eaten. They are high in vitamins C and A.

Ways to Prepare for Eating: Gather the sweet, tender young leaves in the spring. Add them raw to mixed salads or steam them for a short time and serve them as a green vegetable.

Spring Beauty Salad

2 cups spring beauty leaves and stems
½ cup dandelion leaves
1 tomato, chopped
2 or 3 small green onions, chopped
Green pepper, chopped (optional)
Cucumber, chopped (optional)
1 clove garlic, minced
Salt and pepper
Blended salad herbs
Dressing
12 to 15 violet blossoms.

Chop spring beauty, dandelion, and wild cucumber into small pieces and combine with chopped vegetables and garlic. Season with salt, pepper, and blended salad herbs. Add oil and vinegar or creamy dressing and toss. Sprinkle with violet blossoms.

> **Sasha:** When we were little, grown-ups used to tell us not to pick spring beauty blossoms or it would rain. We called them "rain flowers".

To Complete the Meal:

Salmon Ring with Cheese Sauce
Chris Abell

Chris was by birth an Olson. Her father was a fisherman. Her Russian-Aleut mother was active in working to preserve Native culture, and taught the Aleut language in her later years. Chris had relatives in at least three villages, Port Lions, Old Harbor, and Ouzinkie. Before the tidal wave destroyed the old village of Afognak, she had relatives there. Chris's parents lived in Kodiak during the years when Chris was growing up. Favorite recipes traveled the village family circuit through family members.

Chris has made many a guest happy with this salmon ring as her main supper dish.

1 egg
1 cup cooked salmon
½ cup chopped onion
½ cup sharp cheddar cheese
1 teaspoon celery salt
¼ teaspoon pepper
Parsley or petrushki
2 cups buttermilk baking mix
½ cup cold water

Heat oven to 375 degrees. Beat egg slightly; set aside 2 tablespoons. Stir salmon, onion, cheese, celery salt, pepper and parsley into remaining egg. Stir baking mix and water into a soft dough; knead 5 times on floured, cloth-covered board. Roll into rectangle, 15 by 10 inches. Spread with salmon mixture.

Roll up, beginning at the long side. With sealed edge down, shape into ring on greased baking sheet; pinch ends together. With scissors or knife, make small cuts on top of ring about every 1 ½ inches. Brush with remaining egg. Bake 25 to 30 minutes. Serve with hot cheese sauce.

Cheese Sauce:

¼ cup butter or margarine
¼ cup buttermilk baking mix
¼ teaspoon *each* salt and pepper
2 cups milk
1 cup shredded cheddar cheese

Melt butter over low heat. Blend in baking mix, salt and pepper. Cook over low heat, stirring, until smooth and bubbly. Remove from heat; stir in milk. Heat to boiling, stirring constantly. Boil and stir 1 minute. Stir in cheese until melted.

DEVIL'S CLUB
GINSENG FAMILY
Echinopanax horridum
Oplopanax horridus
Cukilanarpak (Aleut)
Nizamynik (Russian)

Description: Devil's club is the only Alaskan member of the ginseng family. This plant is a very prickly shrub with long stems, heavy with sharp spines. These stems are erect or sprawling, 1 to 3 meters tall. They are thick and crooked, but tangled together in mature plants. The numerous large, yellowish, nasty spines, up to 1 cm long, cover the stem. The devil's club plant has a sweetish odor – very pleasant – it reminds me of domesticated geraniums.

The very large leaves are shaped something like maple leaves and are alternate, deciduous, and have 7 to 9 sharply pointed lobes with many teeth. The underside of the leaves is also thick with fine spines.

The flowers are small and whitish. These are arranged in pyramid-shaped terminal clusters. Later the red berries form along the same pyramidal structure. These fruits are bright red, flattened, and shiny.

Devil's club is well armed; however, this armor protects a very valuable plant. References list it as having antifungal, antiviral, antibacterial, and antimycobacterial properties. Related to the famous Asian *Panax ginseng*, it has an illustrious ancestor. Its Latin name, *Panax*, comes from the Greek word for "panacea", or cure-all. In the Orient, ginseng is regarded as the ultimate herb for enhancing general wellness. Ginseng is best known as an energy booster and, indeed, traditional Alaskan Native uses of devil's club indicate that this role is one assigned to our Alaskan relative.

Habitat: Devil's club is found in the woods.

Edible Parts: For an emergency winter food supply in deep snows, dig to the roots and eat the new growth at the root tops. These new shoots may be used in omelets, casseroles, and soups.

Uses in Native and Traditional Folk Medicine

This valuable plant has had a long and varied history of medicinal use by Native Alaskans. Many hold a belief that devil's club is a source of healing and spiritual powers. The plant has been used in the following ways:

Stems and branches: These were cut into pieces and boiled into tea to treat fever.

Berries: The Haida Indians rubbed berries on their heads as treatment for lice and dandruff and to make their hair gleam.

Inner bark of the stem and root: Different Native Alaskan groups have found that the white pulp between the green cambium layer of bark and the stem acts as a laxative when chewed. Natives also used the pulp both internally and externally as a treatment for staph infections and as a remedy for venereal disease.

Devil's Club
Echinopanax horridum

The inner bark, either from the stem or roots, is also applied to cuts. One method is to bake the root until very dry, then rub the pulp between the hands until it is broken up and quite soft. It is said to provide relief for swollen glands, boils, sores, and other infections. Leave the pulp on the area being treated for 3 to 4 hours only. It will burn if left on too long.

Roots: The British Columbia Indians prepared a strong tea from the root bark to treat diabetes. When clinically tested, it was found that an extract of devil's club lowered the blood sugar in rabbits.

The same tea, made by boiling the inner bark of the root in water, was used to treat people with tuberculosis, coughs, colds, stomach troubles, and fever. It is recommended that the tea be taken in small doses, as it seems to act as a strong stimulant. It is also suggested that this tea be made as a spring tonic.

CAUTION: Tea made from roots gathered in autumn or winter, especially after hard frosts, may have toxic amounts of the active ingredients.

Devil's club roots, peeled of their stout outer layer, heated in the oven, and then mashed, can be placed on a sore area for purported relief from arthritis. The root and stem pulp can be put in bath water as they are said to ease rheumatism pains.

For a soothing pack for inflamed eyelids, the Native healer would burn devil's club roots and scrape off the resulting charcoal-like substance. It is then sieved through gauze to make a fine powder. This powder is moistened with milk to make a poultice.

It is said that when the bark is burned inside a house it purifies the air of disease.

Other Uses: The oven-dried roots, ground fine, have been used as snuff.

Spring Tonic
Janice Schofield

For a spring tonic that is believed to balance the body and strengthen the system, try this blend (a favorite of mine) from Janice Schofield's book, *Discovering Wild Plants*:

½ cup shredded devil's club root
1 cup chopped dandelion root and young leaves
1 cup nettle leaves
3 tablespoons poplar (cottonwood) buds
¼ cup willow leaves
1 cup spruce tips

Blend dried herbs. Store in a dark place in an airtight container. Steep 1 teaspoon herb per cup of very hot water for 5 to 10 minutes. Strain and serve. Add honey if desired.

Sasha S: "Nizamyniks (devil's club) are good for colds. Leo (my grandson) was telling me his uncle used to let him drink that juice after he makes it…They take the roots and then boil them, and then he put it in a jug, and when they had a cold, he'd let them drink it kind of warm…and it loosens the chest cold. But you only use a little bit, because it can make you kind of drunk-like."

ELDERBERRY, Red-berried Elder
HONEYSUCKLE FAMILY
Sambucus racemosa
Boozinik (Russian)

Description: The elderberry shrub can grow up to 14 feet tall. Its soft-barked stems grow straight. The large leaves are opposite, with an uneven number of leaflets. The leaves have fine teeth along their edges and downy undersides. The bell-like flowers, which grow in dense conical or pyramidal clusters, are pleasantly scented, small, and white. These clusters of blossoms grow at the ends of the branches. The fruits are bright red berry-like drupes that are unpalatable raw. (Alaskan elder is red-fruited. The blue- to black-fruited varieties may be found as near as British Columbia.)

Sambucus comes from "Sambuke", a Greek instrument. To make the instrument, the poisonous pith is pushed out of the stem with a hot stick. The hollow stem is then made into a flute. If you wish to try your hand at flute making, boil the stems after pith is removed to make sure all poisonous substances are cleansed from it.

CAUTION: The seeds, leaves, twigs and roots are poisonous. They contain a cyanogenic glucoside, which can cause diarrhea and vomiting. There is a chance of cyanide poisoning if too much is ingested.

Habitat: Elderberry is found in woods and open areas.

Edible Parts and Nutritional Value: Only the fleshy part of the berries should be eaten.

Always cook these berries before eating to avoid upset stomach. The berries are rich in vitamin A, calcium, thiamine, and niacin, and are higher in calories and protein than other berries. Blossoms are also edible, and useful for making tea or wine.

Ways to Prepare for Eating: Boil the fleshy part of the berry for jelly. These berries are good mixed with more acid tasting fruit – try them with strawberries.

Try a tea blend using elder flowers – or use them as an ingredient in pancakes, waffles, or cakes. The dried flowers can be ground and added as a baking mix ingredient. Janice Schofield lauds her elderberry fritters, which call for 4 cups of elder flowers. She blends 2 eggs, 1 cup milk, and 2 tablespoons melted butter. Flowers are dipped in this batter and then in a mix made with 1 cup flour, 1 teaspoon baking powder, and ½ teaspoon salt. The flowers are then fried until golden, drained on a paper towel, and served with honey or maple syrup. What an exotic and flavorful breakfast!

Elderberry
Sambucus racemosa

Uses in Native and Traditional Folk Medicine

Early herbalists prescribed elder for over 70 diseases, from plague to toothache. It is probable they commonly used the black-fruited elderberry, although this family member also contains harmful alkaloids and poisons, especially in the root, leaves and bark. The Susitna people made a wash for infections by boiling the stem bark. Although the root is said to be poisonous, Upper Inlet people boiled the inner root and drank the tea for colds, flu, high fever, and tuberculosis.

Local sources say that a tea made from elderberries is good for colds. The flowers are also good for this purpose. Dry the flower parts, boil them, and let the mixture cool. Drink this tea, a glassful twice daily, until the cold is gone. Another Kodiak area remedy is to make a tea from the flowers to use as eyewash.

A local lady says this tea is also just the thing when you get chilled and can't warm up. She says to drink the tea, stay inside, and cover up.

She says that if the berries or blooms aren't available, cut the stem and peel away the outer bark. She uses the orange part inside to make into a tea for the same purposes.

Other Uses: Elderberry leaves make a yellow dye. The berries produce red, lilac blue, and plum to lavender dyes.

The elder has a history of mystical symbolism. In Scandinavia, by custom one would ask permission of the Lady of the Elder before cutting the plant. Some cultures believe the elder to be the chosen home for devas, or plant spirits.

Elderberry Jelly
Cooperative Extension Service,
Wild Berry Recipes

4 ½ cups elderberry juice
7 ½ cups sugar
½ bottle liquid pectin

Pour juice into a preserving kettle. Stir in the sugar. Place on high heat and, stirring constantly, bring quickly to a full rolling boil. Add the pectin and bring again to a full rolling boil; boil hard for 1 minute. Remove from heat. Skim off the foam quickly. Pour jelly immediately into hot, sterilized containers and seal with paraffin and lids.

Elderberry Wine
Fran Kelso

Pack a 1-quart measure with elderberry blossoms, pressing down firmly. Boil 3 gallons water with 9 pounds granulated sugar for 5 minutes, until a thin syrup forms. Add blossoms and mix well. Cool to lukewarm. Add 3 pounds chopped seedless raisins, ½ cup strained lemon juice, and 1 cake compressed yeast. Put into a large crock and let stand for 6 days, stirring 3 times daily. Strain and let stand for several months. Bottle or put into fruit jars. This light wine has the suggestion of a delicate champagne and keeps well for several years.

FIR CLUB MOSS, Club Moss
CLUB MOSS FAMILY
Lycopodium selago

Description: Fir club moss, or club moss, as it is sometimes locally known, is a low perennial plant that has been around since prehistoric times, when its ancient ancestors grew to the size of trees. Coal was formed from this plant.

The branches of this plant stick up from the stem with leaves that are lance-shaped and look like spruce needles. In the summer, some branches have spike-like ends that look like miniature clubs.

Despite its name, this plant is not a moss; rather, it is a vascular plant. It has a cellular network that moves water and nutrients through its tissues. However, unlike flowering plants, it reproduces from spores that form in the axils of its needle-like leaves, near the tip of the branch, in bands that alternate with bands of sterile leaves.

WARNING: All parts of this plant except the spores are poisonous when eaten. Fir club moss is safe when used externally.

Habitat: Fir Club moss grows in acid soil in the woods and grasslands.

Uses in Native and Traditional Folk Medicine

This plant is poisonous when eaten. Only its spores should be taken internally.

Traditional healers boil the whole plant in water for eyewash. A piece of club moss placed on one's head is said to get rid of a headache.

It is reported that a powder made out of the spores will stop nosebleeds and bleeding from a wound. This powder has also been used for absorbing fluids from damaged tissues in different kinds of injuries. In the past, pills were coated with this spore powder to prevent them from sticking together. Also, the spore powder can serve as a dusting powder for various skin diseases. Recent research indicates it may be helpful in treating herpes.

Fir club moss spores have been used to treat uterine problems, knee problems, swollen thighs, water retention, and dropsy (excessive fluid collected in the body). The whole plant was placed in a cloth and applied externally to an aching area.

Fir Club Moss
Lycopodium selago

Other Uses: Fir club moss is also called Christmas greens because it stays green all winter and can therefore be picked for Christmas decorations.

The club moss plant may be substituted for alumroot as a natural mordant for setting color in yarn or fabric when dyeing. (See mordanting recipe under wild alum.)

The plant's spores flash with a hissing noise when ignited. They are used in the manufacture of fireworks.

This plant was probably the "cloth of gold" of the ancient Druids, as it was supposed to provide protection against black magic.

HORSETAIL, Scouring Rush, Joint Grass
HORSETAIL FAMILY
Equisetum arvense

Description: A perennial, horsetail is the only living member of a prehistoric family. Two of its several species flourish on Kodiak Island. Some of its ancestors grew to the size of trees. These mid-Paleozoic plants were in their prime 350 million years ago.

Horsetail is a spore-bearing plant, and has two growth forms. The spore-bearing stem, with a brownish cone that reminds me of asparagus in appearance, comes up first, and dies down after its spores are released. The green, vegetative stem grows from the same rhizome, often growing at close intervals with other stems. These stems develop many small branches and look something like horse's tails or miniature evergreen trees.

The young horsetail stems are made up of a series of hollow joints, giving it one of its common names of "joint grass".

WARNING: If used as an internal medicine, take in small doses – a mouthful at a time, and no more than a cup a day. If taken in larger doses over a long period of time, horsetail can act as a poison due to some of its constituents. Livestock feeding on a steady diet of horsetail have been shown to suffer vitamin D depletion.

Horsetail
Equisetum arvense

Habitat: Horsetail grows in damp woods and on gravelly hillsides. Because it prepares the soil for the trees that follow later, horsetail may often be found in open forest clearings. However, it also loves to invade your garden and its root runners make it hard to annihilate.

Edible Parts and Nutritional Value: In the very early spring just after the ground is thawed, dig underneath the stalks from the previous year. The new shoots, wrapped in a brown protective cover, resemble berries growing on top of the roots. Peeled, these are good to eat. In later spring the cone on the brown stem can be eaten, but not the brushy green growth. Do not eat this plant raw. Horsetail contains an enzyme that destroys thiamine. Cooking destroys this enzyme.

This plant contains trace minerals.

Ways to Prepare for Eating: Peel the buds from the top of the roots and add to salads or stews. The aboveground brownish stem and head can be eaten boiled. The head should be peeled and the inner core used. Do not eat brushy green stems.

Uses in Native and Traditional Folk Medicine

Herbalists give very exact instructions for harvesting and using horsetail. For internal medicinal use, horsetail is gathered when young, while its branches are very short and curved upward. At this stage of life the herbalists call it "shavegrass". The damaging silica is not yet fully developed. Once the branches droop downward, the plant should no longer be collected for medicinal use.

According to natural practitioners, the silica in horsetail makes it beneficial as a wash for sore eyes. For this purpose, the juice is squeezed out from the part above the root (rhizome) and from the stem.

Another use suggested by herbalists is to make a tea and use it as a wash for wounds, sores, and skin problems, and as a gargle for mouth sores and inflamed gums. The plant can be dried and burned and the ashes put on mouth sores.

A tincture may be prepared from shavegrass. It has been used for bronchitis, tuberculosis, urinary tract infections, or to promote the flow of urine.

The acid from the silica in horsetail is said to stabilize the scar tissue in the lungs in mild tuberculosis cases. Horsetail also promotes blood coagulation and was a medicine for the internal bleeding of stomach ulcers. It is also said to help slow a heavy menstrual flow, assist in preventing water retention, and ease discomfort from urinary tract problems. It has been taken to treat and cure arthritis. The standard tea preparation for horsetail is to steep 2 teaspoons dried shavegrass in 2 cups water.

Diedre Bailey of Kodiak gave us a recipe with horsetail that is beneficial to nursing mothers. This tea helps start the flow of milk. Again, it is the silica in the horsetail plant that makes it useful in this recipe. Mix together equal amounts of dried horsetail, chamomile, borage, and comfrey. Measure desired amount into a container: 1 heaping teaspoon of herbs per cup of tea. Add boiling water and steep 45 minutes. Add a dash of honey to sweeten, if desired. Drink in small sips; do not consume in large quantities. Diedre says the tea is tasty and effective.

Other Uses: When the treelike part of the plant, called "scouring rush", appears, it makes an effective plate and pan scrubber for campers. This part also makes a greenish-yellow dye.

The horsetail performs a valuable service in open forest areas. It prepares the soil with nutrients beneficial to the seeding of new trees.

> Prehistoric horsetail trees often fossilized into the coal that was later burned as fuel. Horsetail carries the dubious honor of being older than cockroaches. The first horsetail trees appeared over 350 million years ago; cockroaches have only been around for 300 million years.

MOUNTAIN ASH
ROSE FAMILY
Sorbus sitchensis

Description: Our type of mountain ash is a shrub that grows from 2 to 15 feet tall. It is an attractive and ornamental plant, with 7 to 11 leaflets springing directly from each leaf stalk. These leaflets have saw-toothed edges. The bark is thin and gray. Vivid clusters of reddish-orange berries replace many of the tiny flat, white flower clusters. These berries will stay on the mountain ash all winter if not picked. The leaves and berries have a strong smell.

Mountain Ash
Sorbus sitchensis

Habitat: The mountain ash likes moist or wet soil, and can be found on shaded slopes and in swampy areas.

Edible Parts and Nutritional Value: Berries can be used as an emergency food supply. They contain vitamin C, vitamin A, and some carbohydrates.

Ways to Prepare for Eating: Some Indians ground dried berries into meal and flour in years when food was scarce. The berries can also be made into jams, jellies and marmalades, though preferably mixed with other fruits. Try mixing with apples. For a wilderness lemonade, soak the crushed berries in a like amount of water for 2 hours; strain and sweeten; serve over ice. The berries can also be fermented into wine.

Uses in Native and Traditional Folk Medicine

Because of their vitamin C content, the berries have been gathered to give to those with scurvy. These berries also contain an antibiotic, parasorbic acid, and the juice has been used as a gargle for sore throats and tonsillitis for some Alaskan Natives. They drink the juice also for stomach and intestinal disorders.

The Tlingits boiled the inner bark and took the tea as medicine. They considered it the very best thing for tuberculosis and severe colds. Kenai people soaked dried berries in hot water to make a tea for the same purposes. Others have reported the bark, leaves, and dried berries helpful in treating ulcers, hemorrhoids and sores.

Mountain Ash
Sorbus sitchensis

Other Uses: Because of its astringent qualities, mountain ash has been used in tanning. The branches have been made into barrel hoops. Many people plant this shrub in gardens as an ornamental plant.

In Europe, the mountain ash was known as the rowan tree, venerated by the Druids.

Raspberry
Rubus idaeus

RASPBERRY
ROSE FAMILY

Recent research shows that raspberry is an antioxidant food containing ellagic acid, which helps prevent unwanted cell damage by neutralizing free radicals. According to these reports, raspberry's high content of flavenoid molecules helps prevent the over-growth of certain bacteria and fungi in the body. An example of these is the Candida yeast, which can cause vaginal infections or irritable bowel syndrome. Research also suggests that raspberries may have the potential to inhibit cancer cell growth and the formation of tumors.

In the June 2004 issue of the Archives of Ophthalmology is a study showing that eating 3 or more servings of raspberries per day may lower age-related macular degeneration (ARMD) by up to 36 per cent. ARMD is the primary cause of vision loss in older adults.

Following is a discussion of 3 types of raspberries found in our area.

1) AMERICAN RED RASPBERRY
Rubus idaeus
Malina (Russian)

Description: A shrub with canes (stalks) 2 to 4 feet tall, this plant is an Alaskan favorite that has been transplanted to our area by immigrants from other parts of the state. Its branches are woody and brownish red. Its leaves have 3 to 5 roughly toothed leaflets that are whitish and hairy underneath. Its five-petaled white to pink flowers form in clusters. The red fruit is made up of many balls, or drupelets, formed into the traditional raspberry shape.

Habitat: Raspberries grow in thickets, clearings, and along the edges of woods. Here on Spruce Island, various patches have been planted. These patches are assigned by a sort of seniority system to the local berry pickers, with no trespassing allowed. I did have a rare opportunity to help harvest an abandoned patch on Afognak Island one summer, and found the experience gratifying.

Edible Parts and Nutritional Value: Berries are very high in vitamin C. They spoil easily and must be used or frozen quickly after picking. When freezing, add a bit of lemon juice to help preserve their color. The leaves can be used for tea.

Recent tests on raspberries show that a one-cup serving supplies 62% of the daily requirement of manganese, 51% of our day's requirement of vitamin C and 33% of necessary dietary fiber.

Ways to Prepare for Eating: Use any raspberry recipe. Try these serving suggestions as well: Top cereal, yogurt, or cottage cheese with fresh raspberries. Try a handful in your salad with a little balsamic vinegar. Blend frozen raspberries with a spoonful of honey and some vanilla soymilk, freeze for 20 minutes, and serve for an elegant, healthy treat.

Uses in Native and Traditional Folk Medicine

Pregnant women have used raspberry leaf tea for hundreds of years to ease labor pains, prevent miscarriage, and increase their milk supply. The method of use is to steep 1 ounce leaves in 1 pint boiling water for 15 minutes, and strain. The prescribed amount is two cups of the tea a day.

The tea has been taken to relieve diarrhea and has also been used as a gargle for mouth sores and as a wash for cuts and sores. Eating the berries is said to help stop diarrhea.

Other Uses: Raspberry leaf tea may be beneficial as a hair rinse – it is said to be especially good for brunettes.

2) CLOUDBERRY
Rubus chamaemorus
Maroshka (Russian)

Cloudberry
Rubus chamaemorus

Description: On this low perennial plant, the stems stand erect from a creeping root and grow to 8 inches tall. Two or three leaves grow from each stem. Each leaf has 3 to 5 rounded lobes with toothed edges. Single white flowers with 5 white petals form at the ends of the stem. The pinkish-yellow, soft and seedy berry is made of several small ovals clustered together like a raspberry.

Habitat: Cloudberry can be found in bogs and moist, relatively open areas.

Edible Parts and Nutritional Value: The fresh berry is a very rich source of vitamin C. It should be cooked, eaten, or frozen right after picking.

Ways to Prepare for Eating: Use cloudberries raw, in berry desserts, or in jelly.

Uses in Native and Traditional Folk Medicine

As with American red raspberry, cloudberry is high in antioxidants and can be used to promote a good, healthy diet.

Wild Fruit or Berry Sauce
Nancy and Walter Hall,
The Wild Palate

2 cups whole raspberries (any kind)
1 cup wild fruit or berry juice
¼ cup honey
2 ½ tablespoons cornstarch
1 tablespoon lemon juice

Combine berries with juice, honey and cornstarch in saucepan. Place over medium heat. Stir in lemon juice, cook and stir 3 minutes. Chill thoroughly. Serve as dessert topping, over pancakes, or use in recipes calling for pureed fruit.

3) **TRAILING RASPBERRY,** Mossberry
Rubus pedatus
Kostianika (Russian)

Description: The trailing raspberry has a slender trailing stem. It roots at the stem joints. There are five toothed leaflets, each completely separated from the others, on each mature leaf. White-petaled, solitary flowers later form into 1 to 6 fruits shaped like small red balls. These berries are hard to pick in quantity because they are small, grow in the moss, and are spread out over a large area.

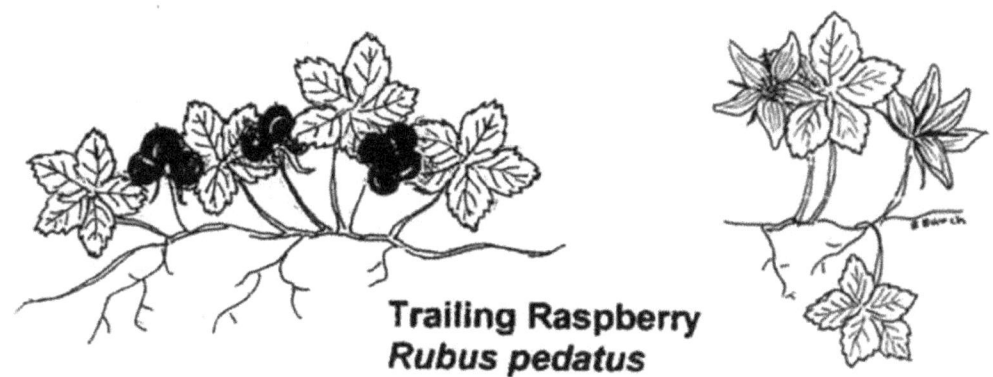

Trailing Raspberry
Rubus pedatus

Habitat: Mossberries, as they are called locally, are found in woods and mossy areas.

Edible Parts: The berries are good to eat.

Ways to Prepare for Eating: These small berries make a delicious jelly, if one has the patience to pick enough of them.

Uses in Native and Traditional Folk Medicine

As with other raspberry family members, trailing raspberries are reported to be high in antioxidants and make a healthy addition to the diet.

Mossberry Jam
Georgia Smith

It takes someone with Georgia's patience and perseverance to pick enough mossberries for this recipe. The result is well worth the effort.

4 cups mossberries, or trailing raspberries
2 cups sugar
Water

Combine berries and sugar in saucepan, adding enough water to keep mixture from sticking. Boil 10 to 20 minutes, depending on the ripeness of the berries. Pour into hot, sterilized jars and seal with lids. Process 15 minutes in a boiling water bath.

SHY MAIDEN, Single Delight, Wax Flower
Star of Bethlehem (local name)
WINTERGREEN FAMILY
Moneses uniflora
Kilitayka (Russian)

Description: The "star of Bethlehem", as it is known locally, is a low plant with a cluster of leaves close to the ground. From this cluster grows a single stem with a dainty 5-petal white flower that faces down. The flower has a faint perfume. The fruit is a 4-5 chambered erect capsule that looks like a tiny pumpkin atop the stem.

Habitat: Shy maiden grows in the moss in the woods.

Edible Parts and Nutritional Value: The whole plant, which contains vitamin C, may be brewed for tea.

Uses in Native and Traditional Folk Medicine

This plant was used extensively in our area by Native healers, for a number of conditions. Here are a few of its uses:

Locals prepared the whole plant, dried or fresh, as a general cold remedy. For this purpose, they added 2 or 3 plants to 1 cup boiling water and steeped for 5 minutes. They also used this tea as a gargle for sore throat or as a drink for relief from other cold symptoms.

One local source says to bathe a sore or wound with tea from the plant, then cover the sore place with old, mildewed leaves dug from under salmonberry bushes.

The dried leaves and flowers have also been made into tea given for stomach disorders and lung troubles. It was known as a good medicine for treating tuberculosis. It was recommended, though, that it be used sparingly!

Anna Opheim (Pleasant Harbor, Spruce Island) says she was taught that star of Bethlehem was good for rashes, bunions and corns. Pick the flowers, place them on the affected area, and tie them in place with a cloth bandage.

Shy Maiden
Moneses uniflorum

> **Jenny C:** I was taught that star of Bethlehem was used for 12 sicknesses. Imagine! I know one lady here…that was the only thing that helped. They went to the woods and got some and they dried them by the stove. And they made a tea and she drank it, and, oh, she vomited blood. After that she got well…

SPRUCE
PINE FAMILY
Picea sitchensis
Shishki (Russian) – Cones

Description: The spruce tree is an evergreen, having needles for leaves. These needles are stiff and sharp and point out on all sides of the branch. There are heavy stands of Sitka spruce in the Kodiak area. Spruce Island got its name because a spruce forest covers a large portion of it.

Sitka spruce is a large tree. It can grow to 220 feet tall and up to 7 feet in diameter. Its main branches are often long and horizontal, with smaller drooping branches growing from it. Spruce bark is thin and brown with a reddish or gray shading. This bark breaks up into small scales. The pollen cones are red; seed cones are long and cylindrical, and brown when mature. Cone segments are thin with toothed edges.

Habitat: Spruce trees grow in all forests in the Kodiak area. Spruce prefers moist, well-drained sites. These trees are commonly found at lower elevations.

Edible Parts and Nutritional Value: The spruce tree contains vitamin C. The cambium, or inner layer of the bark, can be eaten. Indians in British Columbia used to mix this inner pulp with cranberries to form cakes that they ate either fresh or dried. Hunters traditionally mashed this layer into pulp and made it into cakes that could be boiled in camp for an evening meal.

This cambium layer may be eaten raw, boiled in noodle-like strips, or dried and ground into flour. Young spruce tips can be steeped for tea. Orange slices and cinnamon and cloves may be added for spices. Add a little honey and enjoy!

Spruce
Picea sitchensis

Uses in Native and Traditional Folk Medicine

There is a long history of spruce tree use for medicinal purposes, among both the Native people of our area and those in other parts of the state. Some of the uses are:

Sap: Has been prepared as medicine for tuberculosis. The user would peel off a small section of bark in the spring, scrape off the sap, and chew it. They say that this sap can also be placed on a burn or cut to help heal it.

Cambium, or white inner layer of bark: The outer, coarse bark is cut off. Strips of the white inner bark are cut, then boiled or soaked in hot water. The tea made from the strips is said to be good for colds, sore throat, or mouth sores. It has also been a remedy for heart problems, kidney disorders, ulcers, and other stomach illnesses. It can be used as a wash for new babies. Users are warned not to drink this tea in large amounts unless they are in need of a laxative. Spruce syrup or tea is also popular for coughs, colds and urinary tract infections.

These white strips of the inner bark have also been used as temporary bandages to stop bleeding from cuts.

Needles: These are boiled for a tea that is said to cleanse your system. In smaller doses this tea is reportedly an effective cough medicine.

From the new growth of the needles, a spruce beer can be made that is said to be good for cold sufferers or for tuberculosis patients. The needles are boiled and strained and beer brewed from the resulting liquid. This beer was a popular alcoholic beverage with the early sourdoughs. They collected the soft green tips of spruce boughs in the spring and fermented the brew from them. As it was high in vitamin C, they could always claim that they drank it "for medicinal purposes only."

The uncooked juice from these new needles can be squeezed into sore eyes.

Cones: When the new cones of the spruce are almost prime, they are light green and soft.

These were boiled and made into tea for chest colds.

Other Uses: Boiling the item to be dyed with peeled spruce bark can produce a brown dye. Boiling with chopped twigs yields a camel tan shade. "A long time ago, before there were kickers (outboards)," says a local man, "fishnets were dyed this way."

The shishki, or spruce cones, are fine fire-starters. The soft pitch can serve as a caulk for boats, while the hardened pitch makes a chewing gum. Baskets and hats can be formed from the small rootlets. Bow stems and knees for wooden dories can be cut from the above-ground curved root pieces.

Spruce wood has the highest strength-to-weight ratio of any wood. Therefore, it is in demand by many carpenters. It was used for building airplanes during World War II.

An excellent paper can be made from spruce because its long fibers create a strong newsprint.

> **Jenny C:** ..."Then, the spruce, I know. When the spruce first gets cones...you see, they're kind of red at first, and then when they're almost prime, they'll get light green. They're soft, see? That's good when you have a chest cold, and so forth. You got to brew it."

FERNS

Ferns are a group of vascular plants that reproduce by spores, not by seeds. They can thus be placed in a class between "lower plants", such as bryophytes or lichens, and the "higher plants", such as flowering plants. Because they reproduce by spores, they require abundant moisture to reproduce. For this reason, most are absent from dryer areas. The North Pacific is home to approximately 40 species of ferns.

The "true" ferns have creeping or erect rhizomes. These are often very scaly. They have stalked, erect, or spreading fronds, or leaves, often very large. These fronds are curled in a bud, or "fiddlehead", when they first come forth in spring. Fronds are usually lobed, divided, or variously compound. Most often, fertile and sterile fronds are alike; however, in some genera they are dissimilar. Spore sacs (containers for the spores, which are the reproductive parts) are grouped together in sori. These are clusters of small spore cases on the underside of the frond.

Following is a description of the specific ferns included in this book: Bracken, licorice, maidenhair, and shield fern.

BRACKEN FERN
BRACKEN FAMILY
Pteridium aquilinum
Paparotnik (Russian)

Bracken fern does not grow on Kodiak Island, but may be found in coastal areas of Southeast Alaska. Bracken is the world's most widespread fern. People from many parts of the world have gathered it in the "fiddlehead" stage as a food source. However, it is best not to eat this fern, as recent research has indicated that eating it may lead to stomach cancer.

Description: Bracken fern's single fronds are large, erect, and deciduous. Rhizomes are deeply buried and are spreading and branched below the surface. The blades of the fronds are triangular and hairy, with stout stems, or stipes. The fronds are compound and feathery with light green or straw-colored stipes. Leaflets form 10 or more pairs, mostly opposite. The lowest pair is triangular; the pairs become progressively more lance-shaped in the upper part of the frond. The final segments are round-toothed, with margins that curl under.

Habitat: The bracken grows in dry, open places and woods or in cleared or burned areas at low to sub-alpine elevations. Its adaptability to a range of habitats makes this species the world's most widespread fern. According to Eric Hulten (1968), author of *Flora of Alaska and Neighboring Territories,* the bracken fern is not found in the Kodiak area. However, it does grow in Southeast Alaska. It is included here for clarification purposes, as it is the only fern that is considered dangerous to eat.

CAUTION: Recent findings recommend that this fern is not a good addition to one's diet, although people all over the world have eaten bracken since ancient times. The young fronds are eaten while still coiled; they are known as "fiddleheads" because of their appearance. Indian tribes as well as early white settlers in Alaska cooked it as a vegetable. It has long been an important food in Japan, and is still sold as a commercial vegetable there.

However, research has demonstrated that bracken can be toxic. It contains a substance that stops the body from absorbing thiamine. If large quantities are eaten over a long period of time, death could result.

Bracken Fern
Pteridium aquilinum

LICORICE FERN
DEER FERN FAMILY
Polypodium vulgare

Description: The licorice fern is a small to medium-sized evergreen that grows from a rhizome that is creeping, reddish-brown, and scaly. This rhizome has a licorice flavor. Licorice ferns often grow on deciduous tree trunks and branches. In our area this fern is often found growing on the trunks of alder trees.

The stipes of the fronds are straw-colored and smooth, and usually shorter than the blades. Blades are once-pinnate, with leaflets usually longer than 3 cm. with pointed tips and finely scalloped or toothed margins. Licorice fern is easily recognizable because its smooth fronds are less finely cut, with more space between "fingers" than those of other ferns.

Habitat: This fern likes wet, mossy ground. It might grow on logs and rocks, as well as on tree trunks and branches. In the Kodiak area look for it on the trunks of alder trees. Licorice fern is found at low elevations.

Uses in Native and Traditional Folk Medicine

Licorice fern stems contain the same chemical that gives licorice candy its flavor. Tired hikers often pick these ferns and chew them as a refresher. They have been used raw or roasted as a cough medicine. The stems have been chopped, boiled, allowed to stand until cool, and taken for diarrhea or as a worm medicine.

Licorice Fern
Polypodium vulgare

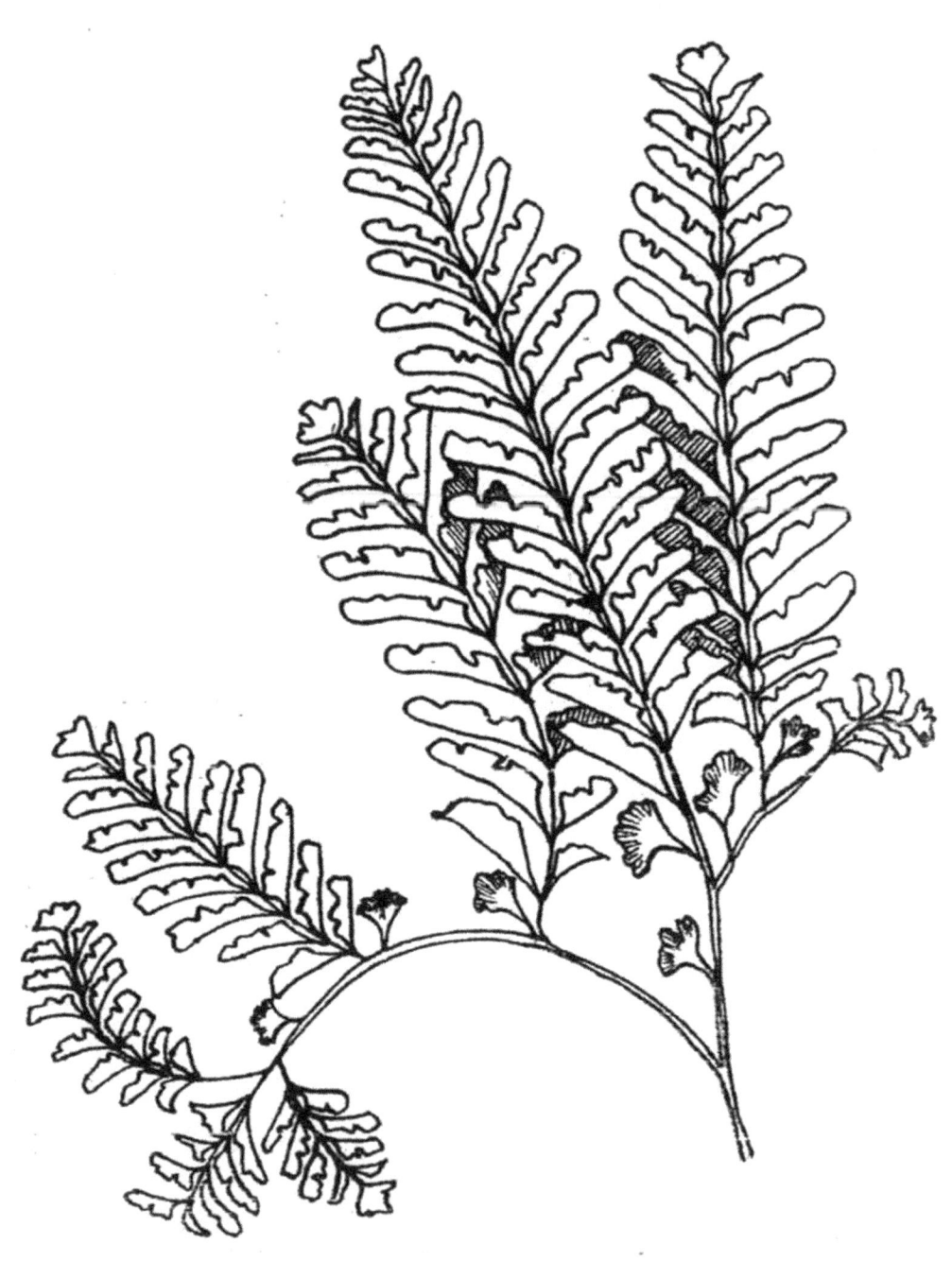

Maidenhair Fern
Adiantum pedatum

MAIDENHAIR FERN
MAIDENHAIR FAMILY
Adiantum pedatum

Description: The maidenhair fern ranges in height from 6 to 24 inches tall. The grayish-green fronds of this fern have a tufted appearance. *Adiantum* comes from a Greek word meaning "waterproof." The fern has the name because the fronds will not absorb much water. *Pedatum* means "having feet": the branching fronds of this fern look like birds' feet.

The delicate, palmately branched fronds of the maidenhair fern are solitary or few. These grow from a stout, scaly rhizome. The fronds have lustrous, dark-brown to purplish-black erect stipes. The top of the stipe is divided into two; then these divisions are divided again. The blade is set nearly at right angles to the stipe, and more or less parallel to the ground. Leaflets have oblong or fan-shaped segments.

The sori are oblong, and found on the edges of the upper lobes of leaflets, and are protected by a flap-like indusium that is formed by the rolled margin of the frond.

Habitat: Maidenhair grows in shady sites in soil rich in humus. This fern is often found in forests, along stream banks or cliffs, and near the spray of a waterfall. Maidenhair grows in low to middle elevations for the most part, but is occasionally found at subalpine elevations.

Uses in Native and Traditional Folk Medicine

It is reported that maidenhair fern leaves can be chewed to help stop internal bleeding. A tea from the leaves is said to be good for treating coughs, hoarseness, and difficult breathing.

Spreading Wood Fern
Dryopteris dilitata

SPREADING WOOD FERN
SHIELD FERN FAMILY
Dryopteris dilitata

Description: The fronds of the shield fern are clustered, erect, and spreading. This fern has stout rhizomes that are covered with the bases of the old leaf stems. This underground part resembles a bunch of bananas. When the fronds first appear in the spring, they are tightly coiled and are called "fiddleheads". Full-grown, they can be up to 1 ½ feet long. These fronds have stipes that are usually shorter than the blades and scaly at the base. The fronds are broadly triangular or egg-shaped and oblong. Leaflets are pinnate, with the lowest pair broadly triangular and asymmetrical. These frond segments, or pinnae, have toothed margins.

Shield fern sori are rounded and partially covered by an indusium.

Habitat: This fern grows in moist forests and openings, in low to subalpine elevations.

Edible Parts: *D. dilitata* has long been an important food source. The banana-like part, which is underground, and the fiddlehead part, up to about 6 inches tall, can be eaten. **NOTE:** Fiddleheads from lady fern (*Athyrium filix-femina*) and ostrich fern (*Matteuccia struthiopteris*) have also commonly been used as a food source. Lady fern has fronds that are narrow at top and base, and broad in the center portion. Ostrich fern is symmetrical and vase-like in shape.

Other Uses: The fibrous, dark brown roots are used for a brown dye. Fine roots are found lining nests of certain songbirds, such as thrushes.

Ways to Prepare for Eating: Dig under the plant for the banana-like parts of the old stem that grow right on top of the root. Roast them, remove the brown covering, dip the inner part in butter, and eat. This part of the fern is best in autumn, because it is juiciest then.

The fiddleheads are gathered in spring, before they get too tall. As they unwind, they tend to become bitter. Remove the brown skin from very young fiddleheads. Try steaming fiddleheads and dipping them in a sauce of butter, lemon, salt, pepper, chili powder, and onion salt. Or, boil or steam fiddleheads and serve like asparagus, with butter or cream sauce. They are also good boiled 1 minute, drained, then sautéed. They may also be used in cream soups or tempura.

The edible parts can be canned, blanched and frozen, or boiled, dried, and stored in a cool place until needed, then reconstituted with water.

Always cook fiddleheads, as they contain an enzyme that robs the body of vitamin B. This enzyme is destroyed by heat. The cooked vegetable is high in iron, potassium, and vitamins A, B, and C.

Uses in Native and Traditional Folk Medicine

My friend, Teddy Panamarioff, taught me that the crushed, fresh plant could be rubbed on nettle rash or bee stings. I received this lesson when I had just been stung by a bee. Rubbing the burning spot with the crushed fern leaves that were conveniently growing nearby took the sting away effectively, so I am not likely to forget this remedy.

Easy Fiddlehead Cheese Bake

For a quick and easy woodland vegetable dish, try this one. It was a popular early spring dish at my house!

4 cups fiddleheads
1 cup bread crumbs
2 eggs, beaten
1 cup grated cheese

Cook fiddleheads, draining and replacing water after it reaches a boil. When fiddleheads can be pierced easily with a fork, place in a casserole and mix in eggs, bread crumbs, and ½ cup of the grated cheese. Sprinkle remaining ½ cup cheese on top and bake at 325 degrees for 20 minutes.

To Complete the Meal:

Baked Halibut with Mushrooms
Georgia Smith

Before the introduction of refrigeration in the village, its residents often dried or smoked halibut or salmon for winter use. When canning became commonplace, it was customary to put in a good supply of canned fish. Now, a supply of halibut or salmon is a "must" for the winter freezer.

1 cup mushrooms, cooked and drained
½ cup chopped onion
3 tablespoons diced green pepper
1 teaspoon lemon juice
1 (8-ounce) can tomato sauce
1 teaspoon salt
½ teaspoon sugar
⅛ teaspoon black pepper
1 ½ pounds halibut steaks

Preheat oven to 350 degrees. Place mushrooms, onion, green pepper, lemon juice, tomato sauce, salt, sugar, and black pepper in medium saucepan. Bring to boil, stirring constantly. Reduce heat and simmer, uncovered, for 2 to 3 minutes. Spoon half of mixture into lightly greased 8 by 12-inch pan. Top with fish. Cover with remaining mushroom mixture. Bake, uncovered, until fish flakes – about 20 minutes. Arrange fish on heated platter. Spoon mushroom sauce over fish.

PLANT LORE
OF AN
ALASKAN
ISLAND

INDEX

Beach Strawberry *(Fragaria chiloensis; F. virginiana)*
Fireweed *(Epilobium latifolium; E. angustifolium)*
Jacob's Ladder *(Polemonium pulcherrimum, P. acutaflorum)*
Kinnikinnik *(Arctostaphylos uva-ursi)*
Wild Sweet Pea *(Hedysarum mackenzii)*

GRAVEL BARS AND RIVERBEDS OR DRY SLOPES

Beach Strawberry
Fragaria chiloensis

BEACH STRAWBERRY, Wild Strawberry
ROSE FAMILY
Fragaria chiloensis
Zemlyanika (Russian)

Description: A perennial plant, the beach strawberry has stout, thick, scaly roots. It starts new plants by runners, just like the cultivated strawberry. The leaves also look like those of its familiar garden cousin. They grow on long, slender stems and have 3 leaflets with deeply toothed margins. The leaves are smooth on top and silky underneath. The flower, with its 5 white petals, also blooms on a long, slender stem. The fleshy, juicy red fruit grows up to 1 inch long.

Habitat: We have heard that *F. chiloensis* grows on the beaches on the Shelikof side of Kodiak Island. Before the tidal wave in 1964, this wild strawberry was found on Spruce Island near the big beach behind the village called "Otherside".

Edible Parts and Nutritional Value: Leaves, stems, and berries are edible. Wild strawberries contain a great deal of vitamin C, iron, potassium, sulphur, calcium, and sodium.

Ways to Prepare for Eating: Traditionally, wild strawberries are eaten raw with sugar or used for jams, jellies, and other desserts. For a tasty tea, gather over 2 handfuls of fresh green leaves and stems, put into 1 quart of boiling water, and steep 5 minutes. Then serve plain or with fresh lemon juice and sugar. This tea is also good served cold the next day.

Uses in Native and Traditional Folk Medicine

As these plants are very high in vitamin C, they are eaten or used in tea to prevent vitamin C deficiency. This wild berry is reportedly high in antioxidants, as are cranberries, raspberries, and blueberries. They are said to help rid the system of harmful free radicals.

Wild Strawberry-Pineapple Conserve
Cooperative Extension Service,
Wild Berry Recipes

2 cups wild strawberries
2 cups canned crushed pineapple
2 cups sugar
1 cup pecans or walnuts

Mix strawberries, pineapple, and sugar and let stand 3 to 4 hours or overnight. Simmer slowly to develop the juice, and then boil rapidly for 1 minute, stirring constantly. Remove from heat. Add nuts. Spoon into hot, sterilized jars and seal with paraffin and lids.

Fireweed
Epilobium angustifolium

FIREWEED, Great Willow Herb
EVENING PRIMROSE FAMILY
Epilobium angustifolium
Epilobium latifolium
Cillqaq (Aleut)
Kipray (Russian)

Description: Fireweed is a perennial plant with a long, single stem from 1 ½ to 8 feet tall. Its leaves are alternate, long and narrow, smooth on top and a paler shade of green underneath. The leaves grow all along the stem, top to bottom. Large, showy flowers grow in spikes at the end of the stem. The four-petaled flowers are rose, pink, or white. A smaller fireweed, *E. latifolium*, is also plentiful and useful in the same ways as its larger cousin. There are many *Epilobium* species in our region, but these two are the best known and most commonly used.

This plant is useful to humans from the time it first appears throughout its entire growing season, and even after its dried stalks fall to the ground.

Habitat: Fireweed can be found in meadows, open forests, sunny hillsides, grassy areas near the beach, burnt-over areas, and recent clearings. *E. latifolium* grows in profusion in the gravel of the river bed near my present Kodiak home.

Edible Parts and Nutritional Value: Young stems, leaves, and blossoms are good to eat.

Fireweed is a good source of vitamins C and A.

Ways to Prepare for Eating: The young stems and leaves can be eaten raw in salads or boiled. They are good with fish eggs. If needed, peel the stems first. It is best to eat young plants, as they tend to get bitter when they grow older. Try this wonderful salad (recipe compliments of Stacy Studebaker) in the spring when the red shoots of the fireweed first appear. Gather a cup or two and chop into bite-sized pieces. Marinate for at least an hour in a vinegar and oil dressing, adding a clove of chopped garlic, a little minced onion and a few mint leaves. Chill and serve.

Very young shoots taste something like asparagus when cut in pieces, dropped into boiling, salted water, and cooked until they can be easily pierced by a fork. Once leaves appear the plants may be bitter. Bring them to a boil, drain, and boil again. Or, peel the stems of older plants and add them to soups. They will thicken the broth.

Green or dried, the leaves can be used to stretch tea, or a tea can be made from them alone.

Uses in Native and Traditional Folk Medicine

Fireweed leaves and stems can be made into tea. The drink is quite refreshing, and is considered to be a tonic.

Traditional folk healers say that a piece of raw fireweed stem, cut in half lengthwise and placed on an infected area, will drain a boil or a cut with pus in it. The plant draws the pus out and keeps an infected cut from healing too quickly.

Other Uses: The down from fireweed seeds has been combined with wool to make blankets, and mixed with cotton or fur to make clothing. It also makes a good fire-starter for campers. The old, fallen stalks can be split into narrow strands and woven into a strong twine. Traditionally, fireweed twine was used to make fishnets.

To Complete the Meal:

French Fried Sea Bass
Georgia Smith

Georgia's menfolk referred to the several varieties of rockfish as "tirpuk". This simple recipe works well with any "tirpuk" you fry, including the hungry sea bass that feed in the shallows near Spruce Island.

> 2 pounds sea bass fillets, cut in 1-inch pieces
> Very thin pancake batter

Dip pieces of fish in batter. Fry in hot fat and drain on paper towels.

Fireweed Honey
Betty Blackshear

> 10 cups sugar
> 2½ cups water
> 1 teaspoon alum
> 18 pink clover blossoms
> 30 white clover blossoms
> 18 fireweed blossoms

Put sugar and water in pan. Add alum and place over high heat. Stir. Bring to a rolling boil and boil 6 minutes. Remove from heat and add blossoms, stirring in well. Strain and pour into hot sterilized jars. Seal.

> Alaskans say that when the fireweed is in full bloom, summer is almost over. An early or late winter is often predicted according to the fireweed blooming cycle.

JACOB'S LADDER
POLEMONIUM FAMILY
Polemonium acutiflorum
Polemonium pulcherrimum
Kushelkok (Aleut)

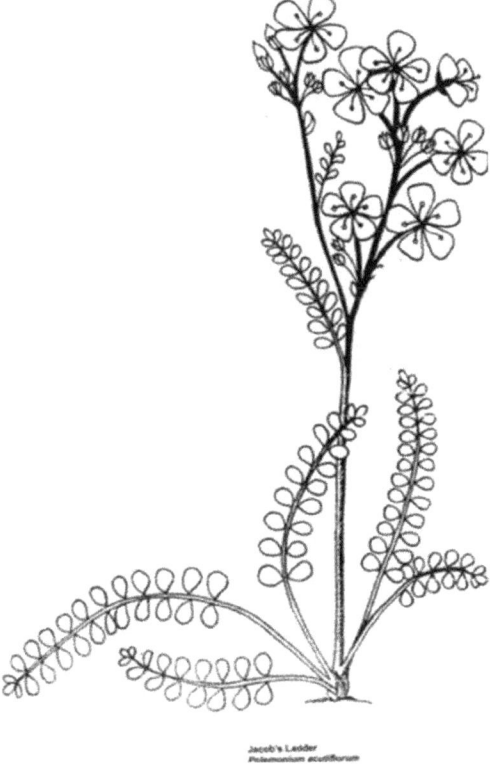

Jacob's Ladder
Polemonium acutiflorum

Description: Jacob's ladder is a perennial plant. Two varieties of Jacob's ladder grow in our area, one taller than the other. Both have violet-blue flowers. The Jacob's ladder flower has five petals. Flowers of tall Jacob's ladder, *P. acutiflorum,* are bell-shaped, while the smaller Jacob's ladder, *P. pulcherrimum*, has 5 rounded violet-blue petals that are white at the base and have a yellow center. The plant got its name because of the ladder-like arrangement of its leaflets.

Habitat: Jacob's ladder can be found in moist areas, but since it likes rocky terrain it is also found in drier soil. The tall Jacob's ladder *P. acutiflorum* be found in open, moist meadows. *P. pulcherrimum* prefers a gravelly habitat, such as riverbeds.

Uses in Native and Traditional Folk Medicine

Tea drinkers, including our "Plants Class", have dried the leaves for tea. To brew this tea, we add 1 ounce leaves to 1 pint boiling water, steep a few minutes, and drink as hot as is comfortable. This tea is said to help cleanse the body by causing sweating.

At one time Jacob's ladder was used to combat rabies.

Sasha and Jenny loved Jacob's ladder for its flowers, and transplanted them to their flowerbeds. They told me of a rare find:

Jenny: One time Sasha and I found a white Jacob's ladder.
Sasha: And then we lost them next.
Jenny: Oh, we got all excited and took roots and all up. And then (laughs) we lost them next. We put them down while we were out in the swamp, and next thing we know we'd lost our plants. We tried to go and look for them but we could never find them.
Sasha: No, we could never find them. Boy, we wanted them. They were nice and white.

THE PLANTS, BY HABITAT

KINNIKINNIK, Mealberry
HEATH FAMILY
Arctostaphylos uva-ursi

Description: Kinnikinnik is a creeping, low-growing shrub with reddish, woody branches that are only inches high. The shrub has leathery, oblong leaves tapered at one end. They are dark green and slightly hairy on top. The pink, urn-shaped flowers usually bloom as the leaves are opening, though sometimes they may bloom earlier, among the old, dried leaves. They turn into a berrylike fruit that is dull orange-red.

The fruits of kinnikinnik and of another related species that is also found in our area, *A. alpina*, or bearberry, are a popular bear snack.

Habitat: These plants like a well-drained, sandy soil. They can be found in gravelly areas or on open hillsides.

Edible Parts: The berries are edible, but tasteless before cooking.

Ways to Prepare for Eating: Though tasteless raw, the flavor of these berries is improved with cooking. Mix with other berries and use the cooked juice for jelly.

Uses in Native and Traditional Folk Medicine

Kinnikinnik
Arctostaphylos uva-ursi

Native healers made the leaves into an astringent tea that was said to cleanse the kidneys. This tea was also used for bladder infections and other urinary tract disorders. The plant reportedly contains substances that hydrolyze in stomach fluids to form urinary antiseptics. Instructions for use were to pick young leaves and dry them at room temperature. Then, 1 teaspoon leaves was boiled in 1 cup water for 5 minutes. Honey was added if desired and the tea was sipped warm.

Kinnikinnik tea has been used as a douche for vaginal inflammation.

Other Uses: Dried kinnikinnik leaves were the principal ingredients in a smoking mixture made by Northwestern American Indian tribes.

CAUTION: Not recommended for internal use by pregnant women. Large quantities could decrease circulation to the fetus.

WILD SWEET PEA
PEA FAMILY
Hedysarum mackenzii

POISONOUS!

Description: This plant is a perennial with a few erect stems up to 1 ½ feet tall, covered with tiny hairs. The leaves, round at both ends, have 9 to 17 small leaflets that are grayish and hairy underneath. The flowers are fragrant and very attractive, rose to violet-purple, arranged as in a sweet pea blossom. The seedpods are flat, usually with 6 oval joints. Each joint contains 1 seed.

Two other members of the *Hedysarum* genus, *H. alpinum* and *H. hedysaroides,* have edible roots. These plants grow in the same type of habitat. They cover an area from northern Alaska and the Yukon to British Columbia. Their range frequently overlaps that of *H. mackenzii*. They have the common name of Eskimo potato or Alaska carrot.

The edible roots of these two species are gathered in fall or spring. They can be washed and eaten raw, grated for use in salad, or cooked as a dinner vegetable. When found, they are often gathered in quantity, and are reported to be highly nutritious.

CAUTION: These plants are all similar in appearance. Unless you are sure you have the correct plant, you would be wise to avoid eating it. If you <u>do</u> know you have the right plant, find a way to mark the spot where it is growing, as it will be unidentifiable in the fall when it is time to dig the roots.

Wild Sweet Pea
Hedysarum mackenzii

Habitat: Wild sweet pea grows in open, gravelly places and sandy riverbeds. This plant is not found as far south as Kodiak.

Poisonous Parts: This plant is reported to be poisonous, as there were cases where it apparently caused sickness in people. It is not to be confused with *Lathyrus maritimus* (beach pea) that grows in our area and is edible.

INDEX

Chickweed *(Stellaria* spp. – 9 species in Kodiak area)
Clover *(Trifolium hybridum; T. repens.)*
Common Plantain *(Plantago major)*
Cow Parsnip *(Heracleum lanatum)*
Dandelion *(Taraxacum* spp. – 3 species in Kodiak area)
Nettle *(Urtica lyallii)*
Pineapple Weed *(Matricaria matricarioides)*
Self-Heal *(Prunella vulgaris)*
Sourdock *(Rumex* spp. – 6 species in Kodiak area)
Spearmint *(Mentha spicata)*
Wormwood *(Artemisia tilesii)*

CULTIVATED AND DISTURBED SOILS; ALONG ROADBEDS

CHICKWEED, Common Chickweed, Winterweed
PINK FAMILY
Stellaria spp.
Makretzi (Russian)
(9 species in Kodiak area)

Description: Chickweed is an annual plant that is found all over the world. It is usually a creeping plant. It has brittle stems, opposite oval leaves, and small, white flowers with 5 petals. The plant is yellowish green to green. Common chickweed is unique because it can start growing in autumn and later be found blossoming in winter. It got the name "chickweed" because it is a source of winter food for birds.

Because chickweed stems are so weak, the whole plant leans on other plants or on any firm, supporting surface. Wherever the stem touches the ground, new roots and stems grow from the stem nodes, often forming a tangled mass.

Habitat: This plant grows in gardens, fields, lawns, waste places, and along roads. Because it is easy to grow, it is a good plant to grow indoors all winter. Use as needed.

Edible Parts and Nutritional Value: The greens are the edible part. They contain copper, iron, phosphorus, calcium, and potassium, and are also a good source of winter vitamin C. Because these greens are low in calories, they are often added to herbal weight-loss teas.

Ways to Prepare for Eating: Chickweed is tenderer than most wild greens, so eat it raw or cooked only slightly. It is a good green for salads when the plant is young. It is an excellent potherb, combining well with dandelions or watercress. It is also tasty wilted with vinegar and bacon. Chickweed is a good addition to soups and makes a flavorful creamed soup or puree. For a different breakfast treat, chop the greens and try them in pancakes some morning.

Fresh or dried, chickweed makes a refreshing tea.

Uses in Native and Traditional Folk Medicine

This herb has been used as a remedy for serious constipation. The herb is boiled (1 ounce chickweed to 1 pint water). It is recommended that one drink a large glass of the tea for this purpose.

It has been a practice among some traditional users to crush fresh leaves and mix with Vaseline for use on bruises, irritations, and other skin problems. Chickweed is a demulcent herb, which means it is soothing to irritated tissue. Chickweed salve has therefore been used on severe burns.

Chickweed has a poor shelf life; thus, it is beneficial to use this herb as a tincture. Prepare by combining fresh chickweed with 80-proof brandy in a

Chickweed
Stellaria species

blender. Store the mixture in a jar in a dark place. Shake daily for 2 weeks; strain and rebottle. Traditional use for this tincture is for bladder, kidney, and urinary tract infections.

Other Uses: Because of its value in soothing the skin, it may be used as a facial steam. Or, it may be added to skin creams and lotions.

Makretzi Soup
Plants Class

A Russian's weed is a vegetable in Ouzinkie! (Makretzi means "weed" in Russian.)

1 small onion, diced
2 tablespoons (or more) butter
2 cups chopped chickweed
½ cup chopped sourdock
2 cups milk
1 potato, minced
Dash paprika
Salt and pepper

Sauté onions in melted butter. Add chickweed and sourdock and cook until wilted. (Add more butter if pan gets too dry.) Mix in milk, minced potato, and seasonings to taste, and simmer until well blended and thickened.

To Complete the Meal:

Fish in French Batter
Fran Kelso

Do you know someone who doesn't like fish? Serve this halibut dish, and perhaps you'll win a convert!

1 egg
1 cup flour
½ teaspoon salt
1 teaspoon salad oil
Up to 1 cup water
1 teaspoon brandy (optional)
Fish fillets (halibut is excellent)
Tartar sauce

Beat egg well. Beat in other ingredients, adding water slowly until desired consistency is reached. Batter should be smooth and quite thick. If a lighter batter is preferred, beat yolk and white separately. Fold in the stiffly beaten egg white after the other ingredients have been well blended.

Cover fish fillets thoroughly with batter and fry in hot oil. Drain well on paper towels. Serve with homemade tartar sauce. I make my tartar sauce with about 2 cups of mayonnaise, generous portions of finely chopped dill pickles and onions, at least a tablespoon of lemon juice, salt, pepper, and a little ground parsley.

CLOVER
PEA FAMILY
Trifolium hybridum
Trifolium repens
Klever (Russian)

Description: Clover is not native to Alaska, but has certainly made itself at home here. Commonly these low perennials have a compound leaf with 3 leaflets growing from the plant stem on a slim stalk attached to the middle leaflet. The leaf edges are minutely toothed. The blossoms of white or pink form dense balls.

Habitat: Clover can grow anywhere that an open garden can be cultivated.

Edible Parts and Nutritional Value: The flowers, leaves, and roots of all clover species are edible and high in protein. Clover roots were a favorite Native food.

Clover
Trifolium species

Ways to Prepare for Eating: It is best to cook the plant, as it might cause gas if eaten raw. Steam the tender greens, use them as a potherb, or add to stews, omelets, or quiche. The blossoms can be saved for brewing tea, making honey, or flavoring foods. The seed-filled dried blossoms can be baked in bread.

It is best to dig the edible clover roots in the autumn or winter. Clean the root and remove the smaller fibrous parts. Chop into ½ inch chunks and boil 5 minutes. Drain, season, and eat as is or in stew.

For another clover recipe, see Fireweed Honey.

Uses in Native and Traditional Folk Medicine

For a good-tasting pick-me-up, make a tea from clover blossoms that have been dried, broken into tiny pieces, and sealed in a jar to keep their fragrance. Add 1 heaping teaspoon of crushed blossoms to 1 cup boiling water and steep 5 minutes. Add honey if desired.

Clover is reputedly good for curing skin diseases and for soothing sore throats and coughs. Clover contains tannin, an astringent.

Mayo Clinic research has shown that clover contains a blood thinner that may be useful for treatment of coronary thrombosis (heart disease).

Other Uses: Clover roots contain bacteria that change nitrogen in the air into soil-improving organic compounds that help other crops to grow. Clover is also a good food for grazing animals.

Clover-Bright Salad

Russ Mohney

(from *Root, Stem and Leaf* by Glen Ray)

1 cup clover blossoms
2 cups dried dandelion leaves
12 mint leaves
1 onion, chopped
½ cup salmonberries or raspberries
1 medium cucumber, sliced
Mint sprigs
Oil and vinegar dressing or lemon

Soak clover blossoms overnight in salted water. Tear dandelion leaves into salad-sized pieces. Mix with mint leaves, onion, and dried clover blossoms. Place in a salad bowl and arrange berries and cucumber slices over the top. Put a sprig of mint on top for effect. Serve with spicy oil and vinegar or other light dressing, or squeeze a fresh lemon over the salad and garnish with the peel. Serves 4.

To Complete the Meal:

Deer Swiss Steaks

Angeline Anderson

Here is a Ouzinkie treat at its finest! This recipe was a Plants Class favorite, fit for a special occasion.

6 medium deer steaks
Salt and pepper
Flour
Cooking oil
1 onion, diced
2 stalks celery, diced
2 cups water
3 tablespoons dried petrushki
   (beach lovage)
1 small can mushrooms
Worcestershire sauce

Season steaks with salt and pepper and roll in flour. Brown on both sides in oil. Remove to roasting pan. Brown onion and celery in oil until tender. Add water, mushrooms, petrushki, browned onion and celery, and Worcestershire. Thicken gravy with flour. Pour over steaks and simmer 45 minutes.

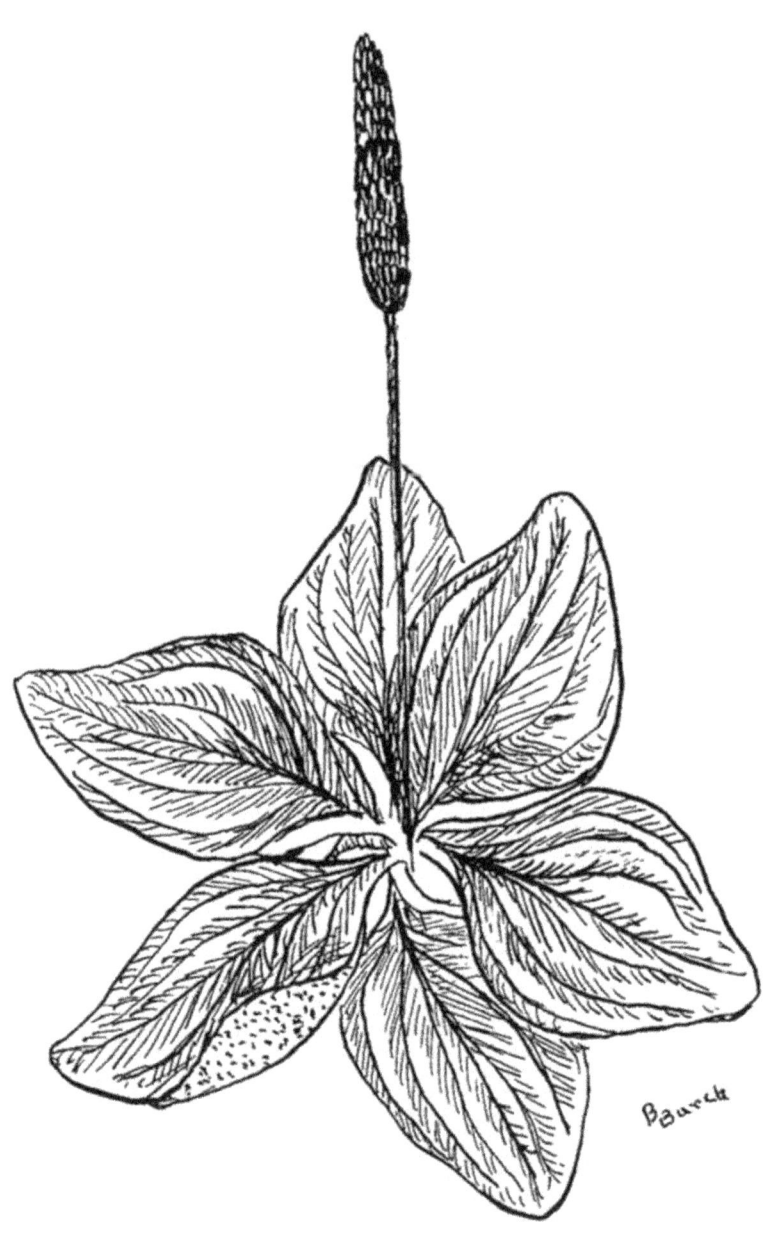

Common Plantain
Plantago major

COMMON PLANTAIN, Broad-leaved Plantain, Snakeweed
PLANTAIN FAMILY
Plantago major

Description: Common plantain is a small perennial plant with broad, oval leaves which form a basal rosette. The leaves have strong veins that are predominately parallel, running from base to tip. Small, inconspicuous greenish-white flowers grow from a brownish spike at the top of a central stem.

Habitat: This plant is often found in waste places, lawns, and along roadsides. It has become known by some as "the mother of all plants", because its origins are so ancient, it is found in so many locations, and it is so hardy.

Edible Parts and Nutritional Value: The edible leaves are rich in vitamin C and many minerals.

Ways to Prepare for Eating: Broad-leaved plantain and the narrow-leaved varieties (see goosetongue) can be prepared in the same ways, although the broad-leaved type is not as tender.

Leaves from any type of plantain are best when picked in the early part of summer.

Eat the tender new leaves raw in salads. Or, cut the leaves into bite-size pieces and boil or steam them until just tender. They may be wilted with vinegar and bacon. If only older plants are available, cook the leaves with a cream sauce after pureeing and pressing through a sieve.

Uses in Native and Traditional Folk Medicine

This plant is considered by many herbalists to be the #1 plant for treating infections. Poultices and teas are used for this purpose. Common plantain is said to destroy a wide range of microorganisms and to stimulate healing.

The whole plant is used as a medicine. For a tea that is reported to be helpful for coughs, hoarseness, and general respiratory problems, or for gas pains: Cover 2 handfuls of chopped leaves with 1 cup boiling water and steep for ½ hour. Measure the same amounts and boil the herb in water for a decoction that is said to help coagulate (clot) blood.

Herbalists also report that the fresh juice can be squeezed from the leaves and taken for stomach problems and worms. The fresh leaves can be crushed and applied to cuts, sores, bites, and even hemorrhoids. Leaves made into salve are also said to be good for eczema and skin problems. Chewing on the rootstalk has been recommended to give temporary relief from toothache.

Sasha Smith tells us her husband had bunions on his feet. Sometimes they would crack and become quite painful. When this occurred, he would wrap his feet with plantain leaves, secure them with a bandage, and leave them on overnight. She claimed that the plantain helped the bunions heal.

For soothing relief for tired feet, try placing plantain leaves in your shoes before a long hike.

Other Uses: According to Glen Ray in *Root, Stem and Leaf,* common plantain leaves can be used for a dye. With alum, chrome, or copper mordant, colors vary from a greenish tint to yellow-brown.

Plantain Pizza

2 cups flour
1 teaspoon baking powder
2 tablespoons milk
¼ pound margarine
1 egg
1 small can tomato sauce
½ small can tomato paste
Salt
12 quarts common plantain or goosetongue, steamed (don't overcook)
1 ½ cups grated Mozzarella cheese.

Make a pizza dough of flour, baking powder, milk, margarine and egg. Spread on cookie sheet. Combine tomato sauce, paste, and salt. Spread over crust. Place alternate rows of plantain and cheese. Bake 30 minutes at 375 degrees.

Janice Schofield tells us that this ancient plant has played its part in the history of civilization. Alexander the Great used plantain for curing headaches. Shakespeare mentioned its traditional healing power in *Romeo and Juliet*. In medieval art, plantain was a symbol of "the holy path to Christ".

Zesty Lemon Roll-ups
Georgia Smith

In a pinch, plantain or goosetongue could be substituted in this recipe for the broccoli.

⅓ cup butter
⅓ cup lemon juice
2 teaspoons chicken bouillon granules or 2 bouillon cubes
2 teaspoons Worcestershire sauce
1 cup cooked rice
5 ounces frozen chopped broccoli, thawed
¼ cup chopped petrushki
1 cup shredded cheddar cheese
8 white fish fillets (halibut, cod, etc.)
Paprika

Preheat oven to 375 degrees. In small saucepan, melt butter; add lemon juice, bouillon, and Worcestershire sauce. Heat slowly until bouillon dissolves; set aside. In a medium bowl, combine rice, broccoli, petrushki, cheese, and ¼ cup lemon butter sauce; mix well. Divide broccoli mixture equally among fillets. Roll up and place seam-side down in shallow baking dish. Pour remaining sauce over roll-ups. Bake 25 minutes, or until fish flakes with fork. Spoon sauce over individual servings; garnish with paprika.

COW PARSNIP, Wild Celery
PARSLEY FAMILY
Heracleum lanatum
Ugyuun (Aleut)
Poochki (Russian)

Description: This perennial plant with hollow, grooved, very stout stems grows up to 9 feet tall. The leaves, large and divided into 3 leaflets, are shaped something like maple leaves. They can measure up to 12 inches across at maturity. These leaves are covered with dense fuzz when young and grow smoother with age. They have a white, woolly look underneath and coarse, irregular edges. They grow from hairy stems that form a large, inflated sheath at the bottom. The small white ray flowers form large, broad flat-topped umbels. These umbels can have from 15 to 30 rays. The fruits are flat, brown, and papery. The plant has a rank odor.

In the Kodiak area this plant is commonly known by its Russian name, poochki.

CAUTION: Cow parsnip contains a chemical that can cause lip blistering and skin irritation. Large blotches, ranging in color from bluish to brown, and sometimes swelling like hives, will mark the area of skin touched by the plant. The blotches often remain for several weeks.

Although this chemical does not cause extreme reactions in everyone, it is best to be safe and gather poochki with gloves. Also, local sources say to gather the plant in morning or evening and not in the sunniest parts of the day. The chemical contained in the plant sensitizes the skin to light; consequently, this ingredient will not be as active when the sun is not as bright. The chemical can, however, be reactivated for a long time after first contact, every time the affected area of skin is re-exposed to sunlight.

Cow Parsnip
Heracleum lanatum

In the November, 1961 issue of *ALASKA SPORTSMAN*, Eudora Preston contributed an article titled "Medicine Women." In the article, she gives a simple cure for the blotches or blisters caused by poochki. She says to bathe the affected skin with a mixture of vinegar and water, claiming it to be "the only sure cure I know."

ADDITIONAL CAUTION: Do not confuse poochki with a similar plant, poison water hemlock (which see).

Habitat: Poochki grows in woods, fields, high meadows, and along the seashore. Though it is sometimes found growing in the shade, it prefers sunny places.

Edible Parts and Nutritional Value: The inner stem and roots are reportedly high in sugar and contain some protein.

Ways to Prepare for Eating: When the plant is young, peel the outer layers of the stem and leaf stalks and eat the inner part the same way you would eat celery. The stem can also be cooked (some sources say cooking improves the flavor). A good way to serve it is as a replacement for celery in soup or stews. Or use it in creamed soups and purees.

Poochki leaves can be added to foods as a seasoning. Gather them in the autumn and dry them, then burn them by placing them on a wire screen and holding the screen over a fire. Powder the ashes and store until ready to use.

West Coast Alaska Indians once ate the root as a vegetable. It is said to taste something like rutabaga when cooked. A Larson Bay man told us his mother dug the roots each spring and pickled them in vinegar.

Uses in Native and Traditional Folk Medicine

The root is the medicinal part. Here are some ways it has been prepared:
1) For colds, sore throat, mouth sores and tuberculosis: The raw root is chewed or boiled for a tea.
2) For arthritis, other body aches, swelling, cuts, and sores: The root is boiled or soaked in hot water. Poochki water may be applied as a wash for the sore area, or the boiled root may be mashed and placed on the sore spot.
3) For toothache: A piece of root is heated until very hot and pushed into the sore tooth. It is said to kill the pain by deadening the nerve.

The seeds of cow parsnip make an effective tincture. Suggested use for this tincture is as a rub for sore gums or for toothache, with clove oil added, if so desired. Another suggested use is to take 5 drops under the tongue for nausea or seasickness.

Other Uses: Poochki can also be used as a dye, according to Glen Ray in *Root, Stem and Leaf*. He says, "When used with alum, chrome, or copper mordant, the flower heads yield a range of colors from light brown to yellow or gold."

Parsnip a la Hercules
(from *Root, Stem and Leaf* by Glen Ray)

6 cow parsnip (poochki) stalks, peeled
¼ cup boiling water
1 tablespoon sugar
Large dash salt
1 teaspoon lemon juice
2 tablespoons butter

Cut the peeled stalks into ¼-inch cubes. Put in a saucepan with all other ingredients except butter. Cook over high heat until all the water evaporates, keeping tightly covered all the while. Lower the heat, add the butter, and let the stalks brown. Serves 4.

When she was a girl, Sasha used to like to eat poochki in the spring, as it was really quite crunchy and tasty, just like celery. She said she used to wonder how her mother always knew she'd been eating the plant. One day after eating some poochki, she looked in the mirror and saw that she had a red mark all the way 'round her lips, and then she understood…

DANDELION
COMPOSITE FAMILY
Taraxicum spp.
Odoovanchik (Russian)
(3 species found in Kodiak area)

Description: The dandelion is a perennial. The stem is erect and the plant often has many flowers. The leaves grow in a rosette at the base of the plant. They are long and narrow with deep teeth. "Dandelion" comes from the French name, "dent de lion" (tooth of the lion), so called because of the shape of the leaves and of the yellow petals. The bright yellow flowers grow in a head. These flowers are replaced by a puffy seedpod. A milky juice comes from the hollow flower stem when it is broken. The plant root looks something like a carrot.

Habitat: Dandelions grow in fields, along roadsides, and in your lawn.

Edible Parts and Nutritional Value: Roots, crowns (parts between roots and ground surface) and tops, from young leaves to flower buds and full blooms, can be eaten.

The fresh leaves are an excellent source of vitamins B, C, and A, and of calcium, potassium, phosphorous, and sodium. (Dandelion is especially high in calcium.)

Ways to Prepare for Eating:

Roots: Scrape, slice, and boil the roots in salted water until just tender when pierced with a fork, then serve as a vegetable. Dandelion is related to chicory, and like its relative, its roots are also suitable for a coffee stretcher or substitute.

Crowns: Boil with leaves or prepare alone as a vegetable.

Flowers: Make dandelion wine, or put in pancakes, fritters, or pies.

Leaves and Buds: Prepare as greens – can be eaten raw or cooked (good wilted with vinegar and bacon). If older leaves are bitter, drain well after they reach a boil, cover with fresh water, and bring to a second boil. Or, pick leaves late in the year – the first frost kills the bitter taste. Hang larger plants by the roots to dry, then crumble and use like parsley.

For a coffee stretcher, (believe us – it's better as a stretcher than as a substitute): Warm 3 cups of cleaned roots on a baking sheet in a preheated (275 degree) oven. Heat until they are brown as a nut all the way through. (Check after 10 minutes.) Grind in a coffee grinder. Mix half-and-half with your morning blend, adjusting dandelion quantity to taste. If you're short of provisions, you could find this recipe of great value.

Dandelion
Taraxicum species

Uses in Native and Traditional Folk Medicine

Many herbalists know dandelion as the "liver plant". They claim that it has two important uses:
1) It helps cause the formation of bile.
2) It removes excess water from the body.

These traditionalists tell us that we can remove poisons from the body, provide a tonic or stimulant, or supply a mild laxative by drinking freshly squeezed juice.

For rheumatism, gout, and stiff joints, folk healers recommend trying the following cure for 8 weeks:
1) Add 2 tablespoons fresh roots and leaves to 1 cup water.
2) Boil, and then steep 15 minutes.
3) Take 1 cup, morning and night.
4) Also take 1 to 2 glasses of water each day with 3 tablespoons of juice pressed from the roots and leaves per glass. Eat fresh dandelion greens daily in salad.

For colds, a tea is prepared in the following manner: Add 2 packed teaspoons fresh, chopped greens per 1 cup of boiling water. Let stand 8 hours and drink 1 cup at a time.

Other Uses: Dandelion is the friend of the soil of our earth. Its roots reach deep and draw nutrients up close to the surface, where they can be beneficial for other growing things.

Mother's Dandelion Recipe
Elizabeth Insley

My mother gathered young dandelions and made this recipe every spring. I believe it served as her wild spring tonic.

3 cups young dandelion leaves
2 tablespoons butter
3 slices bacon, cut in small pieces
Salt
Pepper
1 egg
¼ cup vinegar (more to taste)
1 hard-cooked egg

Wash dandelion leaves well; let drip, but do not dry. Crisp the bacon pieces. Melt butter; add dandelion leaves and bacon. Cook, turning often, until leaves are wilted. Add salt and pepper to taste. Beat egg and vinegar together and add to cooked greens. Slice hard-boiled egg over top.

Dandelion Blossom Pie
Jim Woodruff

Jim took a class at Kodiak Community College from Stacy Studebaker. He contributed this dish to their potluck at the end of their class.

Pick enough dandelion blossoms to fill a 3-quart saucepan ¾ full. Wash blossoms thoroughly and cover with water. Cook 45 to 60 minutes, until blossoms are tender and water is permeated with dandelion flavor. Separate blossoms from liquid.

Measure the following:

> 2 cups dandelion liquid
> 1 cup sugar
> 3 tablespoons quick-cooking tapioca
> 2 cups (packed) cooked dandelion blossoms
> ½ teaspoon nutmeg

Cook liquid, sugar, and tapioca until tapioca is transparent. Fold in the blossoms. Add nutmeg. Place in an 8-inch graham cracker crust or baked pie shell. Garnish with whipped topping and serve.

To Complete the Meal:

Fisharoni Surprise
Georgia Smith

When you reached the season when the only meat remaining in the larder was canned salmon, you became creative…

> 2 cups cooked macaroni
> 1 medium onion, chopped and sautéed in butter
> 1-pound can of salmon, flaked
> 1 medium-size can baked beans
> Salt and pepper
> 1 small can (10 ½ ounces) tomato soup
> 2 tablespoons butter or margarine

Place half of cooked macaroni in bottom of greased casserole. Combine onion and salmon; place half of this mixture over macaroni in baking dish. Add baked beans, spreading evenly. Add remaining fish and rest of macaroni. Sprinkle with salt and pepper. Top with can of tomato soup. Dot with butter. Bake at 350 degrees for 20 to 30 minutes. Serves 4 to 6.

Dandelion Wine
Fran Kelso

Which shall it be? Wine or pie?

- 15 quarts dandelion blossoms
- 3 gallons cold water
- 15 pounds sugar
- 1 yeast cake or about ½ ounce yeast
- Rinds and juice of 1 dozen oranges
- Rinds and juice of 6 lemons
- 2 ½ pounds raisins

Place blossoms in cold water and simmer for 3 hours, then strain the liquid and mix it with sugar. Bring to a boil and strain through cheesecloth. When lukewarm, add yeast. Let mixture stand for 2 or 3 days, skimming it each day.

Simmer thinly peeled rinds of oranges and lemons in a little water for 2 hours. Add cooked rinds and orange and lemon juice to yeast mixture. There should be 5 gallons. Pour into a 5-gallon cask or crockery container, and add raisins. Leave cask open for 1 day, then seal it tightly and let it stand for 6 months before bottling. The wine improves with aging.

NETTLE, Stinging Nettle, Burners
NETTLE FAMILY
Urtica lyallii
Ungaayanaq (Aleut)
Krapeva (Russian)

Description: A perennial plant, nettle grows from a strong spreading rhizome. It has a single stem and varies in height from a few inches to 7 feet tall. Its leaves are dark green, opposite, coarsely grained, and sharply toothed. Leaf stems, leaves and undersides are fuzzy with fine stinging hairs. In late summer, long, slender, multibranched clusters of green flowers bloom in the angles between the leaves and the stems.

The common Kodiak species of this plant is *Urtica lyallii*. It is often called "stinging nettles" or "burners" because of its stinging hairs. These contain formic acid, which can sting the skin so severely that the sensation in the affected area can last for days.

Nettle
Urtica lyallii

Habitat: Nettles are found in deep, rich soil or near moisture, often in shaded places. Where nettles are found, sourdock or fiddlehead ferns are often growing as well. If you accidentally brush your skin against the nettle plant, you can ease the sting by gathering sourdock leaves, squeezing out some juice, and rubbing it on the skin. Or rub the irritated area with the brown skin from fiddleheads.

Interestingly, around the Kodiak archipelago nettles are found growing *thick* around old barabaras (early Native dwellings) and village sites. These plants seem to have a preference for disturbed soil near human habitation.

My favorite nettle patch is on an open hillside, thick with ferns and false hellebore. The nettles seem to like the shade of these plants.

Edible Parts and Nutritional Value: The greens are edible. The nettle is best early in the spring while it is still young. For the tenderest greens, harvest the plant while it is less than 1 foot high. Whenever gathering nettles, use gloves and scissors. Wash the gloves to rid them of all traces of the formic acid.

Nettles are rich in protein, iron, and vitamins C and A. They contain several minerals, including calcium, potassium, and manganese. This plant is one of the highest sources of plant-digestible iron.

Ways to Prepare for Eating: The entire nettle plant is edible when it is small (up to about 18" tall). Later in the season, cut off the first few inches at the top of the plant. With scissors, cut the plants into pan-sized pieces Boil them, then use like spinach. When cooked in boiling water, they lose their stinging quality in a very short time. Cooking time should be based on the amount of vegetables cooked and size and age of greens. Cook 5 to 15 minutes, just long enough to wilt thoroughly and make tender. Older plants are tougher and take longer to tenderize. If older plants are used, they can be boiled twice to overcome their stronger taste.

Nettle greens are good in fish soup, creamed soup, and purees. They can also be dried thoroughly, which eliminates their sting, and then crushed and measured for tea.

Uses in Native and Traditional Folk Medicine

Herbalists tell us that the nettle has many valuable properties. They say that it acts as a blood coagulant, and, because of this quality, has been used to treat all kinds of internal hemorrhaging. They also claim it is helpful for diabetes, as it has been shown to lower the blood sugar level. A tonic prepared from the leaves can be taken for colds, headaches, and aftereffects of childbirth. Local sources say the tea was also given to aid those with tuberculosis.

For sore muscles and joint inflammation, or for rheumatism, Native healers washed the affected area with hot water, and then wrapped it with raw nettle leaves. The leaves can also be prepared in a liniment for the same purpose.

According to Janice Schofield, nettles has been considered a specific remedy for asthma.

Traditional treatment included drinking the tea and inhaling the burning herb.

Ouzinkie people remember treating a toothache with nettle roots. They washed the roots, pounded them, and held them on the jaw in a heated rag as a poultice. Or, they bit down on the cleaned root, spitting out saliva.

An effective hair tonic has been made from nettles, in the following manner: For dandruff, simmer nettle greens in vinegar, cool, and massage into the scalp. For a hair rinse, make a tea of 5 handfuls of leaves to 1 quart boiling water. Allow this mixture to soak for several hours. Wash the hair and rinse thoroughly with the liquid produced by the nettle infusion. This rinse is said to help restore hair color and promotes hair growth.

Other Uses: The long fibers that run the length of the plant can be made into rope. The nettle has also been used to make paper, and a cloth that is said to be more durable than linen.

Seal hunters once rubbed themselves with nettles before going out to sea in their small boats. The practice kept them awake during the long night.

Nettles will make a dye with color variations from yellow to bright green.

The plant is a commercial source of chlorophyll. It is also a great additive to livestock feed, as dried nettles contain 40% protein.

Alaskan Nettles
Sasha Smith

Sasha liked to join us on our Plants Class hikes to Garden Point, because the old abandoned garden plots were our prime spot for gathering nettles. We made sure to bring our old gloves for gathering. We all went home looking forward to the fresh, nutritious greens as a supper vegetable. Here is how Sasha taught us to prepare them:

> Gather nettles when plants are 2 to 4 inches tall. Wash nettles in several waters. Have saucepan ready. Pick nettles from rinse water and place directly in saucepan. The water clinging to the leaves will furnish sufficient cooking liquid. Cover and cook 5 to 10 minutes. Remove from heat. Season with salt and pepper.
>
> *Variation:* Cook 2 tablespoons chopped onion in 1 tablespoon oil. Add washed nettles and cook until tender.

Nettle Casserole
Deborah McIntosh
(This recipe is a favorite of mine!)

Nettles (3 cups after cooking)
1 package dry onion soup mix
1 pint sour cream
1 cup shredded cheddar cheese
½ cup slivered almonds
1 tablespoon butter

Boil nettles 5 minutes or until tender, drain well, and chop into small pieces. Pack tightly to make 3 cups. Mix with soup mix, sour cream, and cheese. Sauté slivered almonds in butter until golden brown and sprinkle over the top of the casserole. Bake at 350 degrees for 30 minutes.

To Complete the Meal:

Easy Salmon Bake
Fran Kelso

To the village, a sure sign of spring was often the first fresh red salmon served for supper. Fishermen supplied their family with one of their first catches of the season. Then they made sure that all the elders got a fresh fish.

> 1 red salmon, filleted
> Lemon juice
> Mayonnaise
> Dill weed, crushed

Place filleted salmon, skin side down, in a baking dish. Sprinkle liberally with lemon juice and spread with a thin layer of mayonnaise. Sprinkle crushed dill weed on top. Bake at 350 degrees for 20 to 30 minutes, until cooked through.

Jenny: You eat the nettles, don't you?
Sasha and Fran: Yes.
Jenny: That's the best medicine when you have toothache. You get the roots. Wash them real good, and pound them, and use them as a poultice.
Fran: Outside your jaw?
Jenny: Yes. Or you can take pieces of root, wash them real good, and bite down on them. But you spit out the saliva at first. I know that. I heard about it and I've seen it being used…

PINEAPPLE WEED, Wild Chamomile
COMPOSITE FAMILY
Matricaria matricarioides
Aramaaskaag (Aleut)
Romashka (Russian)
Aromashka (In Ouzinkie)

Description: A perennial herb, pineapple weed is a low-growing plant, rarely taller than 9 inches. The plant leaves are dark green, small and finely cut. Unlike those of true chamomile, the flowers have only a greenish-yellow cone. The white ray flowers are absent.

The fresh plant smells somewhat like pineapple, which accounts for its name.

Habitat: Pineapple weed is found in open fields and waste places, or in untended lawn areas or driveways. It likes to grow near people.

Edible Parts: The whole plant can be used as a tea; the flowers may be eaten in salads.

Uses in Native and Traditional Folk Medicine

Herbal guides tell us that pineapple weed has the same properties as chamomile. The yellow flower cones are the most important medicinal part, but the leaves are also good as a tea. The plant is used to soothe nerves, remedy delirium tremens (D.T's), and prevent nightmares, or it is taken as a general tonic.

Pineapple Weed
Matricaria matricarioides

For a pleasant tea, add 1 ounce yellow cones to 1 pint of boiling water. *Always* prepare the tea in a covered vessel to prevent the escape of steam. We are told that the medicinal value of the blossoms is decreased by evaporation. Let the tea steep for at least 10 minutes.

Here is a method of use that I learned from a German friend: For head and chest colds, boil the yellow cones in a covered pan of water. Have the person with the cold bend over the uncovered pan, and place a towel over both the person's head and the pan. Breathing the steam into the lungs is said to help relieve cold symptoms.

This tea is said to be helpful as a mild laxative or to relieve nausea. It is also reportedly a good eyewash and skin wash.

The Latin name of this plant can be translated as "mother dear". In our area, the tea has been given to mothers and newborn babies. The method used was to boil the whole plant (above-ground portion) in water. Strain. The mother gets a cup; the baby gets a few drops. Native sources tell me that it acts as a gentle tonic and helps the mother's milk to start.

Other Uses: Pineapple weed makes a good deodorant. Rub the raw, fresh plant between the hands to remove fish smell.

The tea serves as an excellent rinse for blond hair. Sponge tea over your body for an insect repellant.

Pineapple weed is also valuable for the gardener. Spray the tea on new seedlings to prevent damping-off. Plant it in your vegetable garden as a companion plant. Disperse seedlings around the garden to help sickly plants to health.

> **Jenny:** "Long ago, they used to use this plant to cleanse the new mother's insides. After childbirth, the mother is constipated, so they brew that pineapple weed into tea. Once in awhile I still have it."
> **Sasha:** "I like that kind of tea. Once in awhile, I drink it, too."
> **Jenny:** "When we used to pick them, we'd leave one with lots of blossoms, and after that, it would self-seed, see? Back in the garden there used to be lots of them, and I used to save them…for my tea."

SELF-HEAL, Heal All
MINT FAMILY
Prunella vulgaris

Description: Self-heal is a fibrous-rooted perennial with a short stem. Like most members of the mint family, it has square stems and opposite leaves. These are widely spaced, and egg-shaped or long and oval. A characteristic to watch for is the two opposite leaves that grow just under the flower head. *Prunella* can be a small plant, just a few inches tall, or it may grow to around 20 inches tall, depending on location.

The flowers are purplish-pink, and form in a two-lipped tube. The upper lip shades the lower like a bonnet. A series of these charming blossoms grow in a spike-like cluster at the top of the stem.

Pojar and Mackinnon in *Plants of the Pacific Northwest Coast* state that self-heal apparently consists of native plants (ssp *lanceolata*) and introduced plants from Eurasia. In my 1968 version of Hulten, I learned that *P. vulgaris* apparently had not been found (or identified) in the Kodiak area at the time that book was published. We on Spruce Island can announce that it has very definitely arrived on the scene!

Habitat: This plant likes moist roadsides, clearings, fields, lawns, or forest edges, and is commonly found at low to middle elevations.

Edible Parts: The leaves of self-heal may be eaten raw in salads or cooked in soups, stews, or other dishes. They are somewhat bitter in taste due to the presence of tannin in the leaves. However, this taste can be greatly reduced by washing the leaves thoroughly.

Try *Prunella* as a blend ingredient in your favorite herbal teas. Or, prepare it by itself and serve as a refreshing iced tea.

Uses in Native and Traditional Folk Medicine

Self-heal has a long history in Europe as a medicinal plant. Its Latin name, *Prunella*, derives from a German word referring to a disorder of the throat that the plant was said to cure.

Prunella has been used as a mouthwash for sores and gum problems, and as a gargle for sore throats and thrush. As it is reportedly high in antioxidants, it can be prepared with oregano in a tea as an immune system booster.

Self-heal is a powerfully astringent herb, and has been used extensively to staunch bleeding from wounds. It is also used as a poultice to treat bruises, burns, sprains, cuts and hemorrhoids. Herbalists have prescribed it for treating a variety of liver disorders.

They say that it can also act as a cleansing herb, useful for diarrhea, flatulence, and gastritis, or for the expulsion of intestinal parasites.

Recent research has indicated that a polysaccharide fraction of the plant may be useful in combating both the Herpes Simplex

Self-Heal
Prunella vulgaris

virus-1 and virus-2 infections. One Internet source, www.Plant-Life.org, states that the whole plant is antibacterial, antiseptic, antispasmodic, and has substances that gradually restore health. This source states that "its antibacterial properties inhibit the growth of Pseudomonas, Bacillus typhi, E. coli, and Mycobacterium tuberculi."

Pojar and Mackinnon state that the Nuxalk boiled the entire plant into a weak tea for heart conditions. The Quinault and Quileute used the juice on boils. They also used leaves on cuts, bruises, and skin inflammation, or mashed the whole plant and mixed with grease for an ointment for the same purposes. I have found no reference as to use of the plant by Native groups in our area. Perhaps it is because *Prunella* is too new an arrival here for the older Native peoples to have assimilated the plant into their natural pharmacopoeia.

Use self-heal fresh or dried. For drying, harvest in mid-summer.

> Prunella has a variety of ancient common names. Two of these were "hook-heal" and "carpenter's herb". These names evolved because the plant was often used to heal wounds inflicted by sharp-edged tools.

> *Prunella*, like nettles, seems to follow people. One day on Spruce Island, two nuns came to visit me with a plant they wished me to help them identify. They believed it was *Prunella vulgaris*, and when we consulted a few references, we agreed that the plant was, indeed, self-heal.
>
> The nuns had discovered it growing in profusion along the 3-wheeler trail between their mountaintop "skete" and the beach at Sunny Cove. When my friend, Rebecca, later bought the Ed Opheim house close by, with plans to start a wellness center, she considered it a good omen when we found a large colony of self-heal growing along the roadside between the main house and the old boat-building shop. I suspect that Ed's wife, Anna, planted them in her extensive flower gardens, and one year they jumped the fence and journeyed into the wild world beyond.
>
> We later learned the plant flourishes in Southeast Alaska. By some amazing journey, this hardy and adaptable plant arrived in the Kodiak area. In fact, self-heal has now settled on every continent!

SOURDOCK, Arctic Dock, Dock, Curly Dock, Sheep Sorrel
BUCKWHEAT FAMILY
Wild Spinach, Wild Rhubarb
Rumex spp.
Kislitsa (Russian)
(6 species found in the Kodiak area)

Description: Several species of *Rumex* grow in Alaska. All are edible. Each of these perennial plants has a stem that can grow to 3 or 4 feet tall, sprouting from the center of the plant. The stem grows from long, yellowish roots. Sometimes the roots resemble fat carrots, except that they grow sideways instead of up and down. The leaves are long and arrowhead-shaped, with wavy or curly edges. Usually dark green, they are sometimes reddish close to the stem. Most of the leaves grow close to the ground in a basal rosette, with a few climbing the stem in an alternate pattern. The flowers, clustered at the top of the stem, form tiny, thin-winged reddish seeds that are released on windy days.

Sourdock is called "wild rhubarb" by people in the Kodiak area. Another wild rhubarb, *Polygonum alaskanum*, does not grow in our area, though both plants are in the buckwheat family. The *Polygonum* plant is used in much the same way as domesticated rhubarb.

One *Rumex* species, sheep sorrel (*R. acetosella*), has rather small leaves and, though edible, is more commonly used for making dye. It is smaller and more branching and delicate-appearing than sourdock.

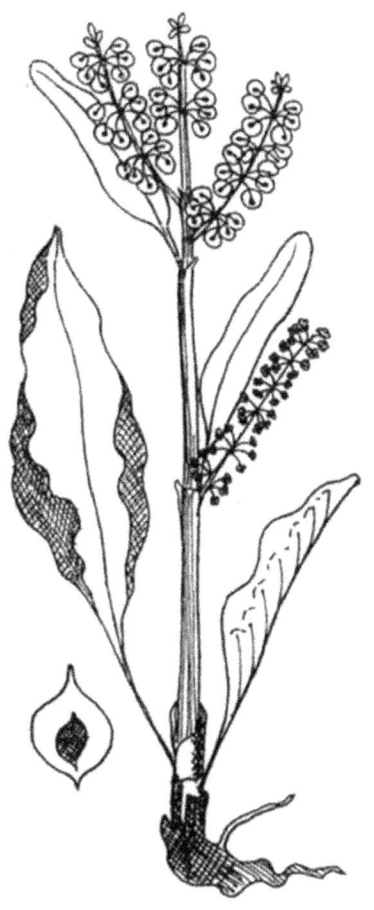

Sourdock
Rumex species

Habitat: Sourdock grows in wet meadows, fields, along roads and slopes, drainage ditches, and vacant lots.

Edible Parts and Nutritional Value: Stems, leaves, seeds, and roots can be eaten.

This plant has more vitamin C than oranges and more vitamin A than carrots. It contains calcium, iron, potassium, phosphorous, thiamine, niacin, and riboflavin.

Sourdock contains oxalic acid, which can be dangerous if consumed in large quantities. However, many other domesticated vegetables also contain oxalic acid and are not harmful if eaten in normal amounts. As long as it is used in moderation, sourdock is a healthful and beneficial wild vegetable.

Ways to Prepare for Eating: Eat leaves and stems raw or boiled. Prepare leaves like spinach and stems like rhubarb. Raw leaves, with their pleasant lemony flavor, are very tasty in salads. They also make a good lettuce substitute for sandwiches.

We suggest steaming young leaves, cooking only until tender. They take just a short time to cook. If left in the pot too long, sourdock becomes quite mushy. Young sourdock leaves are also good wilted with vinegar and bacon.

THE PLANTS, BY HABITAT

When cooking older plants, bring to a boil, drain water away, and add more water. Cook just until tender.

Sourdock can be used in creamed soups and purees. Cook 2 cups sourdock, drain, chop and set aside. Combine ½ cup rich milk with one tablespoon flour, stirring thoroughly. Add sourdock; stir and cook until slightly thickened. Add salt and pepper and serve.

Grind sourdock seeds and make into cakes or cereal.

The Eskimos cooked, chopped, and mixed sourdock leaves with other greens, then stored them in kegs in a cool place for later use.

Uses in Native and Traditional Folk Medicine

Our references report that sourdock leaves and roots can be used for medicinal purposes in the following ways:

Leaves: May be applied as a dressing for blisters, burns, and scalds. Rub the leaves on the skin to remove the sting of the nettle plant. The juice squeezed from fresh leaves is said to provide relief from ringworm or other parasites and fungi. Old-timers recall that sourdock leaves were eaten in large quantities to purge the system and clean the blood.

Roots: These were used by boiling or soaking in hot water. A very strong root decoction was said to bring on vomiting. A brew of a weaker mixture was suggested for a gentle tonic, astringent, and laxative. People have taken this tea for stomach and bladder trouble, tuberculosis, and for relief from a hangover. The roots can be dug in the fall and dried for tea in winter. For an ointment for skin problems, the common usage was to boil the root in vinegar, then mix the softened pulp with lard or petroleum jelly.

Other Uses: The root can be used to make dye ranging from tan to deep gold.

Clam Soup
Bradford Angier,
Feasting Free on Wild Edibles

1 onion, chopped
4 tablespoons butter
2 cups finely shredded young sourdock leaves
2 cups cleaned clam meat, fresh or canned
2 cups rich milk
Pepper

Brown onion in the butter until soft tan. Add sourdock leaves and stir for about 60 seconds – until leaves wilt. Add clam meat and milk. Bring to a slow simmer and cook for no longer than 1 minute (overcooking toughens clams). Sprinkle with pepper to taste and serve.

SPEARMINT
MINT FAMILY
Mentha spicata

Description: Spearmint is a rapidly spreading perennial that greatly resembles its peppermint relative. It has a square stem and opposite leaves, a bright green color, and gives off a definite minty smell. It is called spearmint because the leaves are pointed, like spear tips. Spearmint is not native to Alaska, although it grows well here when planted. This particular species was introduced due to its delightful aromatic qualities. It probably originated in Europe and was brought to North America by early European settlers. Spruce Island has its own large wild spearmint patch that jumped the fence from Sasha Smith's garden one year and has been flourishing in its new home ever since.

Habitat: Mints like moist, rich soil.

Edible Parts and Nutritional Value: The leaves are the edible part. They contain vitamin A.

Ways to Prepare for Eating: Fresh or dried spearmint leaves can be enjoyed as tea (either alone or blended with other ingredients), in salads, sandwich spreads, with vegetables, for mint sauce and jelly, with soups and stews, and as a general seasoning.

Mint Tea: Infuse about 1 ounce dried spearmint in 1 pint water. (When using fresh leaves, more than 1 ounce of the leaves is needed.) You can also add 1 handful fresh mint to your "sun tea" for a delicious blend.

Salad: Mix 1 cup chopped leaves in a salad, tossing well. Dress with oil and vinegar.

Open Sandwich: Mix chopped spearmint leaves with cream cheese and spread on whole-grain bread.

Vegetable: Stir 2 tablespoons minced mint into 1 quart peas, or boil with new potatoes or cabbage.

Simple Mint Sauce: Combine 1 cup well-chopped spearmint leaves with just enough hot water to moisten them thoroughly. After the mass has cooled, stir in 1 cup orange marmalade.

Blender Mint Sauce: In a blender, combine the juice of 2 lemons, 2 cups water, 2 tablespoons sugar, and 1 cup (packed) fresh spearmint leaves. Blend until smooth, chill for about 1 hour, and serve.

Soup and Seasonings: Add powdered, dry leaves. Try these in potato salad or poultry dressing.

Uses in Native and Traditional Folk Medicine

Spearmint has the same properties as peppermint, although spearmint is a little less powerful. Traditionally, it is steeped in tea to alleviate stomachache, gas pains, heartburn, and nausea, and to aid digestion. It is said to help calm nerves or prevent

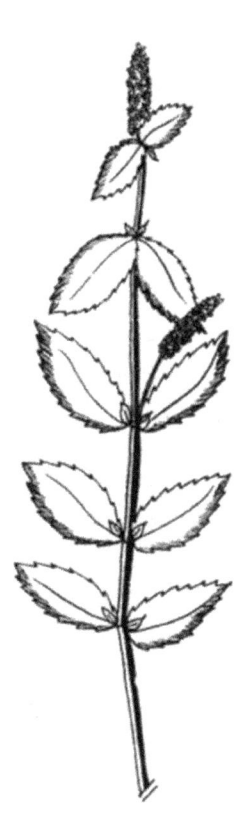
Spearmint
Mentha spicata

sleeplessness. It is also said to be helpful in easing menstrual cramps. Spearmint is excellent to give to children because it is mild.

To prepare, pour 1 pint of boiling water over about 1 ounce of the dried herb (make an infusion), steep for 5 minutes and take ½ to 2 cups a day.

Other Uses: Spearmint and peppermint are often grown as commercial crops. The oil from these mints is used in medicines, kitchen products, cigarettes, cosmetics, toothpaste, bath items, candy and chewing gum.

Spearmint Candy
Noreen Zeine

Dip fresh spearmint leaves in slightly whipped egg whites. Dip in sugar and place on wax paper on a cookie sheet. Dry in warm oven. Peel candy from wax paper and serve.

WORMWOOD, Caribou Leaves, Stinkweed, Silverleaf
COMPOSITE FAMILY
Artemisia tilesii
Polin (Russian) – Noun form
Polinya (Russian) – Adjective form

Description: Polinya, as this plant is known in the Kodiak area, is a perennial plant that grows on a single stem up to 2 or 3 feet tall. Its leaves, which grow close to the stem, are green on top and silver-green underneath. They are shaped something like the foot of a raven: narrow, with 3 to 5 "toes". These leaves have tiny hairs on both the bottom and the top. In late summer, clusters of small flowers grow in a spike at the top of the stem. The plant is most easily recognized by the pleasant smell it gives off if brushed against: pungent and rather sweet. "Almost like spearmint", says Sasha Smith.

For three years, our "Plants Class" knew this plant only by its local name, "polinya". Then, Angeline Anderson discovered a picture of wormwood and an article titled "Medicinal Leaves of the Tahltans" in the April, 1983 *ALASKA* magazine. From this article we learned the plant's Latin name and a British Columbia common name, "caribou leaves".

Wormwood
Artemisia tilesii

Habitat: In our area wormwood is usually found on the mountainside in sunny places and in a few garden spots where local people have transplanted it. On Kodiak Island, Sandra Coen discovered it flourishing along creek banks in the Buskin River area. It also grows in abundance along the road near the top of Pillar Mountain in Kodiak. Recently, I have also found it growing in the gravel flats of the riverbed near my present home in Bells Flats, a few miles from Kodiak city. In this habitat, its growth is a bit stunted by the difficult environment.

Uses in Native and Traditional Folk Medicine

The name for this genus, *Artemisia*, comes from Artemis, Greek goddess of the moon and of female energy. As its name suggests, *Artemisia* has traditionally been used for those conditions that are specifically female.

Wormwood is a common medicine across Alaska for Native people. Tahltans and other people of their area in British Columbia take "caribou leaves", as they name it, as a tea for colds, as a gargle for sore throats, or as a wash for sore eyes or cuts. They also drink the tea to relieve constipation, stop internal bleeding, and alleviate kidney problems. People in other parts of Alaska have used the plant for similar purposes. For a tea, the Inupiaq healer, Puyuk, recommends boiling the leaves for 15 to 20 minutes in water (1 ounce leaves to 1 pint water is a fairly standard herbalist's measure), straining out the leaves, cooling the liquid in a nonmetal container, and then drinking. The taste is bitter but Puyuk says the tea is a "good medicine." Use this tea sparingly; a large dose could upset your system. (See CAUTION, following.)

Locally, the fresh leaves are steeped in boiling water and the tea taken in small doses as a blood-purifying tonic. It is said to help blood circulation and to dissolve lumpy varicose veins. A Ouzinkie lady drank polinya tea for this purpose, and said it helped make the varicose veins go away. Jenny Chernikoff reported that "polinya is used if you're crippled up with arthritis or something, and you can't walk. Then you heat up the plant and put it on wherever it is hurting."

Among the elders in Ouzinkie, wormwood was used for old infected cuts that wouldn't heal. Dried or fresh leaves were steeped in boiling water for a few minutes; then the infected area was dabbed with the wet leaves. Using the leaves in this way would sting, but if the process was continued regularly the infection would be stopped and the wound would be healed. We were told about a small boy in Ouzinkie who had sores on his face that wouldn't heal. The polinya leaves were tried and the sores went away.

Another local lady told us that she learned to chew the leaves for relief from various ailments, including colds and flu. I've tried chewing the leaves – they are strong tasting but not unpleasant. They remind me of eucalyptus. Puyuk also recommends chewing polin leaves or "stinkweed", as she calls it, for colds, flu, fever, headaches, and ulcers. She says chewing the leaves also helps insure a healthy pregnancy.

Julia Pestrikoff in Port Lions said the seeds from polin used to be a remedy for heart troubles. She called it "silverleaf".

At a workshop given by Janice Schofield, I learned the value of wormwood tincture. As it boosts the immune system, Janice suggested taking it in place of expensive *Echinacea*. This tincture is also said to be effective in relieving colds. To prepare the tincture, use fresh or dry leaves; flowers if desired. Fill container with well-chopped herb and add brandy to fill the jar to the top. Store in a dry place out of sunlight for two weeks; shake bottle twice daily. Decant and take, as needed, ½ teaspoon up to 6 times a day.

CAUTION: For internal use, take in small quantities, as the volatile oil, absinthol, is present in some degree in many *Artemesia* family members. Taken in large doses repeatedly, this substance can cause coma and convulsions. It is safe to use the plant as tea in small amounts.

> "Wormwood" gets this common name because it has traditionally been used as a wormer, both for animals and humans. The treatment recommended for people is to drink a couple of cups of wormwood tea a day for two weeks. For animals, mix the powdered flower tops in their food. Practitioners say that the herb may be used to treat roundworms and pinworms.

PLANT FAMILY INDEX

PLANT FAMILY INDEX

The "Plant Family Index" is intended to give you some general characteristics of the plant families represented within this book. If you seek to learn more about a specific plant in the book, look for its family in this section to give you further clues as to its make-up. It is hoped that you will become acquainted with a new friend in the plant kingdom through this process.

These family descriptions are organized as follows: The first paragraph under **General Information** gives data about the worldwide family. Some general remarks about Alaskan family members may follow. The remaining subheadings, with a few exceptions noted in the text, contain information about the family as it occurs in Alaska. If statements are made about a plant or plants specific to our region, it is so noted. In some cases, species information is presented here because it is not found elsewhere in the book, and may be of general interest. (Example: *Betula* (birch).

My source for Latin names used in this book is Eric Hulten's 1968 edition, 1981 printing, of *Flora of Alaska and Neighboring Territories*. Mr. Hulten was also my source for determining whether a specific plant was located in our area. I am also indebted to Carolyn Parker, botanist at the University of Alaska, for all her assistance in helping me to describe these families accurately. It has been so very helpful to have an expert available who has been willing to try to steer me in the right direction!

When we started our "Plants Class" study group, none of us was an expert; we were certainly not botanists. We learned about plants from people who used them or knew them by a common name. It was a hands-on process. It was much later when we started learning Latin names and a few queer new scientific words for the parts of the plant. I believe it possible that many others who have a love for growing things do not know the scientific terms used to describe them. So I am starting this index with a basic botany lesson.

Following are three drawings by Kodiak artist, Barbara Burch, showing the principal parts of a vascular plant and the floral organs, and a comparison of 3 types of root systems. (Information for the first two drawings was taken from <u>Botany</u>, third edition, written by Carl L. Wilson and Walter E. Loomis. The original line drawings were by Hannah T. Croasdale, Dartmouth College. Drawings of the root systems were taken from an illustration done by Bonnie K. Walters for <u>Vascular Plant Taxonomy</u>, Fourth Edition, written by Dirk R. Walters and David J. Keil.)

The terms used in the drawings are defined in the abridged glossary that appears immediately following these plant diagrams. There is a more complete glossary at the back of the book. However, by reading this condensed set of definitions, you, the plant seeker, may find the description of the plant families much easier to decipher. Your understanding of these terms will give you a helpful tool toward making a positive plant identification.

Without further ado, first allow me to present your basic botany lesson. Then, please continue on to meet the families of plants found in this book – Residents of Spruce Island, Kodiak Island and elsewhere in Alaska!

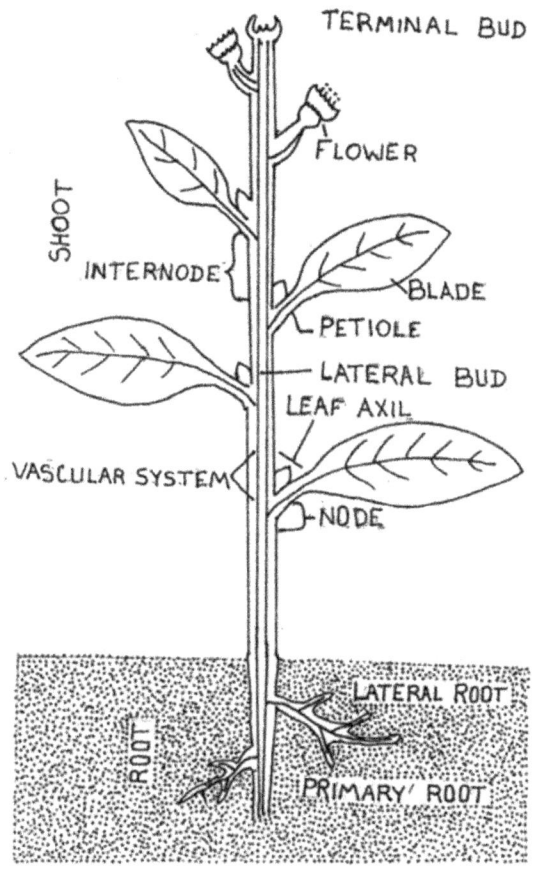

Principal Parts of Vascular Plant

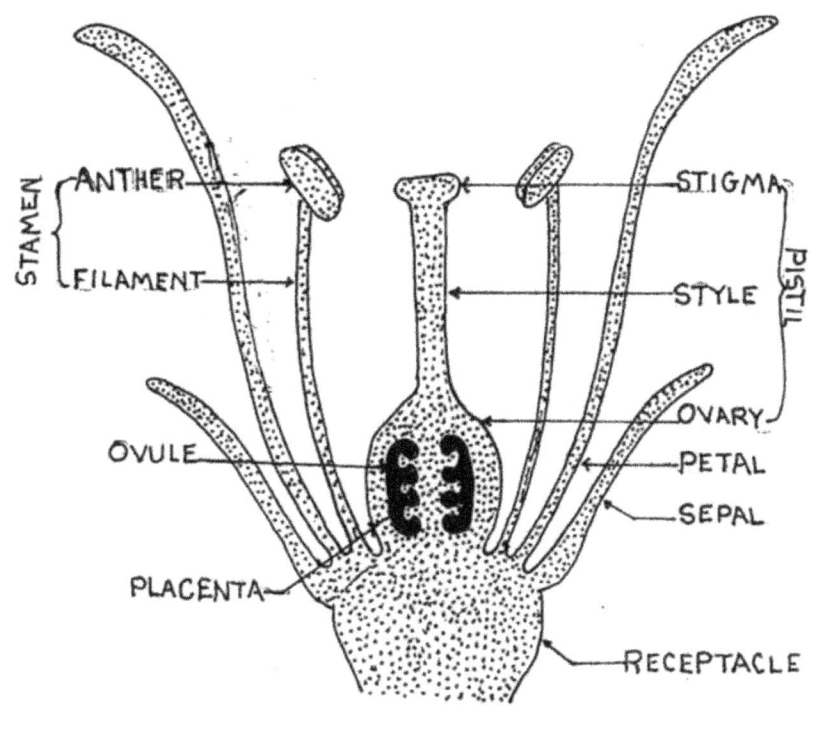

Diagram Showing Floral Organs

Tap Root

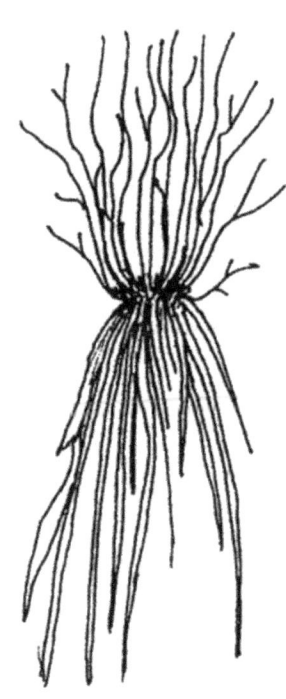

Fibrous Root

Rhizomatous Root
(Adventitious Root)

FLOWER AND PLANT PARTS: ABBREVIATED GLOSSARY

Adventitious root A root that originates from stem or leaf tissue rather than from the interior of another root. Rhizomes usually bear adventitious roots.

Anther Located at the top of the stamen, the anther is an enlarged end of the filament, and contains the pollen grains.

Blade Thin, flat expanded portion of the leaf.

Corolla The collective group of petals.

Fibrous root A thin root arising from another root or from stem tissue. The total root system can be fibrous.

Filament Slender, elongated stalk of the stamen.

Flower The reproductive structure of some seed-bearing plants, often having showy or colorful parts (blossoms). Flowers can be both male and female, producing both pollen and ovule, or one or the other. Flowers are the most commonly used part in identifying a plant.

Internode Area of the shoot between two nodes.

Lateral bud These differ from the terminal bud only in their position on the plant. These buds grow on the sides of the stem, and are responsible for the growth of leaves and side branches.

Lateral root The branching parts of the root which grow from the main root stalk.

Leaf axil Angle where the leaf is attached to the twig.

Node The region of the stem where one or more leaves are attached. Buds are commonly borne in the node.

Ovary Swollen, basal part of the pistil, usually flask-shaped, which contain the ovules, which, after united with the pollen, develop into seeds.

Ovule Embryo sac. Each one contains an egg, and is found within the enlarged, lower part of the pistil. Following fertilization, the ovule develops into the seed.

Petal One of the units of the corolla of a flower. The corolla is the collective name for the white or colored petals.

Petiole Leaf stem.

Pistil Located in the center of the flower; commonly flask shaped, with a swollen, basal part. The pistil is composed of 3 parts: The stigma, the style, and the ovary.

Placenta Region or area where one or more ovules (or seeds) are attached.

Primary root The part of the root system that is the lower end of the shoot, and serves as the main plant anchor.

Receptacle That part of the axis of a flower stem that bears the floral organs.

Rhizome An underground portion of a plant stem, having shoots on top of it and roots beneath it. Though it is underground, it is different from a root in that it has buds, nodes, and scaly leaves. Rhizomes usually bear adventitious roots.

Root Serves to anchor the plant and to absorb water and mineral salts from the soil. It is made up of the primary root and the lateral root.

Sepal The first of four kinds of floral organs, always arranged in the same order. The sepal begins at the base of the flower. These are usually green and leaf-like.

Shoot Made up of stem and leaves, it functions primarily to support, conduct fluids, and manufacture food..

Stamen Located next to the petal. The stamen has two parts: A slender, elongated stalk known as the filament, and an enlarged anther. This latter part contains the pollen grains and terminates the stalk.

Stigma The top, expanded portion of the pistil which receives the pollen. This pollen receptacle may be rough, smooth, sticky, branched, or feathery.

Style Slender and stalklike, the style connects the stigma with the ovary.

Tap root A central main root that descends vertically; it is larger than any branch roots.

Terminal bud The bud that occurs at the tip of a twig, or stem.

Vascular system In plants, refers to the system of channels for carrying life-giving fluids. These channels include plant stems and leaf veins.

BIRCH FAMILY
Betulaceae

General Information: There are 6 genera and about 170 species of this family worldwide. Betulaceae grow in the temperate and boreal areas of the Northern Hemisphere.

In Alaska, the two genera present are *Betula* (Birch) and *Alnus* (Alder). On Spruce Island, the commonly found *Betula* species is *B. nana*, the charming dwarf birch that is found in the bogs. Hulten (1968) mentions that *B. kenaica* also forms a hybrid with this dwarf birch in the Kodiak region. Inland on Kodiak Island, the larger *B. kenaica* trees may be found.

The predominant genus of the birch family found in our area, however, is not *Betula*, but rather, *Alnus crispa*, or alder. *A. crispa* is represented by two subspecies, *crispa* and *sinuata*. (See species information under "Alder" in the habitat section labeled "Stream Banks, Moist, Sunny Hillsides, Rocky Places.")

Leaves and Stems: Leaves of this family are deciduous and alternate. Leaf shapes are a distinguishing feature, as each species has some slight variation of its own. To illustrate: the dwarf birch found in the bogs has leaves that are broader than they are long, with rounded teeth. *B. kenaica* (Kenai birch) has egg-shaped leaves with pointed tips. Birch leaves are dark green on top and paler underneath.

The bark also may differ from species to species. To illustrate again with *Betula*, dwarf birch has smooth bark with dull white markings, and many crooked branches. Kenai birch has dark grey bark, and grows up to 35 feet tall.

Flowers and Fruit: Male and female flowers are clustered in catkins and grow on the same plant. They mature at the same time as the leaves. Male catkins produce pollen. In both birch and alder, the winged seeds (nutlets) are produced later in summer. The cones of *Alnus* are woody, and persistent for 1 to 2 years on the shrub. *Betula* cones are not woody, and disintegrate at the end of the summer.

Alaskan Habitat: The plants of the birch family are found in a wide range of habitats, from lowland bogs to tundra and sub-alpine areas. While the dwarf birch stays in the bogs, the hybrid formed with *B. kenaica* may be found with its alder cousins. Our common large member of the birch family, *A. crispa*, grows close to the forest edge or in wet places, often close to standing or flowing water, commonly at low to middle elevations. The plant becomes smaller as it moves to higher elevations. The subspecies, *sinuata*, occurs in a more distinct subalpine region, along the coast. Alder often forms impenetrable thickets on the mountainsides.

Alder *Alnus crispa*
(alder cone)

Species Found in This Book:
Alder (*Alnus crispa*, ssp. *crispa* and *sinuata*)

BROOMRAPE FAMILY
(Orobanchaceae)

General Information: Members of this family are herbaceous root parasites lacking in chlorophyll. There are about 13 genera and 180 species in this family worldwide. These parasitic plants can be annuals or perennials and are usually somewhat fleshy. Their color can vary, ranging from yellow and brown to violet or red. Hosts for these plants vary from species to species.

In Alaska there are two species. Both of these have been found in the Kodiak area.

Leaves and Stems: The leaves of these plants are simple, scale-like, and alternately arranged on a fleshy erect stem.

Flowers: The flowers are bilaterally symmetrical, and arranged in racemes, spikes, or as a single flower atop a slender stem. Sepals range from 2 to 5, united; 5 petals are united, forming an upper and lower lip. There are 4 stamens. All parts are attached at the base of the ovary.

Fruit: The fruit is a one-chambered capsule.

Alaskan Habitat: Look for the host plant and you may find the broomrape growing close by. Our most common species, *Boschniakia rossica,* is found close to alder, as it is parasitic on alder's roots. The second Alaska species, *Orobanche fasciculata,* is parasitic on *Artemisia.*

Species Found in This Book:
Poque, or broomrape (*Boschniakia rossica*)

Poque
Boschniakia rossica

BUCKWHEAT FAMILY
(Polygonaceae)

General Information: There are about 40 genera and 800 species in this family worldwide. They are found mainly in the temperate areas of the Northern Hemisphere. The members of this family are mostly herbs; in fact, all of our Alaskan species are herbs. In other areas of the world, they are sometimes shrubs or vines with small flowers. Family members can be annual or perennial.

The buckwheats are a food source. Buckwheat grain has been used for hundreds of years in many parts of the world to make flour. In this country, it is popular as pancake flour. Rhubarb is a member of this family. All 3 of the species mentioned in this book are edible.

Leaves and Stems: Leaves are simple, usually alternate. At the stem base they often form a basal rosette. (*Oxyria* has a basal rosette; *Rumex* produces a leafy stem.) Buckwheats are sometimes twining herbs, and their stems commonly have swollen nodes. At the base of the petiole (or leaf stem), there is a distinctive membrane-like sheath around the stem just above the node.

Flowers: Flowers are usually bisexual, but in some species are unisexual. These flowers typically have sepals that are separate and petal-like, sometimes in two series of 3 each. There are 3 to 9 stamens. All these parts are attached at the base of the ovary. Flowers are typically small and numerous. The entire inflorescence is often very showy.

Fruit: The fruits are small, hard, and seed-like, generally 3-sided or lens-shaped.

Alaskan Habitat: Habitat can range from moist to wet areas to dry ridges at high elevations, dependent on the species. *Rumex* species in particular often grow around human settlements or in disturbed areas.

Species Found in This Book:
Mountain Sorrel (*Oxyria digyna*)
Sheep Sorrel (*Rumex acetosella*)
Sourdock (*Rumex* spp.)

Mountain Sorrel
Oxyria digyna

CARROT OR PARSLEY FAMILY
(Apiaceae or Umbelliferae)

General Information: About 300 genera and 3,000 species belong to this medium-sized family worldwide. Most plants in this family are biennial or perennial. Family members include vegetables such as carrots, parsnips, and celery, and seasonings such as parsley, dill, coriander, anise, and caraway. Some species are aromatic herbs. Water hemlock (*Cicuta douglasii*), a species native to the United States and found in Alaska, is very poisonous.

Most members of this family are found in the Northern hemisphere. Nearly one-fourth of the genera are native to the United States. The Umbelliferae are, in fact, well represented in our area.

Leaves and Stems: Leaves are alternate and usually pinnately or palmately compound. Many species have hollow stems; some have fern-like leaves.

Flowers: Small flowers, radially symmetrical, are arranged in simple or compound umbels.

These flowers have 5 small sepals fused to the ovary, 5 petals, and 5 stamens.

Fruit: The small dry fruit splits into two halves, each with one seed.

Alaskan Habitat: Besides the garden habitat of the many cultivated plants in this family, the wild species may be found in a range of locations, from beach sands, marshes, and stream edges to prairies, roadsides, and open fields.

Species Found in This Book:
Angelica (*Angelica genuflexa; A. lucida*)
Beach Lovage (*Ligusticum scoticum*)
Cow Parsnip (*Heracleum lanatum*)
Poison Water Hemlock (*Cicuta douglasii; C. mackenzieana*)

Angelica
Angelica lucida

CLUB MOSS FAMILY
(Lycopodiaceae)

General Information: The club moss family is extremely diverse and ancient, with 10+ genera and 350 to 400 species worldwide. This family is not related to the mosses. Club mosses are vascular plants, with a cellular network for transporting water and nutrients through their tissues. The plants can be trailing or erect; terrestrial or growing upon another plant (though not parasitic).

The genus *Lycopodium* is found throughout Alaska.

Leaves and Stems: The club mosses all have small, narrow, evergreen bract-like leaves that are alternate. These are generally spirally arranged, though sometimes they are arranged in opposite pairs. In most species, the stems are long and creeping with erect branches.

Flowers and Fruit: These plants do not flower and set seed; instead, they reproduce through spores. Spore cases are located in terminal leaf axils. These spore-bearing leaves often form conspicuous 'clubs' at the tip of erect stem branches. These spore-bearing structures vary from species to species. Spores are minute, uniform, and numerous.

Alaskan Habitat: Plants in the club moss family seek habitat in many places, from bogs or moist woods to rocky areas. They may even be found on alpine slopes.

Species Found in This Book:
Fir Club Moss (*Lycopodium selago*)

Fir Club Miss
Lycopodium selago

COMPOSITE FAMILY
(Compositae or Asteraceae)

General Information: The composite family might be called the "Smith family" of plants. It is the largest plant family in the world, with about 920 genera and around 20,000 species. The composites are also known as Asteraceae (sunflower or daisy family).

This family is mostly herbs, and sometimes shrubs and vines. Many species are edibles, domesticated and otherwise. Many medicinals are also members of this huge group. Composites have a fair share of ornamentals, such as dahlias, as well. Of course, some members of any family often seem to have a bad reputation, and the composites are no exception. The current problem plant of the composite family in our area is hawkweed *(Hieracium)*, which has invaded Kodiak on a grand scale. In Ouzinkie, Georgia Smith's back yard turned orange with hawkweed a few years ago, and she is still battling survivors.

Leaves and Stems: The leaves may be simple or compound; alternate or opposite. Stems are herbaceous or sometimes formed into shrubs or vines.

Flowers: Flowers of this family are really an inflorescence. What is sometimes mistaken for a single flower is actually made up of numerous smaller clusters of flowers resting on a single stem – a natural bouquet, as it were. These flowers come in two forms: Disk flowers, which are tubular, and ray flowers, such as in the dandelion, or the daisy one plucks when reciting "he loves me; he loves me not."

The calyx is absent, or modified into hairs, bristles, scales or a crown. Each separate disk flower has a corolla with 5 fused petals, which form a tube; 5 stamens, and an inferior, one-chambered ovary.

Fruit: The fruit is one-seeded and small, with a hard shell.

Alaskan Habitat: Though species from this family may be found in a wide range of habitats, many of them are especially well adapted to a climate that is fairly dry. In cool Alaska, they often grow in the drier areas of the state. However, our area around Kodiak has/supports many species.

Species Found in This Book:
Arnica (*Arnica* spp.)
Dandelion (*Taraxacum* spp.)
Goldenrod (*Solidago multiradiata; S. lepida*)
Pineapple Weed (*Matricaria matricarioides*)
Wormwood (*Artemisia tilesii*)
Yarrow (*Achillea borealis*)

Arnica
Arnica spp.

CROWBERRY FAMILY
(Empetraceae)

General Information: The crowberry family is small, with only three genera worldwide. There are probably six species, though sources disagree.

Our Alaskan crowberry is a low, sprawling evergreen shrub, freely branching, that resembles a miniature fir tree.

Leaves and Stems: Crowberries have slender woody creeping stems. The leaves are needle-like and grow either in whorls of 4 or alternate on the branch. The leaf margins are somewhat rolled under; leaves are grooved underneath.

Flowers: Purplish crimson flowers appear in early spring, with male and female flowers sometimes on separate plants. These flowers are small, with sepals 3; petals 2 or 3 or none; stamens usually 3. The ovary is superior.

Fruit: In Alaska the fruit is a berry.

Alaskan Habitat: Crowberries can be found in bogs or on alpine slopes, dry to wet, sea level to mountaintop. They are often companion plants to species such as lingonberry or Labrador tea.

Species Found in This Book:
Crowberry (*Empetrum nigrum*)

Crowberry *Empetrum nigrum*

CROWFOOT OR BUTTERCUP FAMILY
(Ranunculaceae)

General Information: The crowfoot or buttercup family is a fairly large one, with up to 70 genera and about 2,000 species worldwide. Its members are annual or perennial. They are usually leafy herbs (all Alaska species are herbs.) Members of this family are found chiefly in cooler, temperate regions, especially in the Northern Hemisphere.

Several members of this family are grown as ornamentals, in some cases beautiful but deadly. Some provide drugs. (Example: *Aconitum* is a source of anti-fever compounds that are important to internal medicine.) Several species, including *Aconitum,* are very poisonous. Handle all members of this family with extreme care!

Leaves and Stems: The leaves are mostly alternate; rarely opposite. These leaves are often compound or deeply divided. (Exception: *Caltha,* or marsh marigold.) Stems are usually leafy; sometimes they are vines or shrublike plants.

Flowers: Flowers are usually bisexual and usually radially symmetrical. They can be single or numerous on the plant. Sepals and petals are separate; variable in number; often all are petal-like. The flower usually has many stamens, and pistils may number from one to many. The flowers produce several to many seeds.

Fruit: The fruit may be a capsule, an achene or a berry.

Alaskan Habitat: The cool temperatures of Alaska are ideal for some members of this family. They may be found growing in a wide range of habitats, from the edge of snow beds in mountain meadows to foothills and coastal bluffs. Some species grow in moist forest or grassland. They are often found in wet areas, such as streambeds or seeps.

Species Found in This Book:
Baneberry (*Actaea rubra*)
Buttercup (*Ranunculus* spp.)
Marsh Marigold (*Caltha palustris* ssp. *asarifolia*)
Monkshood (*Aconitum delphinifolium*)
Narcissus-Flowered Anemone (*Anemone narcissiflora*)

Monkshood
Aconitum delphinifolium

DOGWOOD FAMILY
(Cornaceae)

General Information: There are about 12 genera and 100 species in this family, growing in temperate regions of the world. Family members are mostly trees and shrubs and rarely herbs. However, the small species growing in our area is the herbaceous Canadian dwarf cornel. We have no dogwood trees in Alaska.

Leaves and Stems: Dogwood leaves grow on short stems. Some of these leaves survive through one winter: these are referred to as "wintergreen". They are thus distinguished from evergreen leaves, called such because they have survived for two or more years. Dogwood produces new leaves every year. The larger dogwood shrub in the interior has many freely spreading stems with reddish brown bark, while our small Canadian dwarf dogwood has erect stems up to 6 inches high. These stems are somewhat woody at the base.

The leaves grow in terminal whorls, 4 to 7 in number. Atop these leaves are 4 white bracts with a purplish tint; these look like flower petals. However, the true flowers grow in a cluster at the center of the four petal-like bracts.

Flowers: The flowers are small and greenish white or yellowish to purplish, depending on the species. Our Alaska species have 4 sepals, 4 petals, and 4 stamens.

Fruit: The fruit is fleshy, and contains a two-seeded stone. Dwarf dogwood fruits, bright red or orange, are round berries formed in a tight cluster. They are pulpy but have a sweet flavor.

Alaskan Habitat: Dogwood plants grow in moist woods or forest openings. Because many of these plants are often found growing together, they make an excellent ground cover for a woodland garden.

Species Found in This Book:
Canadian Dwarf Cornel or Dwarf Dogwood (*Cornus canadensis*)

Canadian Dwarf Cornel
Cornus canadensis

EVENING PRIMROSE FAMILY
(Onagraceae)

General Information: The evening primrose family has about 17 genera and 675 species. Though relatively small, Onagraceae has representatives sparsely scattered worldwide. Family members include evening primrose, fuchsia, and lopezia, all popular ornamentals. A botanist first used the name "evening primrose" in the 1600's. The sweet-scented *Epilobium* reminded him of the wild primroses of England. Though the two plants are unrelated, the "evening primrose" name has remained.

The numerous species growing in Alaska are all herbs. The two discussed in this book are the two types of fireweed.

Leaves and Stems: Leaves of this family are often opposite, though they can be alternate or whorled. They are commonly alternate in our flora, though they may look superficially opposite. They are simple and sessile (having no petiole, or stem.) The stem is erect and leafy, from top to bottom.

Flowers: The flowers are solitary or borne in terminal clusters or in racemes. The flowers are often radially symmetrical. Typically, they have 4 sepals, 4 petals, 4 to 8 stamens and 1 inferior ovary.

Fruit: Fruits are commonly 4-chambered capsules with several to many hairless or hairy seeds. In the case of the charming ground cover with its heart-shaped leaves that I discovered at the tree line in my yard, enchanter's nightshade, (*Circaea alpina*), the fruits are bristly one- to two-sided nutlets.

Alaskan Habitat: Species may be found in a variety of habitats, from moist, cool soils to dry, sandy slopes or graveled areas such as riverbeds. Consider just the two species in this book: *Epilobium latifolium* grows abundantly in the riverbed near my present home on Kodiak Island. However, *E. angustifolium* thrives in open, sunny areas. In the fall, the hillsides or open fields in our area often appear on fire due to the profusion of fireweed in bloom.

Species Found in This Book:
Fireweed (*Epilobium angustifolium; E. latifolium*)

Fireweed
Epilobium angustifolium

FIGWORT OR SNAPDRAGON FAMILY
(Scrophulariaceae)

General Information: The figworts or snapdragons are a large global family, with about 220 genera and 3,000 species worldwide. They are mostly herbs. However, they may also be shrubs, and, rarely, trees. The plant often has showy flowers. Several family members, including snapdragons and foxglove, are grown as ornamentals.

The species found in our area are all herbs. This family is very well-represented in Alaska.

Leaves and Stems: Leaves may be alternate, opposite, or whorled. In some species, leaves are simple; in others, pinnately divided. Leaf stems may be tinged red. Stems are leafy, erect, or trailing; simple or branched.

Flowers: Typically, the flowers are bilaterally symmetrical, with 4 or 5 united sepals and 4 or 5 united petals, which usually form a two-lipped corolla. There are usually 4 stamens, but sometimes 2 or 5, with the fifth one often sterile and different from the others. All parts attach to a single, superior ovary.

Fruit: Fruits are two-chambered capsules containing numerous seeds, or rarely, a berry.

Alaskan Habitat: Figwort family members are well distributed throughout the state. They may be found in a variety of habitats. Many species occur in sandy soils. Others prefer disturbed soil or moist meadows. Our monkey flower grows in wet places, such as creeks or drainage seeps. It grows near or in the water.

Species Found in This Book:
Monkey Flower (*Mimulus guttatus*)

Monkey Flower
Mimuus guttatus

FORGET-ME-NOT OR BORAGE FAMILY
(Boraginaceae)

General Information: There are about 100 genera and 2000 species in the forget-me-not or borage family worldwide. These plants are generally herbs, and are often covered with bristly hair.

Only a few of the species of this family, all of them herbs, grow in Alaska. Most others are found in a warmer climate. One member of this family, *Myosotis alpestris,* ssp. a*siatica,* or forget-me-not, is the Alaska state flower.

Leaves and Stems: The leaves are simple and may be rough and hairy or smooth. Basal leaves have a long stalk below the leaf blade. Stems are usually leafy. They can be long stalks or low clumps, such as our own oysterleaf..

Flowers: Typically, the flowers are radially symmetrical, and often form in tight coils like a fiddlehead, along one side of the stem. There are 5 sepals, joined at the base; 5 petals fused in a flaring, 5-lobed tube (like a bluebell). Five stamens are attached at the base of the tube, near the ovary. The ovary is superior; the style is attached at the base.

Fruit: Fruits of borage species usually consist of 4 hard nutlets.

Alaskan Habitat: Look for forget-me-nots in moist, open meadows, near seeps, or along stream banks. Oysterleaf grows on ocean beaches.

Species Found in This Book:
Oysterleaf (*Mertensia maritima*)

Oysterleaf
Mertensia maritima

GERANIUM FAMILY
(Geraniaceae)

General Information: Geranium family members are leafy herbs with showy white, pink, or purple flowers in clusters. The family has about 11 genera and nearly 800 species worldwide. Many grow in the northern temperate climates of the world. The cultivated geranium, *Pelargonum,* is a tropical genus that grows especially well in Africa.

Though plants of the geranium family may be annual or perennial, our only Kodiak member, *Geranium erianthum,* is perennial.

Leaves and Stems: Within the entire family, leaves may be alternate or opposite, and simple, pinnately or palmately lobed, or compound. *G. erianthum* has leaves palmately deeply divided into 3 to 5 irregularly lobed and toothed segments. Stems are leafy and hairy.

Flowers: Flowers in the geranium family are usually radially symmetrical, with 5 sepals, free or slightly united at base; 5 petals, free; stamens 5, 10, or 15, with stalks sometimes joined at the base. *G. erianthum* has 5 sepals, 5 petals, 10 stamens, and a 5-parted ovary.

Fruit: Fruits develop from a long-beaked pistil with 5 united chambers. Each chamber has a long style, attached to the central core. This style coils away from the core at maturity, ripping off a segment of the chamber, and ejecting its single seed.

Alaskan Habitat: Our Alaskan species may be found in wet soil from low meadows to sunny alpine mountainsides. Wild geranium can also be found along roadways or trails or in open forests.

Species Found in This Book:
Wild Geranium (*Geranium erianthum*)

Wild Geranium
Geranium erianthum

GINSENG FAMILY
(Araliaceae)

General Information: There are about 70 genera and 700 species in this family worldwide. Members of the ginseng family are trees, shrubs, or perennial herbs. It is interesting that the Latin name for this plant, *Panax,* comes from the Greek word for "panacea", or cure-all. Indeed, the name seems to fit, as the plants in the ginseng family are defined by belief and use as a cure-all by many indigenous groups around the globe.

Devil's club (*Echinopanax horridum*) is the only Alaskan member of this family.

Leaves and Stems: Within the entire family, leaves are alternate or whorled, simple or compound. The stems of the plants in this family are solid, rather than hollow.

Flowers: Flowers are generally in panicled or racemed umbels. There are 5 minute sepals, 5 petals, usually 5 stamens; the ovary is inferior with two or more seed cavities.

Fruits: Fruits are berry-like; these contain nutlets.

Alaskan Habitat: These plants grow on the borders of the forest or in open wooded areas.

Species Found in This Book:
Devil's Club (*Echinopanax horridum* or *Oplopanax horridus*)

Devil's Club
Echinopanax horridum

GOOSEFOOT FAMILY
(Chenopodiaceae)

General Information: There are 105 genera and close to 1500 species in this family worldwide. Annual or perennial plants range in size from herbs to trees. Spinach, beets, sugar beets, and chard are members of this family. Species of the goosefoot family are often found in deserts and especially in saline or alkaline soils.

Leaves and Stems: In some species, the leaves are reduced to scales or teeth. In other species, leaves are alternate, or, rarely, opposite. These leaves are supposedly shaped like the foot of a goose; hence the Latin name, *Chenopodium,* which means "goosefoot". The stems may be erect or decumbent; simple or branched.

Flowers: The flowers are greenish and tiny and form in dense clusters or spikes, both in leaf axils and at stem tips. The flower has a calyx of 1 to 5 sepals, usually small, no corolla; 1 to 5 stamens and 2 to 5 pistils, united, 2 to 5 styles and a one-celled ovary.

Fruit: The fruit is an achene.

Alaskan Habitat: Goosefoot species grow in many areas of Alaska. Some are found on sandy sea beaches. Our regional family members often grow in disturbed soil or along beachfronts.

Species Found in This Book:
Lambsquarter *(Chenopodium album)*
Orach *(Atriplex* spp.)

Lambsquarter
Chenopodium album

HEATH FAMILY
(Ericaceae)

General Information: This family contains at least 50 genera and up to 3,500 species worldwide. Members include numerous shrubs and woody plants, and are often found in temperate regions of the world. The family boasts such ornamentals as rhododendron and azalea, and edible fruits such as blueberries, huckleberries, and cranberries.

Leaves and Stems: Leaves are simple, usually opposite, and often leathery. Stems are often woody.

Flowers: These are radially or bilaterally symmetrical, with 4 or 5 united sepals and twice as many stamens. The 4 or 5 united petals often take the shape of a miniature Chinese lantern. All parts are attached either at the base or at the top of the ovary.

Fruit: These are a capsule, berry, or drupe. Many of these plants typically produce fleshy fruits – the edible berries or capsules. These fruits were a critical food source for many native groups. The berries can be eaten fresh, dried, or stored as jams and jellies.

Alaskan Habitat: Species often prefer acidic soils. This incredibly diverse family dominates the understory of the Pacific Coastal regions. In our state, heath family members may be found in muskegs and woods, or in alpine to subalpine areas.

Species Found in This Book:
Blueberry
    Alpine Blueberry (*Vaccinium uliginosum*)
    Bog Blueberry (*Vaccinium uliginosum* ssp. *microphylum*)
    Early Blueberry (*Vaccinium ovalifolium*)
Cranberry
    Lingonberry or Lowbush Cranberry (*Vaccinium vitis-idaea*)
    Bog cranberry (*Oxycoccus microcarpus*)
Kinnikinnik (*Arctostaphylos uva-ursi*)
Labrador Tea (*Ledum palustre* ssp. *decumbens*)

Bog Blueberry
Vaccinium uliginosum,
ssp. *microphylum*

HONEYSUCKLE FAMILY
(Caprifoliaceae)

General Information: The honeysuckle family is mostly shrubs with some vines and herbs. The flowers are often showy. About 15 genera and 400 species grow in temperate climates or in tropical mountains worldwide. Family members are commonly found in the Northern Hemisphere.

Leaves and Stems: The leaves are opposite, simple, or compound. Stems are erect or twining.

Flowers: The blossoms of the honeysuckle family are radially or bilaterally symmetrical, and are usually in a branched or forked cluster. Flowers have 5 small sepals and a corolla with 5 petals united in a slender tube. They are usually flared into a trumpet-shaped end, or form an upper and lower lip. They usually have 5 stamens. All parts attach at the top of the ovary (ovary is inferior).

Fruit: The fruit is a berry, drupe, or capsule.

Alaskan Habitat: Alaska family members may be found from bogs to foothills. They may grow in meadows, open woods, or along stream banks.

Species Found in This Book:
Elderberry (*Sambucus racemosa*)
Highbush Cranberry (*Viburnum edule*)

Highbush Cranberry
Viburnum edule

HORSETAIL FAMILY
(Equisetaceae)

General Information: This family of perennial plants has only one genus: *Equisetum*. This genus has about 20 species worldwide. The plants do not have flowers, but reproduce by spores. The family is ancient, and is known through fossils from as early as 350 million years ago.

Leaves and Stems: Most horsetail species produce green stems with strobili (spikes, or cones) at the tip. *E. arvense* is an exception in our flora. This species has two growth forms. The first is the spore-bearing stem, which has no chlorophyll, and which arises from the rhizome. The green, vegetative parts of the plant sprout from the same long-creeping underground rhizomes. These produce stems at close intervals, forming a colony of plants. The stems are made up of a series of hollow joints. The round stems are rough in texture, grass-like, and have a grooved surface.

The green stems of some species develop many small branches and look something like horses' tails or miniature evergreen trees. The surface of the plant contains silica crystals and may have projections of the material that give it a harsh, gritty texture. This gritty surface is often so rough that these plants may be used by the camper to scour pots and pans (hence another common name of "scouring rush").

Flowers: The Equisetaceae are spore-bearing plants and do not produce true flowers.

Fruit: The spores are produced in cones at the top of the stem. This spore-bearing portion is brownish in color. Once spores are released, the cone dies away.

Alaskan Habitat: In general, this plant family favors wet areas, and is often found along creeks and seeps. It also loves the disturbed soil of your garden.

Species Found in This Book:
Horsetail (*Equisetum arvense*)

Horsetail
Equisetum arvense

IRIS FAMILY
(Iridaceae)

General Information: The iris family is medium-sized, with about 60 genera and about 1500 species worldwide. Most family members are perennial. Iridaceae grow from rhizomes, bulbs, or corms, and may be found in all but the coldest parts of the earth. Species of iris are quite common in Africa. Family members include iris, crocus, and gladiolas.

Only two genera are found in Alaska. One is *Iris setosa,* or wild flag. The second is *Sisyrinchium*, or the charming blue-eyed grass, which also grows in the Kodiak area.

Leaves and Stems: Leaves are simple and alternate and have parallel veins. In shape they are long and grass-like to sword-shaped. The stems, slender or stout, are cylindrical, though they appear flattened at the base, where the leaves are overlapping one another.

Flowers: These form singly or in clusters at the top of the stem. Sepals and petals are colored.

There are 3 sepals, 3 petals, and 3 stamens. The ovary is inferior.

Fruit: The fruit is a capsule with 3 chambers and many seeds.

Alaskan Habitat: These plants inhabit meadows, bogs, and shorelines.

Species Found in This Book:
Wild Iris, Wild Flag (*Iris setosa*)

Wild Iris
Iris setosa

LILY FAMILY
(Liliaceae)

General Information: The lily family consists of around 250 genera and 3700 species worldwide. Most lilies are perennial herbs, growing from rhizomes, bulbs or fleshy roots. They are found mostly in the warm, temperate, or tropical climates of the world.

Edible lily family members include onions, garlic, leeks, and asparagus. More traditional edibles in Alaska include Indian rice or chocolate lily, wild chives, and wild cucumber.

Caution needs to be taken with this family, as two species found in our area, death camas (*Zygadenus elegans*) and false hellebore (*Veratrum viride*) are both quite poisonous.

Leaves and Stems: Close examination of this family reveals parallel veined leaves. They are either all basal, or they are alternate or whorled along the stem. Stems may be very leafy, or may have few or no leaves.

Flowers: The flower parts are generally in threes; rarely in twos. The sepals and petals are often similar in appearance. Number of stamens is 6 or fewer. The ovary is superior, and generally has three compartments.

Fruit: The fruit of a lily is a capsule or berry. The latter is sometimes edible.

Alaskan Habitat: Lily family members are widely distributed in Alaska. They dwell in a wide range of habitats, from forest edges and moist woods or stream banks to dry, open meadows or roadsides.

Species Found in This Book:
Death Camas (*Zygadenus elegans*)
False Hellebore (*Veratrum viride*)
Indian Rice or Chocolate Lily (*Fritillaria camschatcensis*)
Wild Chives (*Allium schoenoprasum*)
Wild Cucumber (*Streptopus amplexifolius*)

Chocolate Lily
Fritillaria camschatcensis

MADDER FAMILY
(Rubiaceae)

General Information: This large family, with 500 genera and 6,000 species worldwide, is made up primarily of tropical shrubs and trees. Rubiaceae often may be found in the tropical regions of the world. The coffee tree is a valued family member. Gardenias are popular ornamentals from this family.

Our Alaskan family members are herbs: low-growing or sprawling perennials.

Leaves and Stems: The leaves are simple and opposite or whorled along the stem. The herbaceous stems are often sprawling, though our *G. boreale* has stems that are either erect or ascending.

Flowers: Flowers of this family are usually radially symmetrical, with 4 or 5 sepals, 4 or 5 united petals and 4 or 5 stamens. The ovary is inferior, sitting below the flower.

Fruit: The fruits of the Rubiaceae are distinctly 2-lobed. These become dry and then separate into one-seeded nutlets with hooked bristles.

Alaskan Habitat: The Alaska species of this family are widely distributed throughout the state. They may be found along beaches or in open meadows and along roads and trails.

Species Found in This Book:
Cleavers (*Galium aparine*)
Northern Bedstraw (*Galium boreale*)

Northern Bedstraw
Galium boreale

MINT FAMILY
(Labiatae or Lamiaceae)

General Information: Mints are aromatic herbs or shrubs, and rarely trees or vines. The mints are a commonly encountered family, especially in the temperate regions of the world. This family is comprised of about 180 genera and 3,500 species occurring nearly worldwide. Many of the species have been taken into cultivation as ornamentals. Some are highly desirable cooking herbs or flavorings, such as marjoram, savory, peppermint or spearmint.

Spearmint and several other Alaskan species of the mint family are not native; rather, they have been introduced from other places.

Leaves and Stems: Leaves are usually simple, opposite, or whorled. Due to the square stem and opposite leaves, most mint family members are easily recognized. Leaves of some family members emit a minty smell when crushed.

Flowers: The flowers are in long or interrupted clusters along the stem. They are laterally symmetrical, with 5 united sepals and 5 united petals. The petals are usually arranged to form an upper and lower lip. There are 2 to 4 stamens. The ovary is superior.

Fruit: The fruit has 4 lobes. Each forms a hard, single-seeded nutlet.

Alaskan Habitat: Marshes and wet fields are likely spots to find members of this family. Our Spruce Island spearmint grows in rich, sunny soil. Self-heal grows along some of our island trails and roadways.

Species Found in This Book:
Self-Heal (*Prunella vulgaris*)
Spearmint (*Mentha spicata*)

Self-Heal
Prunella vulgaris

NETTLE FAMILY
(Urticaceae)

General Information: There are 45 genera and 700 species in this family worldwide. The nettles are annual or perennial herbs, often with stinging hairs. The plants grow from strong spreading rhizomes.

Leaves and Stems: Nettles have a leafy, upright stem with an average height from 1 to 3 meters tall. Urticaceae leaves are alternate or opposite, simple, coarsely toothed, and lance- to heart-shaped.

Flowers: The nettle flowers are greenish, tiny, and numerous, growing in drooping clusters at leaf axils. Sepals number 2 to 5, distinct or partly united; stamens 2 to 5, nearly separate, or united. Petals are absent. The ovary is superior and one-chambered. There is 1 style and 1 stigma.

Fruit: The fruit is an achene (dry and one-seeded).

Alaskan Habitat: Nettles inhabit a variety of areas, from lowland to subalpine. They can be found in meadows, thickets, along stream banks, and in open forests. They especially prefer disturbed areas, particularly near human habitations. Our Spruce Island nettles grow in abundance in the old abandoned village garden spots. Near my house is a nice stand growing on an open hillside, intermingled with spreading wood fern and false hellebore.

Species Found in This Book:
Nettle (*Urtica lyallii*)

Nettle
Urtica lyallii

PEA FAMILY
(Leguminosae)

General Information: With 60 genera and approximately 13,000 species worldwide, the pea family is probably the third largest in the world. Members of this diverse family are annual or perennial herbs, shrubs, trees or vines.

Leaves and Stems: Leaves are alternate and usually pinnately or palmately compound, generally with conspicuous stipules. Stems vary according to the plant. They may be weak or sprawling; herbaceous and leafy; twining or woody.

Flowers: There are actually 3 types of flowers in this family. The most common type, the "pea flower", which is found in Alaska, has a broad upper petal (banner or standard), two lateral petals (wings), and 2 bottom petals (keel), joined and shaped like the prow of a boat. These flowers are bilaterally symmetrical, with 5 fused sepals, 5 distinct petals, 5 or 10 stamens and 1 superior ovary. They have a 5-toothed calyx, 9 stamens united in a sheath, with the 10th stamen free.

Flowers of the *Trifolium* species are in heads or very short spikes.

Fruit: The fruit is a one-chambered pod (legume) that usually opens along one or two seams. Inside are several to many seeds that are attached to the side of the pod.

Alaskan Habitat: Members of this family can be found in a variety of locations: Open woods and burnt-over land; along the beaches; hillsides, fields or roadsides; waste lands; near streams. The soil might be moist or dry. The family is found from the sea coasts to alpine areas.

Species Found in This Book:
Beach Peas (*Lathyrus maritimus*)
Clover (*Trifolium* spp.)
Nootka Lupine (*Lupinus nootkatensis*)
Wild Sweet Pea (*Hedysarum mackenzii*)

Nootka Lupine
Lupinus mootkatensis

PINE FAMILY
(Pinaceae)

General Information: There are 9 to 12 genera and 210 species in the pine family, worldwide. This family is made up of resinous, gymnosperm trees. They lack a true ovary and bear naked seeds on the upper surfaces of their cone-like scales.

Our Sitka spruce is the most widely distributed spruce in the Pacific Northwest. It is also our most valuable tree, as it is used for construction of buildings and airplanes, and for wood pulp. Pinaceae species present in Alaska include white spruce, black spruce, tamarack and lodgepole pine.

Leaves and Stems: Pine tree trunks can sometimes reach 160 feet or more. The leaves are firm, evergreen, and needle-like. (The leaves are scale-like in other gymnosperm families.) The bark is smooth (younger trees) to scaly or furrowed.

Flowers: Male and female cones grow on the same tree. Scales of both male and female cones are spirally arranged. Each scale has either 2 pollen sacs or 2 ovules. The small male cones disintegrate after the pollen is released. The female cone becomes enlarged and woody, protecting the seeds that need two or more years to mature.

Fruit: Seeds are usually winged, and released from the woody cones formed from the female catkin.

Alaskan Habitat: Pine family members prefer moist, well-drained sites and grow typically at low to middle elevations. Black spruce can tolerate the wettest conditions. It may be found in muskegs, where its growth is stunted.

Species Found in This Book:
Sitka Spruce (*Picea sitchensis*)

Sitka Spruce
Picea sitchensis

PINK OR CARNATION FAMILY
(Caryophyllaceae)

General Information: There are about 80 genera and 2,000 species of this family of annual or perennial herbs worldwide. This mid-sized family prefers the cooler northern regions of the world.

The pink family includes a large number of important ornamentals, such as the carnation and baby's breath.

Leaves and Stems: Caryophyllaceae often have swollen nodes on the stems. The leaves are simple, opposite, and, for most species, narrow.

Flowers: The blossoms grow singly or in a branched or forked cluster. These flowers are radially symmetrical. Most have 5 sepals, free from one another or united; 5 (rarely, 4) distinct petals, often slender at the base and fringed or toothed at the end. Usually there are 10 stamens. There is a single, superior ovary.

Fruit: The fruits are usually one-chambered capsules, often with numerous seeds.

Alaskan Habitat: Some family members, such as seabeach sandwort, prefer to grow in rocky places such as gravelly beach shores. Others might be found on both dry, hard ground and moist soils. They are often found in garden spots or cultivated fields.

Species Found in This Book:
Chickweed (*Stellaria* spp.)
Seabeach Sandwort (*Honckenya peploides*)

Seabeach sandwort
Honckenya peploides

PLANTAIN FAMILY
(Plantaginaceae)

General Information: There are 3 genera and about 270 species in this family worldwide. Most species have small, inconspicuous flowers. They grow in temperate regions.

The ancient *Plantago major* is sometimes called the "mother of all plants", as it has been known since biblical times and is distributed worldwide. *Plantago maritima* is a choice edible.

Leaves and Stems: The leaves are alternate, basal, and simple. They have pinnate veins that may look parallel. Some of these herbaceous plants are stemless. Others are short-stemmed. The flowers grow on a leafless stem.

Flowers: The flowers are radially symmetrical with 4 sepals or 4 petals, and 4 stamens, which often protrude from the flower. These are all attached at the base of the ovary.

Fruit: The fruit is a capsule, usually with two seeds.

Alaskan Habitat: These plants may be found at the seashore or in disturbed soil. *Plantago major* settles near people. *P. maritima* grows in coastal areas. At the beach or along your driveway are good places to look for these plants.

Species Found in This Book:
Common Plantain (*Plantago major*)
Goosetongue, Seashore Plantain (*Plantago macrocarpa; P. maritima*)

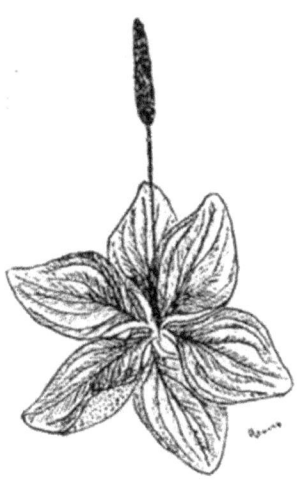

Common Plaintain
Plantago major

POLEMONIUM OR PHLOX FAMILY
(Polemoniaceae)

General Information: This small family, found mostly in North America, has about 18 genera and 300 species worldwide. Usually these are leafy herbs. Occasionally they are small shrubs, which commonly have showy flowers. Some family members grow in desert areas.

The flowers of this family attract pollinators, such as bees, butterflies, and hummingbirds.

Leaves and Stems: Leaves are usually alternate, though in some species they are opposite. They are simple or pinnately compound. Stems may be erect or decumbent.

Flowers: The flowers of this family are often showy, phlox-like, or wheel-shaped, and radially symmetric. These flowers are open or in dense clusters on a forked stem. There are 5 sepals fused into a 5-lobed tube. Petals are also fused into a tube with 5 spreading lobes. There are 5 stamens. These are all attached at the base of a superior ovary.

Fruit: The fruit is a 3-chambered capsule with few to many seeds.

Alaskan Habitat: Numerous species can be found in dry, rocky or open slopes, or in meadows. Gravelly riverbeds are another habitat.

Species Found in This Book:
Jacob's Ladder (*Polemonium acutiflorum; P. pulcherrimum*)

Jacob's Ladder
Polemonium pulcherrimum

PURSLANE FAMILY
(Portulacaceae)

General Information: Purslane family members are found throughout the world, and especially in the Americas. Purslanes are also very common in Africa and Asia. There are about 19 genera and nearly 600 species in this family. The herbs of this small family are often succulent or fleshy, and have delicate flowers. They may be annual or perennial.

A few of the species are grown as ornamentals. Our spring beauty is eaten as a potherb.

Leaves and Stems: The leaves are smooth, simple, alternate or opposite, or in a dense basal rosette. The tender herbs in this family often have succulent leaves and stems.

Flowers: The delicate flowers are radially symmetrical, and either single or in branched clusters. These flowers usually have 2 greenish sepals, united or separate; 4 to 6 distinct petals (usually 5), separate or united at the base; 1 stamen opposite each petal (or many stamens). All are attached to a single superior ovary.

Fruit: The fruit is usually a one-chambered capsule, often opening at the top. Seeds may be one or many.

Alaskan Habitat: Purslanes are often found growing in open, moist places. They may also be found in the loose soil of the forest. Some grow in rocky crevices or on cliffs. Purslane species may also appear on dry slopes in the mountains, shortly after the snows have melted.

Species Found in This Book:
Alaska Spring Beauty (*Claytonia sibirica*)

Alaska Spring Beauty
Claytonia siberica

ROSE FAMILY
(Rosaceae)

General Information: There are about 100 genera and 3,000 species in this worldwide family. Rose family plants may be herbs, shrubs, or trees. Some have prickly stems. In the collection in this book are found representatives of all three types:

1) Trees: mountain ash
2) Shrubs: raspberry, salmonberry, wild rose
3) Herbs: geum, silverweed, marsh fivefinger, beach strawberry, nagoonberry, cloudberry, trailing raspberry, cinquefoil and burnet.

Alaskan ornamentals include roses, mountain ash, spirea, and shrubby cinquefoil.

Leaves and Stems: The leaves of Rosaceae are alternate, simple or compound. These usually have small stipules (leaf-like structures) at the base of the petiole.

Flowers: The flowers are usually bisexual and are radially symmetrical. Typically, they have 5 sepals, united at the base; 5 petals and numerous stamens that are attached to a cup or saucer-like structure atop the flower stalk. Family members may have a few to several simple ovaries. In some species these become enclosed in a fleshy structure (rose hip).

Fruit: The fruit takes a variety of shapes, as can be seen in these family representatives: Apples, pears, quinces, cherries, plums, peaches, nectarines, apricots, blackberries, raspberries, strawberries and almonds.

Alaskan Habitat: Rosaceae may be found in a number of places: Gravelly or rocky slopes and canyons, stream banks, open, moist woods or sandy coastal areas and inland meadows. Many of the species in our area prefer open, moist areas, often in or at the edges of the woods, or sometimes in bogs.

Species Found in This Book:
Beach Strawberry (*Fragaria chiloensis*)
Burnet (*Sanguisorba* spp.)
Cinquefoil (*Potentilla* spp.)
Geum (*Geum macrophyllum: Avens*)
Marsh Fivefinger (*Potentilla palustris*)
Mountain Ash (*Sorbus sitchensis*)
Nagoonberry (*Rubus arcticus*)
Raspberry
    American Red Raspberry (*Rubus idaeus*)
    Cloudberry (*Rubus chamaemorus*)
    Trailing Raspberry (*Rubus pedatus*)
Salmonberry (*Rubus spectabilis*)
Silverweed (*Potentilla egedii*)
Wild Rose (*Rosa nutkana*)

Wild Rose
Rosa nutkana

SAXIFRAGE FAMILY
(Saxifragaceae)

General Information: The saxifrage family is medium-sized, with about 30 genera and 580 species worldwide. Most species flourish in the cooler regions of the Northern Hemisphere. Sometimes shrubs, but usually herbs with small flowers, most saxifrage family members are perennial.

Leaves and Stems: Saxifragaceae have simple leaves that lack stipules. They are alternate or basal. The plant stems can range from herbaceous to woody.

Flowers: Most saxifrage flowers are radially symmetrical, with raceme-like or branched terminal clusters. There are 4 to 5 sepals; 4 to 5 petals (sometimes 10); and 5 to 10 stamens. The most common combination is 5 sepals, 5 petals and 10 stamens. All parts are attached to the edge of a cup-like flower base, with the ovary in the center.

Fruit: The fruit is a capsule or follicle (which is a type of capsule)..

Alaskan Habitat: Saxifrage species often grow in wet places. At times, the plants may be found in an alpine meadow, but often saxifrage species inhabit the rocky places, from slopes to the sides of a cliff. The Latin meaning of "saxifrage" can be roughly translated as "rock breaker", as the plant appears to have split a rock in two so it could grow in the crevice.

This family is distributed throughout Alaska.

Species Found in This Book:
Saxifrage (*Saxifraga punctata*)
Wild Alum (*Heuchera glabra*)

Wild Alum
Heuchera glabra

SEDUM OR STONECROP FAMILY
(Crassulaceae)

General Information: Sedum is a charming family of succulent herbs or small shrubs, either annual or perennial. The family consists of about 35 genera and 1, 500 species worldwide. Many sedums are cultivated as ornamentals. These include jade trees, stonecrops, and air plants.

Leaves and Stems: The leaves are fleshy, and may be opposite, whorled, or alternate. They are usually simple, unlobed and lacking stipules. Stems are usually succulent and herbaceous. They can be decumbent or erect.

Flowers: Commonly, the flowers are star-like and form in branched clusters. Flowers have 4 or 5 sepals, 4 or 5 petals, free or united; at the base of each is a scale-like nectar-producing gland. Stamens may be 4 to 5 or twice as many as the petals; ovaries also number 4 to 5.

Fruit: The fruit is a tiny capsule.

Alaskan Habitat: Sedum may be found in wet places, throughout the state of Alaska. Some species grow in coastal regions. Some find their way to wet alpine meadows. Our roseroot is often found at the very top of a wet cliff, safe from human hands.

Species Found in This Book:
Roseroot or King's Crown (*Sedum rosea*)

Roseroot
Sedum rosea

SUNDEW FAMILY
(Droseraceae)

General Information: The sundew family is small, having only 4 genera and about 100 species worldwide. Most often these are annual, though a few are perennial. This family is noted for its ability to trap insects. The most famous sundew family member is the Venus flytrap (*Dionaea muscipula*). This genus is most abundant in Australia.

Our Kodiak sundew genus is *Drosera*.

Leaves and Stems: The leaves are alternate and simple, but sometimes deeply lobed. The leaves are covered with sticky glandular hairs, which exude a substance that is attractive to insects. The insects become trapped on the leaf's surface and are digested by the plant. According to Pojar and MacKinnon in *Plants of the Pacific Northwest Coast,* it is likely that the nutrients gained are devoted mostly to seed production, as the plant grows in such poor soil.

The leaves can be long-stemmed or the plant can be without stems. Flowers grow on a central stalk.

Flowers: The flowers are radially symmetrical. They have 5 sepals, united; 5 petals, separate; and 5 stamens. All parts attach at the base of the ovary.

Fruit: The fruit is a capsule.

Alaskan Habitat: These plants grow in wet, boggy places that have a sandy, acidic soil.

Species Found in This Book:
Sundew (*Drosera anglica; D. rotundifolia*)

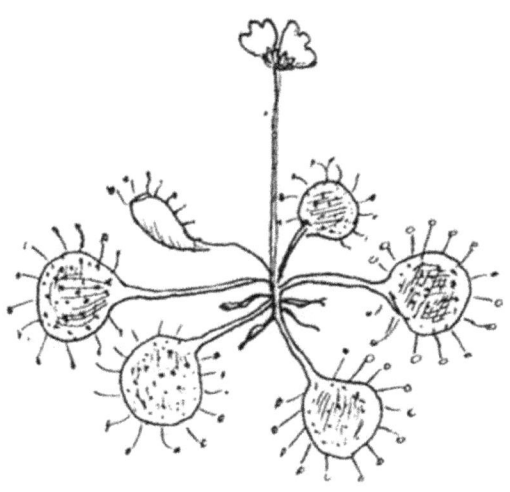

Sundew
Drosera rotundifolia

VIOLET FAMILY
(Violaceae)

General Information: This medium-sized family "gets around", as it occurs on all continents. The family has about 22 genera and 700 species worldwide, mostly perennial herbs. The United States family members are of the more colorful variety. Some tropical family members can be trees or shrubs. Many violet species, including the charming pansies, are cultivated for their flowers.

Leaves and Stems: Leaves are alternate and simple, but sometimes deeply lobed. Some violet species lack aboveground stems. In these, the flower stalks arise from stolons (runners) and thick rhizomes. Other violets have leafy, aboveground stems. Sometimes leaves form only at the upper end of the stems.

Flowers: The flowers are either bilaterally or radially symmetrical. (In our region, they are bilateral.) They are usually single flowers, with 5 sepals and 5 petals. The lower petal is spurred and larger than the others.

Fruit: The fruit is a capsule with numerous seeds. This capsule opens explosively. Curved *Viola* stamens have a finger-like horn that secretes nectar.

Alaskan Habitat: Our Alaskan Violaceae are scattered throughout the state. Violets are often found in wet meadows or along grassy trails. On Spruce Island, purple or yellow violets grow in wet, marshy areas or in open meadows. One large colony of yellow violets flourishes under the salmonberry bushes along a well-used sunny hillside path.

Species Found in This Book:
Violet (*Viola* spp.)

Violet
***Viola* spp.**

WATER LILY FAMILY
(Nymphaeacea)

General Information: This small family grows in watery habitats throughout the temperate and the tropical regions of the world. There are 7 genera and nearly 70 species in the family worldwide. These are perennial aquatic herbs.

Aquatic plants may provide habitat for a wide variety of organisms. The family includes many ornamentals for aquatic gardens.

Leaves and Stems: The leaves are simple with very long stalks. The floating leaf blades are round or heart-shaped. The stems are thick, fleshy, and long and arise directly from submerged rhizomes. Because these plants grow in water, their stems are flexible, rather than rigid, so they can move with the water currents.

Flowers: Water lilies have large flowers that float above the water on long stems. The flowers are radially symmetrical, with 3 to many sepals, and often with many petals. Stamens and ovaries are 3 to many. Sometimes the ovaries are joined in a common, fleshy disk.

Fruits: Fruits in this family are various. In our yellow pond lily, it is a large fleshy capsule which has several chambers, ruptures with age and frees the numerous seeds, which are held in a jelly-like matrix.

Alaskan Habitat: Pond lilies may be found in the quiet, fresh water of a pond or slow-moving stream.

Species Found in This Book:
Pond Lily (*Nuphar polysepalum*)

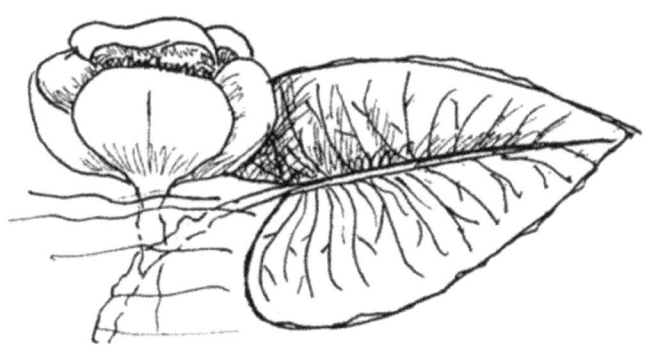

Pond Lily
Nuphar polysepalum

WAX MYRTLE FAMILY
(Myricaceae)

General Information: This small family has 3 genera and about 35 species worldwide. Wax myrtle can be a shrub or a small tree, with fragrant, resinous leaves. The popular bayberry scent that is often used in candles comes from a *Myrica* species.

According to Hulten (1968), *Myrica gale* is the only member of this family found in Alaska.

Leaves and Stems: The leaves are alternate, simple, fragrant, and dotted with resin. Crumple a leaf in your hand and smell the pungent odor that remains on your skin. The stems of *Myrica* shrubs are slender and woody.

Flowers: Simple flowers are found in the axils of bracts that form small catkins. Sepals and petals are absent. Stamens and pistils are in separate catkins and on separate bushes. The pistillate flower is surrounded by several very small bracts. The one-chambered ovary is superior. Stigmas are slender, and number 1 to 4.

Fruit: The fruit is a drupe or achene.

Alaskan Habitat: Wax myrtles prefer a moist to wet habitat. Species of this family are often found in swamps and lake margins. Our Spruce Island sweet gale grows in profusion in swampy meadows or bog edges.

Species Found in This Book:
Sweet Gale (*Myrica gale*)

Sweet Gale
Myrica gale

WILLOW FAMILY
(Salicaceae)

General Information: There are 3 genera and around 400 species in the willow family, worldwide. Willows are deciduous trees or shrubs with alternate leaves and characteristically bitter bark. Willows can vary in size from tiny shrubs to 30-foot trees. A very large family, the Salicaceae have over 3 dozen species in Alaska. Hulten (1968) listed 14 species of *Salix* on Kodiak Island.

The cottonwood tree (*Populus balsamifera*), another member of the willow family, is also found in abundance on Kodiak Island.

Leaves and Stems: Leaves are simple and alternate, with petioles. They may vary in shape and color, but are generally smooth above, and can be short or long. They sometimes have a gray-green cast or hairs, especially on the lower surface.

The leaves and bark of *Salix* contains a natural painkiller, salicylic acid, which is a precursor to aspirin. This herb has been used since early times as a pain reliever.

Flowers: Male and female flowers are held in catkins on separate plants. These catkins, which are often known as "pussy willows", can appear before, after, or with the leaves. Catkin size and shape may vary, but the "pussy willow" look is quite common. Stamens release a golden pollen when mature in the spring.

Fruit: The fruit is an ovoid, oblong or conic capsule with 2 compartments. It contains numerous minute seeds suspended in a dense mass of white silky hairs.

Alaskan Habitat: Many willow species are a good indicator that there is water nearby. Willows or cottonwoods often grow at the edge of streambeds or near standing water. They can be found near beaches or in wet meadows. The range of growth is from sea level to the alpine.

Species Found in This Book:
Willow *(Salix* spp.)
At least 14 species are found in the Kodiak area.
Cottonwood (*Populus balsamifera*)

Cottonwood
Populus balsamifera

WINTERGREEN FAMILY
(Pyrolaceae)

General Information: There are 4 genera and about 40 species in this family worldwide. Members are located mostly in temperate northern areas of the world. Plants of this family are perennials.

Once included as part of the larger heather family (Ericaceae), wintergreens can be distinguished by their petals, which are not fused, but separate. This family also includes some unusual fleshy, chlorophyll-lacking plants, such as Indian pipe (*Monotropa uniflora*) and candystick (*Allotropa virgata*), which are saprophytic (feeding or growing upon dead or decaying organic matter).

Leaves and Stems: The leaves are simple, alternate or opposite, or nearly whorled. They are often dish-shaped. Leaves on some species are evergreen or wintergreen; others are reduced and lacking chlorophyll. Stems are herbaceous or sometimes have a woody base.

Flowers: Flowers are radially symmetrical, borne on a single stem, in racemes, or in a branched cluster. They have 4 to 5 more or less distinct sepals. Petals number 4 or 5, and are separate. Most of the Alaska species have flowers in parts of 5. There are usually 10 stamens. All parts attach at the base of the ovary.

Fruit: The fruit is a 4 to 5 chambered capsule, more or less spherical, that produces numerous tiny, dust-like seeds.

Alaskan Habitat: Wintergreen family members are found in the moist, rich soils of coniferous woods, sometimes near the sunny edges and sometimes in deeply shaded areas. Our shy maiden grows in the moss under the spruce trees.

Species Found in This Book:
Shy Maiden (*Moneses uniflora*)

Shy Maiden
Moneses uniflora

COLOR INDEX

THE INDEXES AND SUPPLEMENTAL INFORMATION

FORGET - ME - NOT

POND LILY

NARCISSUS-FLOWERED ANEMONE

MONKEY FLOWER

TALL FIREWEED
Insert: **DWAFT FIREWEED**

COW PARSNIP

YARROW

TALL JACOB'S LADDER

VIOLET

MOUNTAIN ASH

GEUM

ELDERBERRY

BLUEBERRY: BLOSSOM, BUSH, AND FRUIT

SALMONBERRY: FRUIT AND BLOSSOM

MONKSHOOD   **DEVIL'S CLUB**   **SHY MAIDEN**

LUPINE   **CHOCOLATE LILY**

WILD GERANIUM

BEACH LOVAGE   **BEACH GREENS**   **BEACH PEA**

GOOSETONGUE   **SILVERWEED**

MARSH FIVEFINGER

SUNDEW

FLOWER COLOR INDEX

Flowers greenish to crimson

Mountain Sorrel

Flowers green

Death Camas (greenish white)
Devil's Club (greenish white)
False Hellebore Goosetongue (greenish white)
Lambsquarter (gray-green)
Nettles
Seabeach Sandwort or Beach Greens (greenish white)
Spearmint

Flowers white

American Red Raspberry
Baneberry
Beach Strawberry
Bunchberry (Canadian Dwarf Cornel)
Chickweed
Cloudberry
Clover (white or pink)
Common Plantain
Cow Parsnip
Elderberry
Highbush Cranberry
Mountain Ash
Narcissus-Flowered Anemone
Northern Bedstraw
Poison Water Hemlock
Saxifrage
Shy Maiden
Sundew
Trailing Raspberry
Watermelon Berry / Wild Cucumber
Wild Alum
Yarrow (white; rarely pale lavender)

Flowers yellow

Buttercup
Dandelion
Geum
Goldenrod
Marsh Marigold
Monkey Flower
Pineapple Weed
Pond Lily
Silverweed
Stream Violet

Odd colors: silvery to brown to purplish black

Caribou Leaves (Wormwood)
Cottonwood (Catkins)
Poque (Brownish red)
Sourdock (reddish hue)
Sweet Gale (Brown and yellow-green catkins)
Green first; then brown cones
Willow (Catkins turn to silvery color)

Flowers rose or pink

Alaska Spring Beauty (Rose, white, or rarely pale lavender)
Blueberry (pink)
Bog Cranberry
Early Blueberry (pink)
Fireweed (Rose, pink, or white)
Kinnikinnik
Labrador Tea (pink or white)
Lingonberry (pink)
Lowbush Cranberry (pink)
Nagoonberry (Dark rose)
Salmonberry (Deep pink)
Wild Rose

Flowers rose-purple or lavender

Marsh Violet
Wild Chives
Wild Geranium

Flowers purple to black

Chocolate Lily
Crowberry
Marsh Fivefinger

Flowers bluish-violet

Alaska Violet
Beach Peas (Bluish-violet wings and keel; red banner)
Iris (Rare: white)
Wild Sweet Pea (Rose to violet-purple)

Flowers blue

Jacob's Ladder (Rare: white)
Lupine (Sometimes shaded to pink; rarely white)
Monkshood (Blue; occasionally white)

Flowers Maroon

Roseroot

No Flowers: Spore-Bearing

Ferns
    Bracken Fern
    Licorice Fern
    Maidenhair Fern
    Spreading Wood Fern
Fir Club Moss
Horsetail

MEDICINAL INDEX

MEDICINAL INDEX

This index catalogues all the plants discussed in *Plant Lore of an Alaskan Island* according to their medicinal uses, from ancient times to the present day. This list is not all-inclusive, but it covers those uses included in this plant guide.

The primary purpose of the index is to provide an interesting look at the many and varied ways in which these plants have achieved importance as folk remedies, by both Native and non-native peoples. In some cases modern research has shown the truth to these remedies. However, this list is in no way intended to usurp the position of your personal medical doctor. In fact, if you are under a doctor's care and wish to try one or more of these plants, seek your physician's advice first, before adding the plant to any medication program you may be following. However, if you find yourself in a survival situation, or if you are unable to reach a medical facility, you may find some relief from using these plants as an emergency measure.

As you read, you will notice that often the plant is used as a tea, and you are instructed to make an "infusion" or a "decoction". It is important to know the meaning of these terms. You make an "infusion" by boiling water and placing the plant in the water to steep, just as you would use a teabag to make a cup of tea. (If the instructions in this index tell you to "brew into tea", prepare an infusion.) You make a "decoction" by placing the part or parts of the plant to be used in water and boiling them together. Normally, this second method yields a much stronger solution. When using dried plants to make a tea, use one rounded teaspoon of the plant to one cup of boiling water. For a decoction, a rule of thumb is to use approximately an ounce of plant parts to a pint of water, and heat them together. You can then strain and use as needed.

Here, then, is a list of medical conditions, the plants believed to help relieve them, and a very brief description of how to prepare them. Read on, and marvel at their diversity of historic use!

Alzheimer's
Blueberries   Eat up to 3 servings per day as a preventative
Cranberries   Eat up to 3 servings per day as a preventative

Anemia
Labrador Tea   Decoction of leaves and branches

Appetite increase

Geum	Brew into tea; makes a bitter tonic
Yarrow	Brew into tea

Arthritis relief

Cow Parsnip	Boil root; apply water as wash, or mash root and place on sore spot
Devil's Club	Peel outer layer of roots, heat root and mash and place on sore spot
Horsetail	Brew into tea
Labrador Tea	Decoction from leaves and branches for tea
Willow	Decoction or tincture of inner bark
Wormwood	Poultice of leaves

Asthma

Highbush Cranberry	Decoction of inner bark or tincture
Nettles	Drink tea and inhale the burning herb
Silverweed	Add teaspoon of leaves to cup of warm milk
Sundew	Use as tincture in small doses
Yarrow	Brew into tea

Bad breath

Geum	Brew leaves into tea and gargle

Bee and insect stings

Common Plantain	Crush fresh leaves and apply
Goldenrod	Crush fresh leaves and flowering tops and apply
Monkey Flower	Mash leaves and stems; apply as poultice
Northern Bedstraw	Tea or fresh squeezed juice as wash
Roseroot	Apply leaves
Sourdock	Rub with leaves
Spreading Wood Fern	Crush leaves and apply

Bladder infection

Chickweed	Prepare as tincture
Horsetail (shavegrass)	Brew into tea
Kinnikinnik	Make a decoction of leaves; take ½ cup every half hour
Northern Bedstraw	Drink tea to relieve painful urination

Blisters, burns, scalds

Roseroot	Apply leaves
Salmonberry	Chew leaves and place on burns
Self-Heal	Prepare whole plant as poultice or salve
Sourdock	Use leaves as dressing
Spruce	Peel section of bark; scrape off sap; place on burn

Blood circulation

Wormwood	Brew tea from fresh leaves

Blood circulation (steam bath switch)

Alder	Small branches
Goldenrod	Use whole stem and flower
Sweet Gale	Branches

Blood poisoning

Angelica	Cut and heat root, or mash and boil root; use as poultice
Northern Bedstraw	Tea or juice as wash; destroy cloth with which applied

Boils

Devil's Club	Inner bark, root or stem. Bake until dry; rub between hands until soft. Leave on 3-4 hours.
Sweet Gale	Boil leaves into tea; use as wash

Breathing problems

Maidenhair Fern	Brew tea from leaves for difficult breathing

Bronchial

Marsh Marigold	To loosen dried mucus, take a scant teaspoon of chopped dried plant once or twice daily
Sundew	Use as tincture in small doses

Bunions

Common Plantain	Wrap leaves around cracked and painful bunions
Shy Maiden	Poultice of flowers
Sundew	Apply fresh leaves

Cancer

Alder (Red Alder)	Recent tests: Contains two anticancer agents (Only found in SE AK)

Blueberries	Eat berries (optimum servings: 3 per day) as a preventative; destroys free radicals
Cleavers	For lymphatic cancer, brew tea from fresh plant; take a sip or two every 20 minutes
Clover	For stomach cancer, drink 4 cups of tea daily on an empty stomach
	For throat cancer, gargle with a strong red clover tea 4 or 5 times daily
Lingonberry; Cranberry	Eat berries or drink juice up to 3 times daily as a tumor suppressant

Cataracts
Canadian Dwarf Cornel	Leaves were placed over eyes overnight; in the morning cataracts were removed
Crowberry	Remove cataracts with bark of stems

Chapped hands
Cottonwood	Apply Balm of Gilead (see recipe with cottonwood)
Yarrow	Use tea as wash

Chest ailments
Labrador Tea	Decoction from leaves and branches
Spruce	Boil new cones of spruce while still light green and soft; make tea and drink

Chills
Elderberry	Boil dried flowers into tea
Elderberry	Use orange part of bark (cambium) to brew tea

Cold
Cottonwood	Prepare decoction from bark or from buds
Cottonwood	Prepare tincture from inner bark
Cow Parsnip	Chew raw root or boil and drink tea
Dandelion	Brew into tea
Devil's Club	Boil inner root bark for tea
Elderberry	Boil inner root; drink tea
Elderberry	Brew tea from berries or dried flowers
Highbush Cranberry	Boil inner bark; gargle
Highbush Cranberry	Save pulp from jelly: Two large tablespoons in cup of boiling water and drink
Labrador Tea	Brew tea from leaves and branches
Mountain Ash	Boil inner bark for tea
Mountain Ash	Soak dried berries in hot water for tea

Nettles	Brew into tea
Pineapple Weed	Boil; breathe steam to relieve head, chest colds
Roseroot	Tea of roots or leaves
Shy Maiden	Brew tea from whole plant
Spruce	Boil strips of cambium layer of bark as tea
Violets	Brew whole plant into tea
Wild Rose	Boil broken-up stems and branches to dark tea
Wormwood	Brew into tea or chew leaves
Yarrow	Tea + honey + 3 drops Tabasco for severe colds

Colic

Silverweed	One teaspoon dried or fresh leaves to one cup warm milk

Colonic spasms

Marsh Marigold	Use hot poultice of leaves

Constipation

Monkey Flower	Drink infusion
Wild Cucumber	Eat berries (watermelon berries)

Convulsions

Marsh Marigold	Prepare tea from dried leaves; use sparingly

Corns

Shy Maiden	Poultice of flowers
Sundew	Apply fresh leaves

Coughs

Clover	Brew into tea
Common Plantain	Brew tea from leaves
Devil's Club	Boil inner root bark for tea
Licorice Fern	Chew raw or roasted leaves
Maidenhair Fern	Brew tea from leaves
Marsh Marigold	Prepare tea from dried leaves; use sparingly
Spruce	Boil needles into tea; take in small doses
Sundew	For severe cough, use as tincture in small doses, taking regularly until cough goes away
Wild Rose	Brew petals and rose hips into tea

Cysts and cystitis

Northern Bedstraw	Brew tea from fresh herb (*G. aparine*)

D. T's

Pineapple Weed	Brew into tea

Dandruff

Devil's Club	Crush berries and rub on head
Nettles	Simmer leaves with vinegar, cool, massage into scalp

Diabetes

Devil's Club	Decoction from root bark
Nettles	Brew into tea: helps lower blood sugar level

Diaper rash

Wild Alum	Use as ingredient with arrowroot, as antiseptic: one cup arrowroot, 3 teaspoons alum root powder

Diarrhea

Alder	Boil green cones into tea; take in small quantities
Crowberry	Brew a tea from leaves & stems, or eat berries
Geum	Brew a tea from whole plant
Goldenrod	Brew tea from flowering tops
Licorice Fern	Boil and cool stems for tea
Raspberry	Brew tea from leaves or eat berries
Wild Alum	Boil 1 teaspoon chopped root in 1 cup water for 20 minutes and drink
Wild Geranium	Decoction from root

Digestive aid

Beach Lovage	Brew into tea
Chocolate Lily	Boil and eat bulblets
Marsh Marigold	To stimulate flow of mucus in digestive tract, take a scant teaspoon or less of chopped, dried plant once or twice daily
Salmonberry	Chew young shoots
Salmonberry	Steep bark and leaves into tea
Self-Heal	Drink tea from decoction of leaves and flowers
Silverweed	Add teaspoon of leaves to one cup warm milk
Spearmint	Brew into tea

Dementia

Blueberries	Eat up to 3 servings per day as preventative

Dizziness

Labrador Tea	Decoction from leaves and branches

Draining pus from boils or cuts

Fireweed	Split and apply raw stem

Dysentery

Burnet	Root decoction
Wild Geranium	Root decoction

Eyes

Blueberries	To improve night vision and to protect against vision loss, eat daily (3 servings optimum)
Crowberry	Boil roots, cool liquid, wash
Devil's Club	Burn roots; scrape off charcoal-like substance; sieve to make powder; moisten with milk for poultice
Elderberry	Use tea from flowers as wash
Fir Club Moss	Boil whole plant for wash
Horsetail	Squeeze juice from rhizome and stem for wash
Pineapple Weed	Brew tea for wash
Raspberry	To combat age-related macular degeneration (ARMD), eat 3 servings per day
Roseroot	Brew tea of leaves or roots; cool for wash
Spruce	Squeeze uncooked juice from new growth of needles into eyes
Wild Geranium	Brew tea from leaves for wash
Wild Rose	Soak petals in hot water for wash
Wormwood	Brew tea for wash
Yarrow	Brew tea for wash

Facial paralysis

Marsh Marigold	Apply hot poultice of leaves

Fever

Alder	Boil inner bark into tea
Cottonwood	Prepare decoction from inner bark or buds or tincture from inner bark
Devil's Club	Boil inner root bark into tea

Devil's Club	Boil pieces of stems and branches into tea
Elderberry	Boil inner root for tea
Silverweed	One teaspoon leaves to one cup warm milk
Wild Rose	Boil broken-up stems and branches for tea
Willow	Peel bark from new growth and chew inner layer; prepare tincture from inner bark
Wormwood	Chew leaves
Yarrow	To yarrow tea, add honey and Tabasco; drink 3 times a day; stay covered

Flatulence aid

Goldenrod	Drink cold tea
Self-Heal	Make decoction of leaves and flowers and drink
Yarrow	Brew into tea

Flu

Elderberry	Boil inner root into tea
Wild Alum	For stomach flu, boil 1 teaspoon chopped root in 1 cup water for 20 minutes and drink
Wormwood	Chew leaves

Gall bladder

Yarrow	Brew into tea

Gas pains

Alder	Boil inner bark into tea
Wild Spearmint	Brew into tea

Genital discharges

Burnet	Decoction from root

Glands, swollen

Devil's Club	Use inner bark of stem or roots. Bake until dry; rub between hands until soft. Leave on 3-4 hours

Gout

Dandelion	Drink tea from roots twice daily; add fresh juice to drinking water; eat leaves

Gums, inflamed (See also mouth sores)

Burnet	Use root decoction as mouthwash

Cow Parsnip	Prepare tincture from seeds; rub on gums
Horsetail	Brew into tea; use as gargle

Hair rinse
Devil's Club	Crush berries and rub on hair to give it shine
Nettles	Rinse with strong tea to restore color; promote growth
Yarrow	Tea used as rinse helps prevent baldness

Hangover relief
Cottonwood	Decoction from inner bark or buds; tincture from inner bark
Labrador Tea	Decoction from leaves and branches for tea
Sourdock roots	Brew into tea
Yarrow	Brew into tea

Headache relief
Cottonwood	Decoction from inner bark or buds; tincture from inner bark
Fir Club Moss	Place a piece on head
Lingonberry	Heat berries; wrap in cloth; use as hot pack
Nettles	Brew into tea
Willow	Peel bark from new growth; chew inner layer; drink decoction from bark or take tincture
Wormwood	Chew leaves

Heart problems
Blueberry	Eat berries (optimum: 3 servings per day)
Clover	Brew into tea (contains blood thinner)
Spruce	Boil strips of cambium layer of bark for tea
Wild Geranium	Tea from root decoction

Heartburn
Labrador Tea	Decoction from leaves and branches
Spearmint	Brew into tea

Hemorrhoids
Common Plantain	Crush and apply fresh leaves
Self-Heal	Prepare whole plant as poultice or salve

Herpes
Fir Club Moss	Spores are used: method not stated

High cholesterol

Blueberries	Eat fruit or drink juice; optimum servings 3 per day

Hoarseness

Common Plantain	Brew tea from leaves
Maidenhair Fern	Brew tea from leaves

Immune System, to boost

Self-Heal	Add small amount of oregano to decoction; drink
Wormwood	Use tincture: 5 drops under tongue twice daily

Infections, healing old cuts

Angelica	Cut and heat root or mash and boil root; use as poultice
Common Plantain	Make poultice of fresh leaves; brew tea for wash
Cottonwood	Crush leaves and apply to injury
Devil's Club	Bake inner bark from stem and root until dry; rub between hands until soft; leave on wound for 3 to 4 hours
Elderberry	Boil stem bark for a wash
Fireweed	Apply raw split stem
Northern Bedstraw	Use tea or fresh-squeezed juice as wash
Salmonberry	Dig out old mildewy leaves from under bushes and place over wound that won't heal
Salmonberry	Pound bark and place on wound as painkiller
Wormwood	Dab boiled leaves on sore
Yarrow	Use whole plant in hot pack

Inflammation

Cottonwood	Decoction of buds or inner bark; tincture from inner bark
Lambsquarter	Use boiled leaves as a poultice
Nettles	For joint inflammation, use raw leaves as poultice or prepare as liniment
Self-Heal	Mash leaves and flowers and make salve
Silverweed	Prepare as tincture
Willow	Decoction or tincture of inner bark

Intestinal disorders

Mountain Ash	Drink juice of berries

Irritable Bowel Syndrome

Raspberry	Eat 3 servings of fruit per day or drink fresh juice

Kidney problems

Beach Lovage	Brew into tea
Chickweed	Prepare a tincture
Crowberry	Drink juice from berries or drink infusion of stems and twigs
Goldenrod	Brew tea from flowering tops and leaves
Kinnikinnik	Use dried leaves as tea for cleanse
Northern Bedstraw	Drink tea for kidney stones
Spruce	Boil strips of cambium layer of bark for tea
Wormwood	Brew into tea

Laryngitis

Alder	Boil inner bark; use tea as gargle
Highbush Cranberry	Boil inner bark for gargle
Highbush Cranberry	Save pulp from jelly: 2 large tablespoons to cup of very hot water; drink
Highbush Cranberry	Eat berries raw

Laxative

Chickweed	Brew into tea
Devil's Club	Chew white pulp between green bark and stem
Pineapple Weed	Brew into tea for mild laxative
Spruce	Boil strips of cambium layer of bark and drink until no longer needed
Wild Cucumber	Eat watermelon berries in quantity
Wormwood	Brew into tea
Yarrow	Brew into tea

Leg cramps

Fir Club Moss	Place the whole plant in a cloth and tie around the cramping area

Lice

Alder	Boil inner bark in vinegar and use as wash
Devil's Club	Crush berries and rub on head

Liver problems

Dandelion	Drink tea to aid in formation of bile
Yarrow	Drink tea to stimulate flow of bile

Lower back pain

Marsh Marigold	Apply hot poultice of leaves

Lung congestion

Marsh Marigold	To stimulate mucus flow, take a scant teaspoon or less of chopped dried leaves once or twice daily
Shy Maiden	Drink tea brewed from dried plant

Lung (hemorrhaging)

Willow	Prepare a strong decoction of leaves and inner bark and drink before eating

Menstrual cramps

Highbush Cranberry	Steep 1 teaspoon fresh or dried bark in 1 cup water and sip slowly
Highbush Cranberry	Prepare as tincture; add 10 to 15 drops to 1 cup water (Common name: "Crampbark")
Silverweed	One teaspoon dried or fresh leaves to 1 cup milk; scald and drink warm
Spearmint	Brew into tea
Willow	Combine inner bark with highbush cranberry bark in a tincture
Yarrow	Drink tea with honey and a few drops Tabasco

Menstrual: regulation of

Angelica	Chinese angelica, or dong quai, was a popular herb used for this purpose

Menstrual: to slow flow

Horsetail (Shavegrass)	Brew into tea
Yarrow	Drink tea with honey and a few drops Tabasco

Menstrual: to start flow

Wild Rose	Boil broken-up stems and branches to a dark tea

Mineral deficiency

Labrador Tea	Brew tea from leaves or branches for anemia
Lambsquarter	Eat for calcium deficiency

Mosquito and insect repellant

Yarrow	Crush fresh plant and rub on skin

Mouth sores; sore gums

Cow Parsnip	Chew raw root or boil and drink tea

Geum	Brew into tea
Horsetail	Brew tea for gargle
Horsetail	Dry and burn plant; apply ashes
Raspberry	Brew tea from leaves as gargle
Roseroot	Brew tea from leaves or roots
Self-Heal	Make decoction; use as mouthwash
Silverweed	One ounce dried plant with 1 teaspoon alum and 1 pint white vinegar: boil and gargle
Spruce	Boil strips of cambium layer of bark for tea
Wild geranium	Chew raw root Willow
Willow	Chew the inner bark or drink tea brewed from it

Nausea relief

Cow Parsnip	Prepare tincture from seeds; take 5 drops under tongue
Pineapple Weed	Brew into tea
Spearmint	Brew into tea

Nerve soother

Pineapple Weed	Brew into tea
Spearmint	Brew into tea

Nettle sting

Goldenrod	Rub with crushed leaves and flowers
Sourdock	Rub with leaves
Spreading Wood Fern	Rub with crushed leaves

Newborn babies (general tonic)

Pineapple Weed	Teaspoon of tea at birth
Spruce	Boil strips of cambium layer of bark; use as wash
Wild Geranium	Teaspoon of tea at birth

Nightmare prevention

Pineapple Weed	Brew into tea

Pain Reliever

Angelica	Cut root; heat, or mash, and boil; place over the sore place as a poultice
Willow	Drink decoction from bark or take tincture

Pimples
Sweet Gale	Boil leaves into tea for wash

Pneumonia
Sundew	Use as tincture in small doses

Poison: to remove from system
Dandelion	Brew into tea

Pregnancy and childbirth
Angelica	Chinese angelica, or dong quai, was commonly used to help expel afterbirth.
Horsetail	Steep equal parts horsetail, chamomile, borage, and comfrey: 1 heaping teaspoon to l cup water. Steep 45 minutes and drink.
Nettles	Drink as tea after childbirth
Pineapple Weed	Cup of tea after delivery
Raspberry	Tea of leaves: ease labor pains; prevent miscarriage; increase milk
Wild Geranium	Tea from root decoction as tonic
Wormwood	Chew leaves to help insure healthy pregnancy

Psoriasis
Devil's Club	Make into salve and apply
Northern Bedstraw	Use tea or squeezed juice as wash

Purge system; cleanse blood
Sourdock	Eat leaves
Wormwood	Brew fresh leaves into tea

Rashes
Northern Bedstraw	Brew tea or squeeze juice for wash
Shy Maiden	Poultice of flowers

Respiratory: general conditions
Common Plantain	Brew tea of leaves

Rheumatism
Dandelion	Brew tea from roots; drink twice daily; add juice to drinking water; eat leaves
Devil's Club	Put root and stem pulp in bath water
Lambsquarter	Make a decoction and use as a rub

Nettles	Wash area with hot water; wrap with raw nettle leaves
Willow	Decoction or tincture from inner bark

Ringworm; parasites; fungi

Sourdock	Apply juice from fresh leaves

Scabies

Sweet Gale	Boil leaves as tea for wash

Seasickness

Angelica	Roast roots and inhale steam
Cow Parsnip	Prepare tincture from seeds; take 5 drops under tongue

Sinus – to clear

Marsh Marigold	To loosen dried mucus, take a scant teaspoon of chopped, dried plant once or twice daily
Pineapple Weed	Boil whole plant; breathe steam
Yarrow	Boil whole plant; breathe steam

Skin problems; bruises

Alder	Boil inner bark in vinegar and use as wash
Chickweed	Crush fresh leaves and mix with Vaseline for bruises or skin irritations
Clover	Use tea as wash
Common Plantain	Use as poultice for eczema or other skin problems
Cottonwood	Make Balm of Gilead from buds and apply to affected area
Fir Club Moss	Make dusting powder from spores
Horsetail	Use tea as wash
Monkey Flower	Mash leaves and stems; apply as poultice
Northern Bedstraw	Mix fresh juice with butter or lard for salve
Pineapple Weed	Use tea as wash
Roseroot	Apply leaves
Self-Heal	Prepare whole plant as poultice or salve
Silverweed	One ounce dried leaves; 1 teaspoon alum; 1 pint white vinegar; boil 4 minutes. Apply to freckles, skin blemishes, or sunburn.
Sourdock	Boil roots; mix pulp with lard for salve
Violet	Heat leaves and apply for bruises
Violet	Make into salve and apply to skin inflammation and abrasions
Yarrow	Use tea as wash

Sleep aid

Pineapple Weed	Brew into tea
Spearmint	Brew into tea

Sore or pulled muscles; sprains

Angelica	Cut root and heat, or mash and boil; place over sore muscle or sprain as a poultice
Fir Club Moss	Wrap plant in cloth and place on sore area
Geum	Apply plant to sore area; wrap with wet hot towel
Nettles	Use raw leaves as poultice or make into liniment
No. Bedstraw (Cleavers)	Soak plants in hot water and use as poultice
Self-Heal	Prepare whole plant as poultice or salve

Sore throat

Alder	Boil inner bark; use as gargle
Clover	Brew into tea
Cottonwood	Boil bark and gargle the liquid
Highbush Cranberry	Boil inner bark; gargle
Highbush Cranberry	Eat berries raw
Highbush Cranberry	Save pulp from jelly; add 2 large tablespoons to cup of very hot water and drink
Lingonberry	Chew raw berries
Mountain Ash	Brew tea from berries and gargle
Roseroot	Prepare tea from leaves or roots
Self-Heal	Gargle with a decoction
Shy Maiden	Brew into tea for gargle
Silverweed	One ounce dried leaves; 1 teaspoon alum, 1 pint white vinegar; boil 5 minutes and gargle
Spruce	Boil strips of cambium layer of bark for tea
Violet	Brew into tea
Wild Geranium	Root decoction as tea or gargle
Willow	Gargle a decoction of inner bark
Wormwood	Use tea as gargle

Sores

Angelica	Cut root and heat, or mash and boil root; place over sore as poultice. Leaves also used as poultice
Cottonwood	Grind bark and use as drying powder

Cow Parsnip	Boil root; use water as wash or mash root and use as poultice
Devil's Club	Bake inner bark from root or stem until dry; rub between hands until soft; leave on sore 3 – 4 hours
Goldenrod	Crush fresh leaves and flowering tops and apply
Horsetail	Brew into tea for wash
Raspberry	Brew tea from leaf and use as wash
Shy Maiden	Bathe with tea made from whole plant
Wild Alum	Use pounded, dried roots as a poultice
Yarrow	Brew into tea for wash

Staph infections

Devil's Club	Apply pulp between outer bark and stem externally as poultice or take internally by chewing
Sundew	Use as tincture in small doses

Staunch bleeding externally; stop nosebleeds (Coagulant)

Burnet	Make decoction from root and leaves or dry and powder the root and apply
Fir Club Moss	Apply spore powder
Goldenrod	Crush fresh leaves and flowering tops
Northern Bedstraw	Warm plants in hot water; use as poultice
Self-Heal	Prepare poultice from whole plant and apply
Spruce	Use strips of inner bark as temporary bandages
Wild Alum	Apply pounded, dried roots
Wormwood	Use tea as wash
Yarrow	Brew tea from whole plant or use hot pack of leaves

Staunch bleeding internally (Coagulant)

Burnet	Make a decoction from root
Common Plantain	Decoction
Goldenrod	Tea from flowering tops
Horsetail	Brew into tea
Maidenhair Fern	Chew leaves
Nettles	Brew into tea
Willow	Prepare strong decoction of bark and inner root; drink before eating
Wormwood	Brew into tea
Yarrow	Tea (used especially for lungs)

Stiff joints

Dandelion	Take tea brewed from roots twice daily; add fresh juice to drinking water; eat leaves

Stomach and bladder trouble

Common Plantain	Take fresh juice squeezed from leaves
Devil's Club	Boil inner root bark for tea
Highbush Cranberry	Boil inner bark for tea
Horsetail (Shavegrass)	Brew tea for internal bleeding of stomach ulcers
Labrador Tea	Brew tea from leaves and branches
Mountain Ash	Drink berry juice
Shy Maiden	Brew tea from dried plant
Sourdock	Brew into tea
Spearmint	Brew tea for stomachache
Spruce	Boil strips of cambium layer of bark for tea
Wild Geranium	Use root decoction for stomach ulcers
Wild Rose	Boil broken-up stems and branches to a dark tea
Willow	Peel bark from new growth and chew inner layer for stomachache
Yarrow	Brew into tea for stomach cramps

Strep Throat

Highbush Cranberry	Decoction or tincture for stomach cramps
Sundew	Use as tincture in small doses

Stroke

Blueberries	Eat plenty of berries to lessen brain damage after stroke

Swelling

Cow Parsnip	Boil root; use as wash or mash as poultice
Lingonberry	Heat berries, wrap in cloth, place as hot pack

Tonic, gentle; astringent or laxative

Burnet	Brew leaves alone or mix with dandelion and nettles or other favorite tonic ingredients
Clover	Brew into tea
Dandelion	Brew into tea
Devil's Club	Boil inner root bark for spring tonic tea
Fireweed	Brew leaves and stems into tea
Jacob's Ladder	Brew into tea: cleanses by causing sweating

Pineapple Weed	Brew into tea
Poque	Add 1 teaspoon dried rootstock as ingredient in herb blend
Silverweed	Brew into tea
Sourdock	Drink infused weak tea from roots
Spruce	Boil needles into tea
Yarrow	Brew into tea

Tonsillitis

Mountain Ash	Brew berries as tea or gargle

Toothache

Angelica	Squeeze juice from plant onto sore tooth, or place a piece of root in cavity and leave it until tooth breaks up and falls out
Cow Parsnip	Heat piece of root until very hot, then push into sore tooth: It deadens nerve. Or prepare tincture from seeds and rub on sore area
Common Plantain	Chew on rootstalk
Lambsquarter	Make a decoction and use as a mouthwash
Nettles	Hold pounded roots on jaw in heated rag, or bite down on root, spitting out saliva
Salmonberry	Pound bark and lay on tooth
Silverweed	One ounce dried plant; 1 teaspoon alum; 1 pint white vinegar; boil 5 minutes and gargle
Wild Geranium	Bite down on raw root
Yarrow	Chew fresh leaves or apply to sore spot on jaw

Tuberculosis

Alder	Brew tea from bark
Cow Parsnip	Chew raw root or boil and drink tea
Crowberry	Prepare infusion of stems and twigs
Devil's Club	Boil inner root bark for tea
Elderberry	Boil inner root; drink tea
Horsetail	Brew into tea: Acid from the silica stabilizes scar tissue
Labrador Tea	Decoction from leaves and branches
Mountain Ash	Boil inner bark for tea, or soak dried berries in hot water and drink
Nettles	Brew into tea
Shy Maiden	Brew tea from dried plant
Sourdock	Brew into tea
Spruce	Boil new growth of needles; ferment into beer

Spruce	Peel section of bark; scrape off sap; chew
Sundew	Use as tincture in small doses
Sweet Gale	Boil leaves into tea
Wild Geranium	Brew tea from leaves

Tumors

No. Bedstraw (Cleavers)	Brew tea from fresh herb

Ulcers

Alder	Boil bark for tea
Spruce	Boil strips of cambium layer of bark for tea
Wild Geranium	Decoction from root
Wormwood	Chew leaves

Urinary tract infections

Chickweed	Prepare a tincture
Cranberry; Lingonberry	Drink up to 3 glasses unsweetened juice per day
Horsetail	Prepare young horsetail, or "shave grass", fresh or dried, as tea
Kinnikinnik	Boil into tea; drink ½ cup every half hour

Uterus

Marsh Marigold	To stimulate formulation of mucus, take scant teaspoon or less of dried, chopped plant once or twice daily

Vaginal inflammation

Kinnikinnik	Boil tea and use as a douche

Vaginal infections

Raspberry	Eat 3 servings of berries per day or drink fresh raspberry juice

Varicose veins

Wormwood	Brew tea from fresh leaves

Venereal disease

Devil's Club	Decoction from white pulp between outer green bark and stem or from outer bark; drink

Vitamin deficiency

Beach Greens	Eat for vitamin C deficiency (scurvy preventative)

Beach Strawberry	Eat raw or used in tea for vitamin C deficiency
Lambsquarter	Eat for vitamin A and C deficiency
Mountain Ash	Berries eaten for scurvy

Vomiting, dry, to alleviate

Wild Alum	Boil 1 teaspoon chopped root in 1 cup water for 20 minutes and drink

Vomiting, to induce

Sourdock	Boil or soak roots in hot water and drink
Wild Rose	Soak bark in hot water until tea is very strong; drink

Warts

Sundew	Apply fresh leaves (juice is caustic)

Water retention

Clover	Brew leaves and flowers into tea
Dandelion	Brew into tea
Fir Club Moss	Used against dropsy (excessive fluid collected in body); method not outlined
Goldenrod	Brew into tea
Horsetail	Brew tea to help prevent water retention
Silverweed	Prepare tincture
Wild Geranium	Brew leaves into tea

Weight loss

Northern Bedstraw	Combine with chickweed and bladderwrack (fucus) for tea

Whooping cough

Silverweed	Add 1 teaspoon leaves to 1 cup warm milk; drink
Sundew	Use as tincture in small doses

Worms

Common Plantain	Consume fresh juice from leaves
Highbush Cranberry	Eat raw or cooked berries for tapeworm
Licorice Fern	Boil stems and cool for tea

Wounds or cuts

Canadian Dwarf Cornel	Use poultice for cuts or scrapes
Common Plantain	Crush fresh leaves and apply

Cow Parsnip	Boil root; use water as wash or mash root for poultice
Devil's Club	Bake inner bark from stem or roots until very dry. Rub between hands until quite soft; apply. Leave on 3 to 4 hours only.
Horsetail	Brew tea for wash
Northern Bedstraw	Brew tea or squeeze fresh juice for wash
Raspberry	Brew tea of leaves for wash
Roseroot	Brew tea of leaves or roots; cool and use as wash
Roseroot	Chew raw root and place on cut
Salmonberry	Apply old mildewy leaves as poultice after wash with shy maiden.
Self-Heal	Prepare whole plant as poultice or salve
Shy Maiden	Bathe wound with tea from whole plant
Spruce	Peel section of bark; scrape off sap; place on cut
Wild Alum	Use pounded, dried roots as a poultice
Willow	Bruise leaves and apply to wounds or cuts

PLANT LORE OF AN ALASKAN ISLAND

BERRIES, LOW AND HIGH

BERRIES, LOW AND HIGH

To avoid confusion, we've supplied the following list of Kodiak area berries, giving their names – common, Latin, Aleut and Russian – and showing their relationship to each other.

Closely related berries, such as bog blueberry, black huckleberry, and early blueberry, can often be used interchangeably in recipes calling for these berry varieties.

Many berry recipes call for sugar. In such a recipe, honey in half the sugar amount can be substituted. Since honey will not cause jam or jelly from berries without natural pectin to thicken sufficiently, in these recipes add 1 level teaspoon agar per cup of liquid. (Agar is a kind of dried seaweed, available in most health food stores.)

CROWBERRY FAMILY
CROWBERRY, Blackberry
Empetrum nigrum
Shíksha, Shikshónik (Russian)

DOGWOOD FAMILY
BUNCHBERRY, Canadian Dwarf
Cornel, Airberry, Dwarf Dogwood
Cornus canadensis

HEATH FAMILY
BLUEBERRY
Cuawak (Aleut)
Cherníka (Russian)

1) **ALPINE BLUEBERRY**
   Vaccinium uliginosum

2) **BOG BLUEBERRY**
   Vaccinium uliginosum, ssp. *microphyllum*

3) **EARLY BLUEBERRY,**
   Forest Blueberry *Vaccinium ovalifolium*

CRANBERRY
Kenegtaq (Aleut)
Brusníka (Russian)

1) **LINGONBERRY,**
   Lowbush Cranberry, Bog Cranberry
   Vaccinium vitis-idaea

2) **LOWBUSH CRANBERRY,**
   Bog Cranberry, Swamp Cranberry
   Oxycoccus microcarpus

KINNIKINNIK, Mealberry
Arctostaphylos uva-ursi

HONEYSUCKLE FAMILY
ELDERBERRY, Red-berried Elder
Sambucus racemosa
Boozínik (Russian)

HIGHBUSH CRANBERRY
Viburnum edule
Amaryaq (Aleut)
Kalína (Russian)

ROSE FAMILY
BEACH STRAWBERRY
Fragaria chiloensis
Zemlyaníka (Russian)

NAGOONBERRY, Wild Raspberry,
Wineberry
Rubus arcticus
Puyurniq (Aleut)

RASPBERRY

1) **AMERICAN RED RASPBERRY**
   Rubus idaeus
   Malína (Russian)

2) **CLOUDBERRY**
   Rubus chamaemorus
   Maróshka (Russian)

3) **TRAILING RASPBERRY,**
   Mossberry
   Rubus pedatus
   Kostianíka (Russian)

SALMONBERRY
Rubus spectabilis
Alagnaq, Chughelenuk (Aleut)
Malína (Russian)

WILD ROSE
Prickly Rose
Rosa nutkana
Roza (Russian) – Rose
Shipoynik (Russian) – Wild Rose Bush

LILY FAMILY
WILD CUCUMBER,
Watermelon Berry, Twisted Stalk
Streptopus amplexifolius
Oogoortsi (Russian)

HINTS ON COOKING WILD EDIBLES

HINTS ON COOKING WILD EDIBLES

Very often it seems that the novice at foraging for wild edibles reaches a kind of plateau when it comes to the actual preparation of plants for the dinner table. The new plant enthusiast has learned to identify wild vegetables correctly, discovered where they are growing, harvested them, and brought them home. But what then?

Part of the purpose of this book is to make that next step easier. Specific recipes have been provided throughout the book to help the cook get the wild vegetable on the table. The purpose of the lists that follow is to make that task even simpler. One can see at a glance how the plant in question can be used, and plan the meal accordingly.

In the introduction it was stated that wild edibles generally have a higher nutritional value than commercial vegetables. The best ways to get full benefits of that nutritional value are:

1) Eat plants as soon as possible after gathering.
2) Eat plants without cooking them. Therefore, if used in salads soon after picking, the plants have maximum nutritional value — cooking has destroyed none of their vitamins.

However, not all wild plants can be put in salads. Then, too, the day's meal may call for a dish other than a salad. Many leaves of wild edibles can be cooked as potherbs, which means they are boiled or steamed and served like spinach. Some can be wilted with vinegar and bacon. Or they might replace vegetables like asparagus or green beans.

Some plants are quite tender and should not be overcooked. They can be steamed and eaten as they are, with butter, salt and pepper, or with a little vinegar. Others are coarser-textured and require more cooking time. Use a fork to check for doneness (fork should pierce plants easily).

Still another group of plants tends to be bitter or strong in flavor. Included here is the marsh marigold, which contains a poison that is destroyed by cooking. Place plants listed in this category in a small amount of water, cover, and bring to a boil, then drain. Pour a fresh supply of boiling water into the pan and cook until plant is tender. Some plants, such as marsh marigold, may need the water changed twice to rid the plant of all undesirable properties.

Some wild plants are cooked in soup stocks and stews, or act as seasonings; others appear in purees and creamed soups (see recipes following).

A few Alaskan plants can be served as potato substitutes. The plants in this group are best gathered from autumn to spring because the starch stored in their roots is more abundant then. Also, during the cold months the roots are firm, but in summer roots become mushy.

A few plants growing in the Kodiak area produce seeds that can be ground into flour. Before grinding, it is necessary to remove the husks and separate them from the seeds. Rub the seeds between two boards or two flat rocks, then pour them between two tin cans in a light breeze. The husks will blow away and the seeds will remain.

The seeds can be ground between two rocks to produce flour. However, as they need to be crushed as fine as possible, a knife-type kitchen blender, a hand flourmill or an electric coffee bean grinder might work better.

Seeds can also be boiled for cereal – add sweetener or bacon drippings to taste.

Two plants, dandelion and northern bedstraw, can be roasted and used as coffee substitutes.

Basic Purée Recipe

Simmer greens for 20 minutes, then press through a colander and mash, or use a meat grinder or blender. Add butter and seasonings.

Basic Cream Soup Recipe

Pour 1 quart rich cream in a pan; place over low heat. When cream starts to bubble, add 3 cups pureed greens; season with salt and pepper to taste.

Variations:
1) Reduce the amount of cream and add 1 can cream of mushroom soup.
2) Mince 1 onion, sauté in butter, and add.
3) Add 2 cups grated cheese.
4) Add 2 or 3 beaten egg yolks; blend well.
5) Add various seasonings, such as curry powder or paprika, to top soup.

Wild Salads

(Young plants are best)

Alaska Spring Beauty
Beach Peas
Common Plantain (very young)
Chickweed
Dandelion (leaves)
Fireweed (stems and leaves)
Goosetongue
Lambsquarter
Mountain Sorrel
Petrúshki (Beach Lovage)
Rose (petals)
Roseroot
Salmonberry (blossoms)
Saxifrage
Seabeach Sandwort (Beach Greens)
Sourdock
Spearmint
Wild Chives
Wild Cucumber
Wild Violet
Willow (very young leaves)

Wilted with Vinegar and Bacon

Chickweed
Dandelion
Goosetongue
Lambsquarter
Mountain Sorrel
Saxifrage
Beach Greens (cook with sausage and no vinegar)
Sourdock

Blanched (boiled 1 minute), Drained, Sautéed

Fireweed (shoots)
Spreading Wood Fern (fiddleheads)

I. Cooked Greens
(Tender: Steam and don't overcook)

Alaska Spring Beauty (young plants)
Common Plantain (young plants)
Chickweed
Clover (leaves of young plants)
Goosetongue
Lambsquarter
Mountain Sorrel
Sourdock

II. Cooked Greens
(Cook longer than Group I, but no more than necessary; use fork test)

Beach Peas
Clover (roots)
Dandelion (young roots)
Fern (fiddleheads)
Fireweed (shoots)
Nettle (boil or steam 5 to 15 minutes)
Wild Violet (leaves)

III. Cooked Greens
(May be bitter – boil, drain, boil again)

Common Plantain (older plants)
Dandelion (leaves of older plants)
Fireweed (young plants)
Marsh Marigold (boil in three changes of water)
Northern Bedstraw
Petrúshki (Beach Lovage)
Sourdock (older plants)

Cooked in Soup Stocks and Stews; Used as Seasonings

Clover (roots)
Fireweed (peeled stems of older plants)
Horsetail (new shoots above rootstock)
Petrúshki (Beach Lovage)
Póochki, or Cow Parsnip (leaves dried, burned, and powdered, or peeled stems)
Spearmint
Sweet Gale (leaves or berries, to season meat)
Wild Chives

Creamed Soups and Purees

Common Plantain
Chickweed
Goosetongue
Lambsquarter
Marsh Marigold (boil in three changes of water)
Mountain Sorrel
Nettle
Poochki, or Beach Lovage (peeled stems)
Saxifrage
Sourdock
Wild Cucumber

Edible Roots and Bark

(Source of starch or potato substitute)

Indian Rice
Roseroot (where abundant)
Silverweed
Willow (inner bark)
Yellow Pond Lily (boil twice)

Edible Seeds and Bark

(For flours and cereals)

Clover
Lambsquarter
Sourdock
Willow (inner bark)
Yellow Pond Lily

Coffee Substitutes

Dandelion (roots)
Northern Bedstraw (seeds and roots)

PLANT LORE OF AN ALASKAN ISLAND

DYES FROM WILD PLANTS

DYES MADE FROM WILD PLANTS

Since ancient times, people all over the world have used plants to produce dyes for fibers, woven textiles, and leathers. Early Alaskan people were no exception. Yarns for clothing or ceremonial garments were dyed with plants gathered for that purpose. Dyed bark and grass fiber brightened baskets. Early fishermen in Alaska colored their nets with homemade dyes.

Today, we can imitate the ancients and use natural dyes made from the plants growing around us to produce many pleasing yarn colors.

A great variety of plants in the Kodiak area can be utilized to produce dyes. In this chapter we include a list of those we have researched, with recipes for making dyes from them. We have tried some of these dye recipes; others remain to be tested in future Plants Class (Ouzinkie Botanical Society) sessions. There are other Alaskan dye producing plants and recipe variations not included here, but the ones that follow will give the beginning student a good introductory sample. Use these recipes as guidelines for experimentation.

The Plants

Some plants can be dried and used later for dyeing; others are best when used fresh. Blossoms picked for dyeing, for example, sometimes lose their color when they are dried. Most plants suitable for dyeing produce best results when picked in the late summer or autumn, or at the peak of their growing season.

The usual way to prepare plants for the dye bath is to crush or chop them, cover with water, and let stand overnight. (As a general rule, use a 2-gallon container of plant material to produce 4 gallons of dye bath.) The next day, boil plants 30 minutes to 2 hours, depending on the shade desired. Strain out the plants and add enough water to make 4 gallons; mix well and heat.

Two Processes

Usually, dyeing with plants calls for two processes. The first process is "mordanting"; the second is the dyeing itself. A mordant is a substance used to fix the color – make it permanent. Common mordants are alum, chrome, iron and tin. Other mordants include vinegar or acetic acid, ammonia or urine, blue vitriol, caustic soda or sodium hydroxide, lime, tannic acid, and cream of tartar.

Mordanting and dyeing can be done at the same time, but a clearer color will result if they are done separately. Be sure to allow enough time for each process.

The Yarn

Any natural fiber — not synthetic — can be dyed. Sometimes dyeing different fibers requires differing procedures. The directions given here are for wool yarn.

Use clean yarn. If the yarn is dirty or greasy, wash it in mild soap. If yarn is dry, wet it thoroughly before mordanting or dyeing, and squeeze — don't wring — to remove excess water.

For either mordanting or dyeing, *do not let wool yarn boil* — keep it simmering. Be careful to increase or decrease water temperature gradually. Drastic temperature changes cause wool to be "shocked" and result in shrunken, felted or matted yarn.

Let water cool slowly before removing yarn from either mordant or dye bath. When yarn is cool enough to handle, lift it out and rinse it in water that's the same temperature as the mordant or dye bath you took it from. Let the yarn dry slowly.

Equipment

The pot used for mordanting and dyeing should be copper, stainless steel, or enamel. Have available a cooking thermometer, large heat-resistant glass measuring cups, plastic spoons for measuring mordants, glass rods or wooden sticks for stirring (if sticks are wooden, use a separate one for each color), and plastic or enamel containers for rinsing yarn.

Water

For best results, use soft water for dyeing; rainwater is best. Hard water contains dissolved mineral salts. Because of the minerals, dye colors will be less bright and clear. However, if only hard water is available, the addition of a little white vinegar will help soften it.

Crystals and Salts

If a recipe calls for copperas crystals (iron or ferrous sulfate), purchase the crystals in a drug store or from a chemical company.

Some recipes call for Glauber's salts. Although dyeing can be done without these, they are suggested because they make the dye color uniform. If Glauber's salts are used, it is not necessary to stir the dye bath. The salts can be purchased at a chemical company or a drug store.

Alum Mordant

When using an alum mordant, dissolve 3 ounces alum and 1 ounce cream of tartar in a small amount of water, then add it to 4 gallons lukewarm water. (This quantity is sufficient for 1 pound of yarn.) Then add wet yarn, slowly heat to just below boiling, and simmer 1 hour. Turn the yarn occasionally. Cool; remove from mordant bath.

If you don't plan on dyeing right away, let yarn dry slowly. It might take a few days for the yarn to dry completely. Before putting it in the dye bath, moisten yarn and squeeze gently to remove excess water.

Chrome Mordant

To use a chrome mordant, dissolve ½ ounce chrome in a small amount of boiling water. Pour into 4 gallons of hot water, add 1 pound yarn, and simmer, covered, 1 hour. Cool to lukewarm (see "The Yarn," preceding) and rinse. NOTE: Whenever using chrome mordant, dye immediately after mordanting. Squeeze yarn gently to remove excess water before putting in dye bath.

Copperas Crystals
(Iron or Ferrous Sulfate) Mordants

These mordants color fibers green; they improve green or blue tones in the dyed yarn.

Add 2 ounces iron vitriol to 3 gallons warm water. Immerse 1 pound yarn and simmer 1 hour for dark green, a shorter time for lighter shades.

Dyeing Procedure

For each pound (dry weight) of wool yarn, use 4 gallons dye bath. Immerse moist yarn when the bath is lukewarm. Then heat slowly to a simmer and let simmer for ½ hour, occasionally stirring gently. If the water level gets low: remove yarn, add hot water, mix well, and return yarn to dye bath.

If dyeing and mordanting are done together, dissolve the mordant in the warm dye bath before adding the yarn (add cream of tartar, if used, after yarn has been in the bath 30 minutes). Leave yarn in the bath for 1 hour.

When dyeing time is completed, rinse the yarn several times in water of gradually decreasing temperatures until rinse water is clear. Squeeze out excess moisture and dry yarn in a cool place.

DYES FROM LICHENS

Lichens are one of nature's most mysterious plant forms. These tiny organisms are unique because they are both algae and fungi. (Algae are plants with chlorophyll but no vascular system, such as stem or leaf veins, for carrying essential fluids. Fungi are plants that have no chlorophyll; mushrooms are an example.) Both parts of the lichen cooperate so that the total plant flourishes in what is called a symbiotic union. Because of this alga-fungus cooperation, the lichen is one of the most adaptable and widely distributed plants on earth; there are thousands of species of lichens.

For centuries, lichens have had a variety of uses. Medicinally, they have been sought for treatment of skin ailments, for making antibiotics, and for curing tuberculosis. They are also used in making perfume. However, one of their most interesting uses is as a dye for yarn.

One of the nicest things about dyeing with lichens is that they require no mordanting, although mordants can be added if desired. Lichens also give wool yarn a pleasant smell, and it is said that they make wool mothproof.

The Plants Class has experimented with five different types of lichens, using no mordants. From the pale-green hair-like lichen known as old man's beard, in the genus Usnea, we obtained a tan color. From a member of the genus Cladonia we came up with a rich medium-brown shade. From a genus Parmelia lichen, nicknamed by Stacy Studebaker the "bird-dropping lichen" because of its appearance, we got a deep brown color. From two other Parmelia lichens we obtained a dark tan and a gold.

We urge you to experiment. Just be sure, as you collect, to gather lichens that are all the same type. We also suggest that, for lichens and all other plants used in dyeing, you save a small portion of the plant along with a little piece of the dyed yarn as a record of the color you obtained.

Lichen Dye

Gather about 2 gallons of the type of lichen you wish to try. (You might find it easier to gather the lichens after a rain.) Soak lichens overnight in water to cover. Boil in the same water for 1 hour, strain, add enough water to make 4 gallons, add 1 pound yarn, and simmer for ½ hour or longer. (Adjust amounts of water and yarn to strength of dye material.)

No mordant: Color will vary, depending on type of lichen used.
With alum mordant: Yellow tan.
With 1/6 ounce chrome and 1/16 ounce vinegar or acetic acid (see chrome mordant directions): Rose tan.

NOTE: Mordanted yarn shades might vary with different kinds of lichens.

DYES FROM SMALL PLANTS
Common Plantain *(Plantago major)*

According to references, plantain produces colors from green to yellow brown when mordanted. We do not have the recipe — feel free to experiment.

Goldenrod *(Solidago lepida, S. multiradiata)*
Blossoms

Pick when first in bloom. Gather 1 to 1 ½ pounds flowers and cover with water. Let stand in water overnight. Boil 1 hour or longer. Strain, add enough water to make 4 gallons, add 1 pound yarn, and simmer 1 hour.

With alum mordant: Yellowish tan.
With 1/6 ounce chrome and 1/6 ounce vinegar or acetic acid (see chrome mordant directions):
Old gold.

Whole plant

Gather 4 gallons goldenrod plants in late summer or autumn. Cut into 1 to 3-inch pieces, cover with water, and boil for 2 hours. Add more water as liquid boils away. Cool. Strain and add 4 ounces copperas crystals; stir until completely dissolved. Add enough water to make 4 gallons.

Add damp wool yarn (1 pound, dry) and simmer 30 minutes. Dissolve 4 tablespoons cream of tartar and ½ cup Glauber's salts in 1 pint boiling water and add to dye bath. Keep yarn covered with the bath to prevent streaking and simmer 30 minutes longer. Cool. Rinse until water is clear. Dry yarn in the shade.

Color: Dark green. Re-use dye bath for lighter shades of green.

Horsetail (Equisetum)

Gather 2 or more gallons of the branching stalks (scouring rushes). Put the stalks in a pot and cover them with rainwater. Layer 1 pound wool yarn alternately with the horsetail. Use amount of yarn for each layer equal to about 1/10 of the weight of the wet plant layer. Simmer for 30 minutes, rinse repeatedly in warm water until water stays clear, and dry in the shade.

The horsetail-dyed yarn can be redyed with other plants. Colors seem to improve if the yarn is first dyed with horsetail.

With alum mordant: Greenish yellow.
With copperas crystals (iron or ferrous sulfate) mordant: Gray green.
With copper sulfate mordant: Grass green.

If an aluminum or zinc kettle is used, a green color will result if plants are heated in the dye bath for 2 hours.

Nettles (Urtica lyallii)

Gather mature plants, using gloves and scissors. Chop whole plants into small pieces, cover with water, and boil 1 hour. Strain and add water to make 4 gallons. Heat dye bath to lukewarm. Add wet, mordanted wool yarn, bring to a boil, and simmer 30 minutes. Cool, rinse in warm water until clear, and dry.

With alum mordant: Greenish yellow.

Northern Bedstraw (Galium boreale)

For ½ pound wool yarn, use ½ pound roots and 1 ounce alum. Crush the roots, wrap in cheesecloth, and soak overnight in rainwater to cover. Add enough water to make 2 gallons, then boil for 1 hour, add alum, and stir until dissolved. Add wet yarn and simmer 30 minutes, or until color is satisfactory. Rinse thoroughly and dry.

No mordant: Brownish pink.
With alum mordant: Light red.
With chrome mordant: Purplish red.

For a deeper color, use ½ the quantity of roots and wool yarn, add 4 ounces vinegar or acetic acid with the yarn, and simmer gently for 1 hour.

NOTE: The leaves produce a yellow dye.

Póochki or Cow Parsnip (Heracleum lanatum)

References inform us that póochki makes a dye ranging in color from light brown to yellow or gold, depending on mordants. We do not have the recipe; feel free to experiment!

Sheep Sorrel (Rumex acetosella)

Gather the whole plant. Put chopped plants, 4 gallons lukewarm water, 1 ounce cream of tartar, and 3 ounces dissolved alum in a wooden bowl and allow to steep 2 to 3 weeks. Add 1 pound yarn and leave in dye bath for a couple of days. Stir occasionally for an even color. Hang to dry without rinsing.

Color: Light grayish pink.

NOTE: This method can also be used for willow, mountain ash, alder, birch, and yarrow.

Sourdock (Rumex)

Dig the roots anytime after the plant blooms. Late autumn is okay, if you can locate the plant. The roots, which look something like sweet potatoes, can go quite deep. They can be used fresh or dried.

Chop roots into small pieces. Cover well with water, soak overnight, then boil for 2 hours in the same water. Mash with a potato masher while they are cooking. Strain, add enough water to make 4 gallons, add 1 pound yarn, and simmer 1 hour.

No mordant: Tan.
With alum mordant: Gold.
With chrome mordant: Reddish tan to deep gold.

Silverweed (Potentilla anserina)

Although several references inform us that a reddish dye can be made from the roots of silverweed, we have not found a specific recipe. We would suggest using alum-mordanted wool yarn and following a process similar to that set forth for sourdock roots.

Spreading Wood Fern (Dryopteris dilatata)

We understand that this plant's fibrous, dark brown roots yield a brown dye, but we do not have specific directions.

DYES FROM TREES AND SHRUBS

Tree bark should be collected in the spring, as the sap is highest then. Gather from young trees that are free of moss. (Do not peel bark all the way around the tree; this will kill the tree.) Dry the bark. It can then be kept for several years if stored in a dry place. As almost all tree barks contain tannic acid, the addition of iron salts gives dark colors.

Alder *(Alnus crispa)*

Gather branches and strip off outer and inner bark. (Use 2 pounds bark to 4 gallons water.) Cut bark into small strips and soak overnight in water to cover. Boil for 2 hours in the same water. Strain, add enough water to make 4 gallons, add 1 pound yarn, and simmer 1 hour.

No mordant: Brown.
With 2 ounces alum mordant (2/3 ounce cream of tartar): Shades varying from ice green to orange.
With copperas mordant: Gray brown.

Spruce *(Picea sitchensis)*

Bark

Peel inner and outer bark of the spruce tree and follow the same process as with alder. Simmer until the desired shade is obtained.

Color: Brown.

Twigs

Chop lichen-free twigs and simmer in water to cover, using aluminum or enamel kettle, for 12 hours. Then place yarn on top of the twigs but keep it under water. Heat to 176 degrees. Simmer, stirring to get an even color. When the yarn reaches the desired shade, hang to dry without rinsing. Longer simmering will yield a darker shade.

Color: Camel-hair tan

Blueberry *(Vaccinium)*

Gather berries when fully ripe. Crush ½ pound berries; boil in 1 gallon water for 1 hour to extract color. Strain. Add water to make 1 gallon. Add about 1 ounce alum and boil 5 minutes longer. Add wet wool yarn (1 pound, dry) and simmer for 1 hour

Color: Lavender to purple (fades in sun).

Elderberry *(Sambucus racemosa)*

Boil ½ pound berries in ½ gallon water for 30 minutes to 1 hour. Add 1 tablespoon salt. Strain and add water to make ½ gallon or more. Add wet yarn (1 pound, dry) and simmer for 1 hour.

No mordant: Red.
With alum mordant: Lilac blue.
With chrome mordant: Plum to lavender.

NOTE: Elderberry leaves produce a yellow dye.

Lingonberry *(Vaccinium vitis-idaea)*

Use fresh stems and leaves gathered in summer (use 2 gallons of the plant to produce 4 gallons of dye bath). Cover with water and let stand overnight. Boil 2 hours, strain, add enough water to make 4 gallons, then add 2 tablespoons alum and 1 tablespoon cream of tartar. Add wet yarn, stir, and simmer in the bath for 1 hour or until desired shade is obtained. Rinse repeatedly in warm water until water is clear; hang to dry.

Color: Red.

Sweet Gale *(Myrica gale L.)*

Three different shades of yellow can be obtained from the same dye bath. Divide 12 ounces wool yarn into 3 skeins and mordant with 12 ounces alum in enough water to cover. Let wool cool in the mordant solution. Cover 10 ounces fresh sweet gale leaves with cold water and boil 1 hour. (If dried leaves are used, soak overnight first.) Strain. Add enough water to cover yarn well and heat slowly. When temperature reaches 95 degrees, add all 3 skeins of yarn; simmer 45 minutes. Remove and hang yarn.

Color: Golden yellow.

Now pour half the dye bath into another kettle and add 1/5 ounce copper vitriol; stir until dissolved. Add 1 gallon water. When temperature reaches 104 degrees, drop in 1 of the 3 skeins of yellow yarn and simmer 15 minutes. Remove and hang yarn.

Color: Warm yellow brown.

To the remaining dye, add 1/3 ounce copperas crystals and stir until dissolved. Add 1 gallon water. Heat to 104 degrees and drop in 1 skein of the yellow yarn. Let simmer 15 minutes. Remove and hang yarn.

Color: Cool yellow green.

Wash and rinse the three skeins of wool yarn and hang to dry in a shady place. The three colors will blend very well.

PLANT LORE
OF AN
ALASKAN
ISLAND

GLOSSARY

GLOSSARY

Achene A small, dry one-seeded fruit that does not split at maturity.

Adventitious root A root that originates from stem or leaf tissue rather than from the interior of another root. Rhizomes usually bear adventitious roots.

Algae (Singular alga) Any of a group of lower plants having chlorophyll but no vascular system, such as stem or leaf veins, for carrying essential fluids. Seaweeds and related freshwater plants are examples of algae.

Alternate Refers to a way leaves grow on the stem of a plant. Alternate leaves are arranged singly at different points along both sides of the stem.

Annual Refers to the life cycle of a plant. An annual completes the cycle from seed to death in one year or season.

Anther Located at the top of the stamen, the anther is an enlarged end of the filament, and contains the pollen grains.

Antiseptic An agent or substance for destroying or slowing down germs that cause decay and infection.

Archipelago A group of islands.

Ascending Growing upward; rising.

Astringent An agent or substance that shrinks body tissue, reducing secretions or discharges.

Biennial Refers to the life cycle of a plant. A biennial completes the cycle from seed to death in two years or seasons.

Blade Thin, flat expanded portion of the leaf.

Bract A modified leaf, usually smaller than the true leaves. It forms either on the flower stalk or as a part of the flower head. Bracts are sometimes mistaken for flowers.

Branch The older part of a shoot, behind the twig.

Bryophyte A nonvascular plant, e.g. algae, lichens, fungi, and mosses. Bryophytes are characterized by rhizoids (a slender, rootlike filament), rather than true roots, and little or no organized vascular tissue. Includes true mosses, liverworts, and hornworts.

Buds An unexpanded flower or leaf that can be found at a leaf node or anywhere else on a stem.

Calyx The sepals collectively form the calyx.

Cambium A thin cellular layer of tissue, under the hard outer bark of trees and shrubs, from which new tissues develop.

Carbohydrate Any of various compounds made up of carbon, hydrogen, and oxygen. Sugars and starches are such compounds.

Carpel The part of a plant that holds seeds. The carpel can be single or compound (having two or more sections).

Catkin A spikelike flower cluster (as of a willow) bearing petal-less, unisexual flowers and having bracts, or modified leaves, on or at the base of the flower stalk.

Caulk To make tight against leakage by a sealing substance; to make the seams of a boat watertight by filling with waterproofing materials.

Chlorophyll The green material in plants. When exposed to sunlight, chlorophyll forms carbohydrates in a process called photosynthesis.

Coagulate When a portion of liquid (for example, blood) thickens and sticks together, it clots, or coagulates.

Companion plants Plants which grow together or which are planted together because their physical demands for growth complement each other.

Compound leaf Blade is divided into several or many parts, which are termed leaflets.

Corolla Collective name for the petals of the flower. These are white and colored.

Decoction To make a decoction, place the plant parts to be used in water and boil them together. This method is used to extract mineral salts or bitter substances from plants, or to remove active ingredients from hard materials such as roots, bark and seeds.

Deciduous Refers to trees and shrubs that lose their leaves in the fall.

Decumbent Reclining or lying on the ground, but with the end ascending.

Demulcent Soothing to irritated tissues because of its high mucilage content.

Disc flowers Tubular flowers atop the broadened stem in the Composite family.

Diuretic An agent that increases the flow of urine.

Dropsy An abnormal accumulation of fluid in the body.

Drupe Fruit with a stone.

Evergreen A plant that retains its leaves for two or more years.

Family A group of related plants having common characteristics. A family of plants may include many plant genera (see genus).

Fibrous root A thin root arising from another root or from stem tissue. The total root system can be fibrous.

Filament Slender, elongated stalk of the stamen.

Flower The reproductive structure of some seed-bearing plants, often having showy or colorful parts (blossoms). Flowers can be both male and female, producing both pollen and ovule, or one or the other. Flowers are the part most commonly used to identify a plant.

Follicle A dry fruit developed from a single ovary, splitting along one seam to release seeds.

Frond Leaf of the fern.

Fungus (plural fungi) Any of a large group of lower plants that do not contain chlorophyll. This group includes molds, mildews, mushrooms, and bacteria.

Generic Of or related to a genus.

Genus (Plural genera) A grouping of plants of closely related species. Families of plants are divided into the more specialized groups of genus and species. The division into genus and species is called the "binomial system", and uses a pair of Latin words for each plant name. The first part of this botanical name is the genus of the plant and is always capitalized. The second word is the species name and is not capitalized. The species is the fundamental group that can be consistently identified as being different from other plant groups.

Habitat The place or kind of place where a plant naturally grows.

Hardy Plants that are able to withstand adverse weather and freezing temperatures.

Hemorrhage A large discharge of blood from the blood vessels.

Hemorrhoids A swollen mass of dilated veins situated at or just within the anus.

Herb Plant in which the portion above ground is relatively short-lived and the tissues comparatively soft.

Indentation Notches or deep recesses, as in leaf edges.

Indusium An outgrowth covering and protecting a spore cluster in ferns.

Inferior Beneath. When the floral tube fuses with the ovary, the sepals, petals, and stamens apparently grow from the top of the ovary. Ovary is then said to be inferior.

Inflorescence Flowers growing in a cluster.

Infusion An infusion is a beverage made like tea, by combining boiling water with plant parts (usually the green parts or the flowers). The plant parts are then steeped – left to soak in hot water – to remove their active ingredients. This method, with its relatively short exposure to heat, minimizes the loss of vitamins or other ingredients that are destroyed by cooking.

Internode Area of the shoot between two nodes.

Lateral bud These differ from the terminal bud only in their position on the plant. These buds grow on the sides of the stems, and are responsible for the growth of leaves and side branches.

Lateral root The branching parts of the root which grow from the main root stalk.

Leaf Axil Angle where the leaf is attached to the twig.

Lobe A part or division of a leaf that is curved or rounded.

Mordant A substance used in dyeing for the purposes of fixing the color and making it permanent.

Node The region of the stem where one or more leaves are attached. Buds are commonly borne in the node.

Opposite Two leaves are attached to the same node, on opposite sides of the twig.

Ovary Swollen, basal part of the pistil, usually flask-shaped, which contain the ovules, which, after united with the pollen, develop into seeds.

Ovule Embryo sac; each one contains an egg, and is found within the enlarged, lower part of the pistil. Following fertilization, the ovule develops into the seed.

Palmate Leaves divided into lobes like diverging fingers.

Panicle A branched raceme.

Perennial A plant that lives through three or more seasons.

Petal One of the units of the corolla of a flower. The corolla is the collective name for the white or colored petals. Petals may be missing from some species and the colorful sepals attract the pollinator.

Petiole Leaf stalk.

Photosynthesis The process by which chlorophyll-producing plants form carbohydrates when exposed to sunlight.

Pinnate Feather-formed; compound leaf in which leaflets are placed on each side of a common axis, like the barbs of a feather.

Pistil Located in the center of the flower; commonly flask shaped, with a swollen, basal part.

The pistil is composed of 3 parts: The stigma, the style, and the ovary.

Placenta Region or area where one or more ovules (or seeds) are attached.

Pollinate To carry pollen to the female part of a plant to fertilize the seed.

Poultice A soft, usually heated mass made from medicinally useful plants, then spread on or wrapped in cloth and applied to a sore or injury.

Primary root The part of the root system that is the lower end of the shoot, and serves as the main plant anchor.

Raceme An elongated inflorescence, or cluster of flowers along the main stem. Flowers at the base of the raceme open first.

Radially symmetrical Developing uniformly on all sides, like spokes of a wheel.

Ray flowers The strap-shaped flowers arranged around the edges of the stem top in the Composite family. Often falsely called petals.

Receptacle That part of the axis of a flower stalk that bears the floral organs.

Regenerate To form or create again. Plants regenerate themselves in various ways.

Respiratory Referring to the act or process of breathing. Diseases of the respiratory system would be those which interfere with this breathing process.

Rhizome An underground portion of a plant stem, having shoots on top of it and roots beneath it. Though it is underground, it is different from a root in that it has buds, nodes, and scaly leaves. Rhizomes usually bear adventitious roots.

Root The plant body consists of an axis, which at one end becomes the root, and at the other the shoot, made up of the stem and leaves. The root anchors the plant and absorbs water and mineral salts from the soil. It is made up of the primary root and the lateral roots.

Rosette A circular or spiral arrangement of leaves growing from a center or crown. Many plants have leaves arranged in a "basal rosette," or a circular arrangement of leaves at the base of the plant.

Saprophytic Feeding or growing upon dead or decaying organic matter.

Scurvy A disease caused by a deficiency of vitamin C. Symptoms include spongy and bleeding gums and loose teeth.

Sepal The first of four kinds of floral organs, always arranged in the same order. The sepal begins at the base of the flower. These are often green and sometimes leaflike. In some species the sepals are colorful like petals and replace the petals as an attractant for the pollenator.

Sessile Referring to a leaf attached directly to a stem (having no petiole).

Shoot Made up of stem and leaves, it functions primarily to support, conduct fluids, and manufacture food.

Silica A mineral composed of silicon and oxygen. Silica is found in some plants, and can be useful in treating certain physical conditions.

Simple leaf Blade is single and undivided. Of one piece; not compound.

Sorus (Plural sori) A cluster of small spore cases found on the underside of the fern leaf.

Species The second part of a binomial name in the Scientific Classification Index. The species name is often descriptive of some distinctive quality of the plant. There can be numerous species in a genus of plants, and many genera of plants in a family.

Spore sacs Containers for spores, which are the one- to several-celled reproductive body in ferns, lichen, and mosses.

Stamen Located next to the petal. The stamen has two parts: typically a slender, elongated stalk known as the filament; an enlarged anther, which contains the pollen grains, terminates this stalk.

Steep Allowing herbs to stand in hot water to extract their active ingredients. Herbs should be steeped in an enamel, glass, or porcelain pot, not a metal one. A covered container is best.

Stigma The top, expanded portion of the pistil which receives the pollen. This pollen receptacle may be rough, smooth, sticky, branched, or feathery.

Stipe A supporting stalk, such as the leafstalk of a fern or the stalk of kelp, such as bull kelp.

Stipule An appendage on either side of the base of the leaf of some plant species.

Strobilus (Plural strobili) Comes from the Greek *strobilos,* or cone. A structure characterized by partly overlapping bracts or scales, somewhat like shingles on a roof. Example: pine cone.

Style Slender and stalklike, the style connects the stigma with the ovary.

Succulent A plant having fleshy tissues that conserve moisture.

Superior Above. When the sepals, petals, and stamens attach underneath the ovary, the ovary is said to be superior. Position of ovary in relation to these parts governs the method of reproduction.

Symbiotic A type of association or union of two differing organisms which live together for mutually beneficial purposes.

Tap root A central main root that descends vertically; it is larger than any branch roots.

Terminal bud The bud that occurs at the tip of a twig, or stem.

Textile Any kind of cloth, especially woven or knit cloth.

Tonic An agent or substance that strengthens or invigorates organs or the entire body.

Toxic Poisonous.

Twig Present on all woody plants. The twig is the leaf-bearing part.

Umbels A kind of flower cluster (inflorescence) in which the flower stalks arise from the same point, like the ribs of an umbrella.

Vascular system In plants, refers to the system of channels for carrying life-giving fluids. These channels include plant stems and leaf veins. In the human body, the vascular system carries blood through the body.

Vitamin Any of various organic substances that are essential, in tiny amounts, to most animals and some plants and are mostly obtained from food.

Whorl A circular arrangement of three or more leaves or flowers at the same point or level on the stem of the plant.

Wintergreen Annual leaves that survive through one winter on an otherwise deciduous plant.

BIBLIOGRAPHY

BIBLIOGRAPHY

Aggarival, B.B. "Role of Resveratrol in Prevention and Therapy of Cancer: Preclinical and Clinical Studies." Anticancer Research, 2004; 24: 2783-2840.

Alvin, Kenneth L. *The Observer's Book of Lichens*. London: Frederick Warne Ltd., 1977.

Anderson, J. P. *Flora of Alaska and Adjacent Parts of Canada*. Ames, Iowa: The Iowa State University Press, 1959.

Angier, Bradford. *Feasting Free on Wild Edibles*. Harrisburg, Pennsylvania: Stackpole Books, 1966.

Angier, Bradford, *Field Guide to Edible Wild Plants*. Harrisburg Pennsylvania: Stackpole Books, 1974.

Ball, Georgiana. "Medicinal Leaves of the Tahltans." ALASKA, vol. XLIX, No. 4, April 1983.

Bell, C. Ritchie. *Plant Variation and Classification*. Belmont, California: Wadsworth Publishing Co., Inc., 1967.

Benoliel, Doug. *Northwest Foraging*. Seattle, Washington: Signpost Books, 1974.

Bomser, J., et al. "*In vitro* Anticancer Activity of Fruit Extracts from *Vaccinium* Species." Planta Medica, 1996. 62: 212-216.

Bricklin, Mark. *The Practical Encyclopedia of Natural Healing*, Emmaus, Pennsylvania: Rodale Press, 1982.

Chase, Cora G. *The Weedeater's Cook Book*. Seattle, Washington: Shelton Publishing Co., 1978.

Christiansen, Clyda. "Health Remedies." Kodiak Area Native Association Newsletter, 1982.

Clark, Lewis J. *Wild Flowers of Marsh and Waterway in the Pacific Northwest*. Sidney, British Columbia: Gray's Publishing Ltd., 1974.

Clark, Lewis J. *Wild Flowers of the Sea Coast in the Pacific Northwest*. Sidney, British Columbia: Gray's Publishing Ltd., 1974.

Cobban, Gerry. "Island Edibles and Elixirs." *Memoirs of a Galley Slave*. Fishermen's Wives Auxiliary. Kodiak: Page Photo, 1981.

Coon, Nelson. *Using Plants for Healing*. Emmaus, Pennsylvania: Rodale Press, 1963, 1979.

Cooperative Extension Service. *Wild Berry Recipes.* Fairbanks, Alaska: The University of Alaska, 1973.

Cooperative Extension Service. *Wild, Edible and Poisonous Plants of Alaska.* Fairbanks, Alaska: The University of Alaska, 1966.

Domico, Terry. *Wild Harvest.* Seattle, Washington: Hancock House Publishing Inc., 1979.

Editors of ALASKA magazine. *The Alaska-Yukon Wild Flowers Guide.* Anchorage, Alaska: Alaska Northwest Publishing Company, 1974.

_____. *Alaska Wild Berry Guide and Cookbook.* Anchorage, Alaska: Alaska Northwest Publishing Company, 1982.

Editors of ALASKA magazine and friends. *Cooking Alaskan.* Anchorage, Alaska: Alaska Northwest Publishing Company, 1983.

Furlong, Marjorie and Virginia Pill. *Edible? Incredible! Pondlife.* Happy Camp, California: Naturegraph Publishers, Inc., 1980.

Garibaldi, Ann. *Medicinal Flora of the Alaska Natives.* Anchorage, Alaska: University of Alaska, Alaska Natural Heritage Program, 1999.

Gibbons, Euell. *Stalking the Healthful Herbs.* New York, New York: David McKay Company, Inc., 1966.

Gilkey, Helen and LaRea J. Dennis. *Handbook of Northwestern Plants.* Corvallis, Oregon: Oregon State University Bookstores, Inc., 1967.

Grieve, Mrs. M. *A Modern Herbal.* vols. I and II. New York, New York: Dover Publications Inc., 1971.

Grimm, William Carey. *How to Recognize Trees.* New York, New York: Castle Books, 1962.

Hall, Alan. *The Wild Food Trail Guide.* New York, New York: Holt, Rinehart and Winston, 1973.

Hall, Nancy and Walter. *The Wild Palate.* Emmaus, Pennsylvania: Rodale Press, 1980.

Heller, Christine. *Wild Flowers of Alaska.* Portland, Oregon: Graphic Arts Center, 1966.

Hulten, Eric. *Flora of Alaska & Neighboring Territories: A Manual of the Vascular Plants.* Stanford, California: Stanford University Press, 1968.

Hylton, William H., ed. *The Rodale Herb Book.* Emmaus, Pennsylvania: Rodale Press Book Division, 1974.

Kari, Priscilla Russell. *Dena'ina K'et'una, Tanaina Plantlore.* Anchorage: University of Alaska, Adult Literacy Laboratory, 1977.

Keats, Della. "To Heal the People." A reprint in part from *Northwest Arctic Nuna*, Fall Edition. Kotzebue, Alaska: a Maniilaq Association Publication, 1982.

Kloss, Jethro. *Back to Eden*. Santa Barbara, California: Woodbridge Press Publishing Company, 1975.

Krochmal, Arnold and Connie. *A Field Guide to Medicinal Plants*. New York, New York: Times Books, The New York Times Book Co., Inc., 1984.

Las Aranas Spinners and Weavers Guild. *Dyeing with Natural Materials*. Albuquerque, New Mexico: Las Aranas, 1973.

Leer, Jeff. *A Conversational Dictionary of Kodiak Alutiiq*. Fairbanks, Alaska: Alaska Native Language Arts Center, University of Alaska, 1978.

Lesch, Alma. *Vegetable Dyeing*. New York, New York: Watson-Gupstill Publications, 1970.

Lyons, C. P. and Bill Merilees. *Trees, Shrubs, and Flowers to Know in British Columbia and Washington*. Redmond, Washington: Lone Pine Publishing, 1995.

Lust, John. *The Herb Book*. New York, New York: Bantam Books, 1974.

McMullen, Elenore. "Home Remedies We Have Used." *Fireweed Cillqaq*. Port Graham High School Publication, vol.2, Soldotna, Alaska: Kenai Peninsula School District, 1981.

Meyer, Joseph E. *The Herbalist*. 1918. Reprint. Glenwood, Illinois: Meyer Books, 1975.

Mindell, Earl. *New Herb Bible*. New York, New York: Simon and Schuster Fireside Books, 2000.

Montana Plant Life. www.montana.plant-life.org/Self-Heal. Accessed 14 April, 2006.

Moore, Michael. *Medicinal Plants of the Mountain West*. Santa Fe, New Mexico: Museum of New Mexico Press, 1979.

Oberg, Kalervo. *The Social Economy of the Tlingit Indians*. Seattle and London: University of Washington Press, 1973.

Pojar, Jim and Andy MacKinnon. *Plants of the Pacific Northwest Coast*. Vancouver, British Columbia: Lone Pine Publishing, 1994.

Potter, Louise. *Roadside Flowers of Alaska*. Hanover, New Hampshire: Roger Burt, 1969.

Pratt, Verna E. *Alaskan Wild flowers*. Anchorage, Alaska: Alaskakrafts Publishing, 1989.

Preston, Eudora M. "Medicine Women." ALASKA SPORTSMAN, November, 1961.

Prevention. Emmaus, Pennsylvania.

Ray, Glen. *Root, Stem and Leaf: Wild Vegetables of Southeast Alaska*. Juneau, Alaska: Southeast Regional Resource Center, 1982.

Rimando, A.M.; W. Kalt; J.B. Magie; J. Dewey; J. R. Ballington. "Resveratrol, pterostilbene, and piceatannol in *Vaccinium* Berries". Journal of Agriculture, Food, and Chemistry, July 28, 2004, 52 (15); 4713-9.

Robinson, Peggy. *Profiles of Northwest Plants*. Portland, Oregon: Far West Book Service, 1978.

Rose, Jeanne. *Herbs and Things*. New York, New York: Grosset and Dunlap, 1972.

Schaffer, Boyd J. *The Flora of South Central Alaska*. Soldotna, Alaska: Kenai Peninsula College, Arts and Sciences Division, 1995.

Schetky, Ethel Jane McD. and Carol H. Woodward. *Dye Plants and Dyeing*. Special printing of "Plants and Gardens," vol. 20, no. 3, Brooklyn, New York: Brooklyn Botanic Garden, 1964.

Schofield, Janice. *Discovering Wild Plants*. Bothell, Washington: Alaska Northwest Books, 1989.

____. *Alaska's Wild Plants*. Portland, Oregon: Alaska Northwest Books, 1993.

Sharples, Ada White. *Alaska Wild Flowers*. Stanford, California: Stanford University Press, 1958.

Spellenberg, Richard. *The Audubon Society Field Guide to North American Wildflowers*. New York, New York: Alfred A. Knopf, 1979.

Stuart, Malcolm, ed. *Herbs and Herbalism*. New York, New York: Van Nostrand Reinhold Company, 1979.

The Herb Quarterly. Newfane, Vermont, 1979-1981.

Tufts University. "Researching a Blueberry/Brain Connection": Tufts University Health and Nutrition Letter, March 2001, Vol. 19, Number 1.

Viereck, Eleanor G. *Alaska's Wilderness Medicines*. Edmonds, Washington: Alaska Northwest Publishing Co., 1987.

Viereck, Leslie A. and Elbert 1. Little, Jr. *Guide to Alaska Trees*. Forest Service, United States Department of Agriculture, 1974.

Walker, Marilyn. *Harvesting the Northern Wild*. Yellowknife, Northwest Territories, Canada: Outcrop Ltd., 1984.

Weir, T. Elliot, C. Ralph Stocking, Michael G. Barbour, and Thomas L. Rost. *Botany: An Introduction to Plant Biology.* New York, New York: John Wiley & Sons, 1982.

Wilson, Carl L., Walter E. Loomis and Hannah T. Croasdale. *Botany.* New York, New York: Holt, Rinehart and Winston, 1964.

Walters, Dirk R. and David J. Keil. *Vascular Plant Taxonomy.* Fourth Edition. Dubuque, Iowa: Kendall/Hunt Publishing Company, 1996.

Wren, R.C. *Potter's New Cyclopaedia of Medicinal Herbs.* New York, New York: Harper Colophon Books, 1972.

INDEX

INDEX

A

Abell, Chris 152
Achillea borealis 86, 112, 228
Aconitum delphinifolium 86, 103, 230
Actaea rubra 114, 119, 230
Adiantum pedatum 148, 173
Alagnaq (Aleut) 133, 298
Alaska Miner's Lettuce 151
Alder 114, 117, 118, 130, 171, 223, 224, 276, 279, 280, 281, 283, 284, 287, 288, 292, 311, 312
Allium schoenoprasum 86, 109, 242
Alnus crispa 114, 117, 130, 223, 312
Alnus sinuata 117, 223
Alpine Blueberry 58, 61, 238, 296
Alum Root 139, 279
Alutiiq 4, 24, 56, 65, 326
Amaryaq (Aleut) 125, 297
American Cranebill 111
American Red Raspberry 27, 148, 163, 164, 252, 271, 297
Anderson, Angeline v, 41, 42, 193, 215
Andromeda polifolia 58, 77
Anemone narcissiflora 86, 106, 230
Angelica 3, 28, 31, 32, 33, 129, 226, 276, 282, 284, 286, 287, 288, 289, 291
Angelica genuflexa 28, 31, 226
Angelica lucida 31
Angier, Bradford 57, 127, 212, 324
Aramaaskaag (Aleut) 207
Arctic Dock 211
Arctostaphylos uva-ursi 178, 186, 238, 297
Arnica 86, 89, 90, 101, 102, 228
Arnica alpina 89, 186 *Arnica amplexicaulis* 89
Arnica frigida 89
Arnica-Iris oil 89, 90
Arnica lessingii 89
Arnica montana 89
Aromashka (in Ouzinkie) 207
Arrow Grass 28, 41
Artemisia tilesii 188, 215, 228
Athyrium filix-femina 175

B

Baker Cottage 12, 72
Balm of Gilead 4, 91, 92, 277, 287
Balsam Poplar 91, 92
Beach Greens 38, 51, 53, 271, 292, 301, 302
Beach Lovage 28, 35, 193, 226, 279, 283, 301, 302, 303
Beach Peas 28, 37, 246, 272, 301, 302
Beach Strawberry 178, 181, 252, 271, 292, 297
Berries, Low and High 23, 295, 296
Bibliography 323, 324
Birch Family 117, 223
Blackberry 73, 252, 296
Blueberry 58, 60, 61, 62, 63, 67, 73, 77, 181, 238, 271, 274, 276, 279, 280, 282, 290, 296, 312, 327
Bog Blueberry 58, 60, 61, 62, 238, 296
Bog Cranberry 67, 69, 76, 144, 238, 271, 297
Bog Myrtle 84
Bog Rosemary 58, 77
Bogs, Pond Edges, Damp Terrain, Alpine Slopes 59
Boozinik (Russian) 155
Boschniakia rossica 114, 130, 224
Botany by Carl Wilson and Walter Loomis 3, 218, 328
Bracken Family 170
Broomrape Family 130, 224
Brusnika (Russian) 67
Buckwheat Family 127, 211, 225
Bunchberry 58, 65, 271, 296
Burch, Barbara v, 3, 32, 218
Burners 203
Burnet 114, 121, 252, 279, 281, 289, 290

C

Caltha palustris ssp. *asarifolia* 28, 48, 230
Canadian Dwarf Cornel 65, 231, 271, 277, 293
Caribou Leaves 215, 271
Carrot or Parsley Family 226
Chenopodium album 28, 45, 237
Chernika (Russian) 60
Chernikoff, Jenny v, 2, 10, 12, 13, 14, 35, 99, 106, 216
Chickweed 38, 50, 53, 188, 190, 191, 248, 271, 275, 283, 287, 292, 293, 301, 302, 303

Chiming Bells 28, 51
Chocolate Lily 99, 242, 272, 279
Chughelenuk (Aleut: young salmonberry shoots) 133, 298
Cicuta douglasii 32, 114, 129, 226
Cicuta mackenzieana 129
Cillqaq (Aleut) 183, 326
Ciquq (Aleut) 91
Claytonia acutifolia 151
Claytonia siberica 148, 151
Claytonia tuberosa 151
Cloudberry 27, 148, 164, 252, 271, 297
Clover 184, 188, 192, 193, 246, 271, 276, 278, 282, 287, 288, 290, 293, 302, 303
Club Moss 139, 148, 157, 158, 227, 272, 280, 281, 282, 284, 287, 288, 289, 293
Club Moss Family 157, 227
Coen, Sandra v, 3, 145, 215
Common Chickweed 190
Common Plantain 65, 188, 195, 196, 249, 271, 275, 276, 278, 282, 287, 289, 290, 291, 293, 301, 302, 303, 309
Composite Family 89, 97, 112, 199, 207, 215, 228, 317, 320
Cooperative Extension Service 62, 74, 105, 156, 181, 325
Corn Lily 75
Cornus canadensis 58, 65, 231, 296
Cottonwood 4, 86, 89, 91, 92, 154, 259, 271, 277, 280, 281, 282, 283, 287, 288, 289
Cow Parsnip 188, 197, 198, 226, 271, 275, 277, 281, 285, 287, 289, 290, 291, 293, 303, 311
Cow Parsnip, chemical reaction 197
Cowslip 48
Crampbark 125, 147, 284
Crampweed 56
Cranberry 58, 67, 68, 69, 70, 73, 76, 114, 125, 126, 144, 147, 167, 181, 238, 239, 271, 272, 274, 275, 277, 283, 284, 288, 290, 292, 293, 297
Croasdale, Hannah T. 3, 218, 328
Crowberry 58, 73, 74, 76, 229, 272, 277, 279, 280, 283, 291, 296
Crowberry Family 73, 229, 296
Crowfoot Family 48, 103, 106, 119, 123
Cuawak (Aleut) 60, 296

Cukilanarpak (Aleut) 153
Cultivated and Disturbed Soils; Along Roadbeds 189
Curly Dock 211

D

Dandelion 38, 112, 151, 154, 188, 190, 193, 199, 200, 201, 202, 228, 271, 277, 281, 284, 286, 287, 290, 293, 301, 302, 303
Deer Fern Family 171
Devil's Club 4, 38, 148, 153, 154, 236, 271, 275, 276, 277, 278, 280, 281, 282, 283, 284, 286, 287, 289, 290, 291, 292, 293
Dock 15, 211
Dogwood Family 65, 231, 296
Dong quai 31, 284, 286
Dory knees 4, 10
Drosera anglica 58, 82, 255
Drosera rotundifolia 82
Dryopteris dilitata 148, 175
Dyes from Wild Plants 23, 305
Dyes from lichens 308
Dyes from small plants 309
Dyes from trees and shrubs 312

E

Early Blueberry 58, 62, 238, 271, 296
Echinopanax horridum 148, 153, 236
Elderberry 125, 148, 155, 156, 239, 271, 277, 280, 282, 291, 297, 313
Empetrum nigrum 58, 73, 229, 296
Epilobium angustifolium 27, 183, 232
Epilobium latifolium 178, 183, 232
Equisetum arvense 148, 159, 240
Evangel, the 12
Evening Primrose Family 183, 232

F

Ferns 27, 75, 148, 169, 171, 203, 272, 319, 321
Fialka (Russian) 145
Fibrous Root 82, 221, 318
Figwort or Snapdragon Family 79, 233
Fir Club Moss 148, 157, 158, 227, 272, 280, 281, 282, 284, 287, 288, 289, 293
Fireweed 27, 54, 178, 183, 184, 192, 232, 271, 279, 282, 290, 301, 302, 303, 326

Floral Organs, Diagram 218
Flora of Alaska and Neighboring Territories 3, 24, 170, 218
Flower and Plant Parts: Abbreviated Glossary 221
Forget-me-not or Borage Family 51, 234
Fragaria chiloensis 178, 181, 252, 297
Fritillaria camschatcensis 86, 99, 242

G

Galium aparine 28, 49, 243
Galium boreale 49, 243, 310
Geranium erianthum 86, 111, 235
Geranium Family 111, 235
Getz, Linda v, 3
Geum 86, 95, 252, 271, 275, 279, 285, 288
Geum macrophyllum (Avens) 86, 95, 252
Ginseng Family 153, 236
Glossary 218, 221, 315, 316
Goldenrod 24, 86, 97, 228, 271, 275, 276, 279, 280, 283, 285, 289, 293, 309
Goosefoot 45, 237
Goosefoot Family 45, 237
Goosetongue 28, 38, 41, 42, 43, 195, 196, 249, 271, 301, 302, 303
Grassy Meadows and Forest Clearings 87
Gravel Bars and Riverbeds or Dry Slopes 27, 51, 179, 251
Great Willow Herb 183
Griffin, Jennifer v, 3

H

Hall, Nancy and Walter 164, 325
Heal All 209
Heath Family 60, 67, 76, 186, 238, 296
Hedysarum mackenzii 37, 178, 187, 246
Heracleum lanatum 188, 197, 226, 311
Heuchera glabra 114, 139, 253
Highbush cranberry 114, 125, 126, 147, 239, 271, 275, 277, 283, 284, 288, 290, 293, 297
Hints on Cooking Wild Edibles 23, 127, 299, 300
Honckenya peploides 28, 53, 248
Honeysuckle Family 125, 155, 239, 297
Horsetail 148, 159, 160, 240, 272, 275, 280, 281, 285, 286, 287, 289, 290, 291, 292, 293, 303, 310
Horsetail Family 159, 240

Hudson Bay Tea 76
Hulten, Eric 3, 24, 32, 57, 89, 151, 170, 218, 326

I

Igoria (Russian) 111
Indian Rice 86, 99, 100, 242, 303
Introduction: How to Use this Book 23
Iris Family 101, 241
Iris setosa 86, 101, 241

J

Jacob's Ladder 27, 178, 185, 250, 272, 290
Joint Grass 159

K

Kakoriki (Russian) 107
Kalina (Russian) 125
Kamchatka Lily 99
Kelso, Fran v, 54, 69, 156, 191, 202, 206
Kenegtaq (Aleut) 67, 297
Kidney plant. *See* goldenrod
Kilitayka (Russian) 166
King's Crown 131, 254
Kinnikinnik 178, 186, 238, 272, 275, 283, 292, 297
Kipray (Russian) 183
Kislitsa (Russian) 211
Klever (Russian) 192
Klinkert, Cathy 134
Kodiak Island 1, 3, 9, 10, 11, 12, 27, 75, 89, 107, 159, 170, 181, 215, 218, 223, 232, 259
Kostianika (Russian) 165
Krapeva (Russian) 203
Kulich 71, 72
Kushelkok (Aleut) 185

L

Labrador Tea 58, 76, 77, 229, 238, 272, 274, 275, 277, 279, 281, 282, 285, 290, 291
Lady Fern 175
Lambsquarter 28, 42, 45, 46, 237, 271, 283, 285, 287, 291, 292, 301, 302, 303
Lathyrus maritimus 28, 37, 187, 246
Ledum palustre, ssp. *decumbens* 58, 76, 238
Lettuce saxifrage 137

Licorice Fern 148, 171, 272, 278, 279, 293
Ligusticum scoticum 28, 35, 226
Lily Family 75, 81, 93, 99, 109, 141, 242, 257, 298
Lingonberry 58, 67, 68, 69, 73, 229, 238, 272, 277, 281, 288, 290, 292, 297, 313
Liver plant (dandelion) 200
Lostochki (Russian) 151
Lowbush Cranberry 58, 67, 69, 238, 272, 297
Lund, Chris 5
Lupinus nootkatensis 37, 86, 107, 246
Lycopodium selago 148, 157, 227

M

Madder Family 49, 243
Maidenhair Family 173
Maidenhair Fern 148, 173, 272, 276, 278, 282, 289
Makretzi (Russian) 190, 191
Malina (Russian) 133, 163
Map of City of Ouzinkie 8
Map of Spruce Island 7
Maroshka (Russian) 164
Marsh Fivefinger 58, 78, 252, 272
Marsh Marigold 28, 48, 123, 230, 271, 276, 278, 279, 280, 284, 287, 292, 300, 302, 303
Masking 70
Matricaria matricarioides 188, 207, 228
Matteuccia struthiopteris 175
McIntosh, Deborah 205
Mealberry 186, 297
Medicinal Index 23, 26, 273, 274
Mentha spicata 188, 213, 244
Mertensia maritima 28, 51, 234
Mertensia paniculata 28, 51
Milfoil 112
Mimulus guttatus 58, 79, 233
Mint Family 209, 213, 244
Mogulnik (Russian) 76, 77
Mohney, Russ 100, 193
Moneses uniflora 148, 166, 260
Monkey Flower 58, 79, 233, 271, 275, 278, 287
Mordanting recipe 139, 158
Monkshood 86, 103, 230
Mossberry 165, 298
Mountain Ash 148, 161, 252, 271, 277, 283, 288, 290, 291, 292, 311

Mountain Sorrel 53, 114, 127, 225, 271, 301, 302, 303
Myosotis alpestris, ssp. *asiatica* 234
Myrica gale 58, 84, 258, 313

N

Nagoonberry 86, 105, 252, 272, 297
Nettle 14, 46, 154, 175, 188, 203, 204, 205, 206, 210, 212, 245, 271, 275, 277, 278, 279, 281, 282, 283, 285, 286, 287, 288, 289, 290, 291, 302, 303, 310
Nettle Family 203, 245
Nizamynik (Russian) 153
Northern Bedstraw 28, 49, 243, 271, 275, 276, 278, 282, 283, 286, 287, 289, 293, 301, 302, 303, 310
Northern Ground Cone 130
Nuphar polysepalum 58, 81, 257

O

Odoovanchik (Russian) 199
Old School 11
Oogoortsi (Russian) 141, 298
Open Woods and Forest 27, 149
Opheim, Ed, Jr. 4, 10
Opheim, Ed, Sr. 4, 10
Oplopanax horridus 153, 236
Orach (*Atriplex* spp.) 45, 237
Ouzinkie v, 1, 2, 4, 6, 9, 10, 11, 12, 13, 14, 15, 16, 35, 41, 42, 47, 55, 63, 65, 72, 74, 75, 121, 123, 125, 152, 191, 193, 204, 207, 216, 228, 306
Ouzinkie Botanical Society v, 1, 42, 306
Ouzinkie map 4
Ouzinkie, Then and Now 4, 6, 9
Oxycoccus microcarpus 58, 67, 69, 238, 297
Oxyria digyna 114, 127, 225
Oysterleaf 28, 51, 234

P

Pagook 135
Panax ginseng 153
Paparotnik (Russian) 170
Parker, Carolyn 3, 218
Pea Family 37, 107, 187, 192, 246
Pestrikoff, Nicholas (Nick) 4, 9, 10, 11, 13
Petrushki 35, 36, 38, 42, 47, 50, 52, 80, 152, 193, 196
Picea sitchensis 148, 167, 247, 312
Pigweed 45, 46

Pineapple Weed 188, 207, 208, 228, 271, 277, 278, 280, 283, 285, 286, 287, 288, 290
Pine Family 167, 247
Pink Family 53, 190, 248
Plantago macrocarpa 28, 41, 249
Plantago major 188, 195, 249, 309
Plantago maritima 41, 249
Plantain Family 41, 195, 249
Plant Family Index 3, 23, 26, 27, 217, 218
Plants Class 1, 2, 3, 4, 23, 25, 27, 42, 49, 54, 63, 69, 78, 185, 191, 193, 205, 215, 218, 306, 308
Poisonous Plants 27, 129, 137, 325
    Arrow Grass (*Triglochin* spp.) 28, 41
    Baneberry 48, 114, 119, 230, 271
    Bog Rosemary (*Andromeda polifolia*) 58, 77
    Bracken Fern 27, 148, 170, 272
    Buttercup 48, 114, 123, 230, 271
    Death Camas 93, 109, 242, 271
    False Hellebore 58, 75, 93, 141, 203, 242, 245, 271
    Iris 86, 89, 90, 101, 102, 241, 272
    Monkshood 48, 86, 103, 111, 230, 27
    Narcissus-Flowered Anemone 86, 106, 230, 271
    Nootka Lupine 86, 107, 246
    Poison Water Hemlock 31, 32, 114, 129, 197, 226, 271
    Wild Sweet Pea 37, 178, 187, 246, 272
Pojar and MacKinnon 81, 209, 210, 255
Polemonium acutiflorum 185, 250
Polemonium Family 185
Polemonium pulcherrimum 27, 178, 185
Poleznaya trava (Russian) 24, 112
Polin (Russian) 215, 216
Polinya (Russian) 215, 216
Polypodium vulgare 148, 171
Pond Lily 58, 81, 257, 271, 303
Poochki (Russian) 80, 197, 198, 303
Populus balsamifera 86, 91, 259
Poque 114, 130, 224, 271, 290
Potentilla egedii 56, 252
Potentilla fruticosa 28, 56
Potentilla palustris 58, 78, 252
Potentilla villosa 57
Pratt, Verna 4, 327
Preface 1, 4
Prickly Rose 143, 298
Prunella vulgaris 188, 209, 210, 244
Pteridium aquilinum 148, 170
Purslane Family 151, 251
Puyurniq (Aleut) 105, 297

Q

Qangananguaq (Aleut) 112
Quaccia, Janet v, 3

R

Rain Flower 151, 152
Ranunculus spp. 114, 123, 230
Raspberry 27, 67, 99, 105, 133, 148, 163, 164, 165, 181, 193, 252, 271, 279, 280, 283, 285, 286, 289, 292, 293, 297, 298
Ray, Glen 24, 53, 100, 193, 195, 198, 327
Recipes 2, 4, 23, 25, 38, 60, 62, 67, 72, 74, 77, 105, 109, 144, 152, 156, 164, 181, 296, 300, 306, 307, 325
    Alaskan nettles 205
    Baked deer spareribs 142
    Baked halibut with mushrooms 176
    Basic cream soup recipe 301
    Blueberry jam 63
    Blueberry jelly 61
    Blueberry pie 62
    Cat's salmonberry wine 134
    Clam chowder 109
    Clam soup 212
    Clover-bright salad 193
    Codfish bacon bake 38
    Confectioners' sugar icing 71, 72
    Cranberry jelly 68, 126
    Cranberry muffins 70
    Crowberry pie 74
    Dandelion blossom pie 201
    Dandelion wine 199, 202
    Danny's spicy steamed mussels 80
    Deer roast 57
    Deer Swiss steaks 193
    Deviled eggs with petrushki 35
    Duck soup 100
    Easy fiddlehead cheese bake 176
    Easy salmon bake 206
    Elderberry jelly 156
    Elderberry wine 156
    Elk Mulligan 47

Fireweed honey 184, 192
Fisharoni surprise 201
Fish chowder with petrushki 36
Fish head soup 50
Fish in French batter 191
Franny's favorite Spruce Island weed salad 54
French fried sea bass 184
Highbush cranberry jelly 126
Hot cross buns from kulich dough 72
How to cook a seal 77
Indian rice 100
Lingonberry relish 69
Makretzi soup 191
Mossberry jam 165
Mother's dandelion recipe 200
Mountain sorrel and fish soup 127
Nagoonberry jelly 105
Nellie's halibut supreme 52
Nell's favorite scallop recipe 38
Nettle casserole 205
Octopus salad 36
Ooeduck (baidarka or gumboot) soup 42, 43
Parsnip a la Hercules 198
Pigweed pie 46
Plantain pizza 196
Poached halibut 39
Rose Hip Syrup 144
Roseroot "beach camp" omelette 132
Russian Easter kulich 71
Salmonberry jam 39, 134
Salmon perok 55
Salmon ring with cheese sauce 152
Scallop broth 38
Sea lion pot roast 84
Seasonal herbcakes 38
Silverweed cakes 57
Spearmint candy 214
Spring beauty salad 151
Spruce Island goldenrod tea 97
Violet jelly 145
Wild cucumber salad 142
Wild fruit or berry sauce 164
Wild green soufflé 46
Wild strawberry-pineapple conserve 181
Wildwood fritters 42

Zesty lemon roll-ups 196
Red-berried Elder 155, 297
Red tide 80
Riceroot 99
Romashka (Russian) 207
Rosa nutkana 114, 143, 252, 298
Rose Family 27, 56, 78, 95, 105, 121, 133, 143, 161, 163, 181, 252, 297
Roseroot 114, 131, 132, 254, 272, 275, 277, 280, 285, 288, 293, 301, 303
Roza (Russian) 143, 298
Rubus arcticus 86, 105, 252, 297
Rubus chamaemorus 148, 164, 252, 297
Rubus idaeus 148, 163, 252, 297
Rubus pedatus 148, 165, 252, 298
Rubus spectabilis 114, 133, 252, 298
Rumex spp. 188, 211, 225
Russian Orthodox Church 12, 70

S

Salad greens 137
Salix spp. 114, 147, 259
Salmonberry 39, 43, 54, 114, 133, 134, 135, 166, 193, 252, 256, 272, 275, 279, 283, 291, 293, 298, 301
Sambucus racemosa 148, 155, 239, 297, 313
Sanguisorba stipulata 114, 121
Sarana (Russian) 99
Saxifraga punctata 114, 137, 253
Saxifrage 54, 114, 137, 139, 253, 271, 301, 302, 303
Saxifrage Family 137, 139, 253
Schofield, Janice 4, 32, 38, 82, 83, 84, 91, 92, 111, 129, 130, 132, 137, 139, 154, 155, 196, 204, 216, 327
Scotch Lovage 35
Scouring Rush 159, 160, 240, 310
Scurvy Grass 53, 131
Seabeach Sandwort 28, 53, 54, 248, 271, 301
Sea-Chickweed 53
Sea Purslane 53
Seashore and Beach Marshes 29
Seashore Plantain 41, 249
Sedum rosea 114, 131, 254
Self-Heal 188, 209, 210, 244, 275, 279, 280, 282, 283, 285, 288, 289, 293, 326
Sheep Sorrel 211, 225, 311
Shield Fern Family 175

Shiksha (Russian -- crowberry) 73
Shikshonik (Russian -- crowberry bush) 73
Shipoynik (Russian -- wild rose bush) 143, 298
Shishki (Russian -- cones) 167, 168
Shrubby Cinquefoil 28, 56, 252
    the "Shuyak" 16
Shy Maiden 134, 148, 166, 260, 271, 276, 277, 278, 284, 287, 288, 289, 290, 291, 293
Siberian Spring Beauty 151
Silver Cinquefoil 56
Silverleaf 215, 216
Silverweed 28, 56, 57, 252, 271, 275, 278, 279, 280, 283, 284, 285, 288, 290, 291, 293, 303, 311
Single Delight 166
Sitka alder 117
Skripka (Russian) 131, 132
Smith, Alexandra (Sasha) v, 2, 36, 42, 55, 100, 102, 109, 195, 205, 213, 215
Smith, Georgia v, 14, 35, 41, 57, 68, 70, 126, 142, 165, 176, 184, 196, 201, 228
Smith, Joyce 4, 41
Smith, Kevin 4
Smith, Norman 12, 16, 72
Smith, Timothy 4, 11
Snakeweed 195
Solidago lepida 97, 309
Solidago multiradiata 86, 97, 228
Sorbus sitchensis 148, 161, 252
Sourdock 42, 53, 54, 127, 188, 191, 203, 211, 212, 225, 271, 275, 276, 281, 285, 286, 287, 288, 290, 291, 292, 301, 302, 303, 311
Sourgrass 127
Spatterdock 81
Spearmint 97, 188, 213, 214, 215, 244, 271, 279, 281, 282, 284, 285, 288, 290, 301, 303
Spreading Wood Fern 75, 148, 175, 245, 272, 275, 285, 302, 311
Spring tonic (devil's club and other herbs) 4, 154
Spruce 1, 3, 4, 9, 10, 11, 12, 13, 15, 24, 27, 31, 54, 57, 65, 69, 73, 76, 83, 97, 100, 103, 113, 117, 129, 141, 148, 154, 157, 163, 166, 167, 168, 181, 184, 209, 210, 213, 218, 223, 244, 245, 247, 256, 258, 260, 276, 277, 278, 280, 282, 283, 285, 286, 288, 289, 290, 291, 292, 293, 312

Spruce Island 1, 3, 4, 9, 10, 12, 13, 15, 24, 27, 31, 54, 57, 69, 76, 83, 97, 100, 103, 113, 129, 141, 163, 166, 167, 181, 184, 209, 210, 213, 218, 223, 244, 245, 256, 258
Squartsoff, Rosemary v, 38, 47, 50, 84
Star of Bethlehem 134, 166
Starring 70
Stellaria spp. 188, 190, 248
Stinging Nettle 203
Stinkweed 215, 216
Stoltenberg, Loretta 5
Stonecrop Family 131, 254
Stream Banks; Moist, Sunny Hillsides and Rocky Places 115
Streptopus amplexifolius 114, 141, 242, 298
Sundew 4, 31, 58, 82, 83, 255, 271, 275, 276, 278, 286, 289, 290, 291, 293
Sundew Family 82, 255
Swamp Cranberry 69, 297
Sweet Gale 58, 84, 85, 258, 271, 276, 286, 287, 291, 303, 313

T

Tap Root 222, 322
Taraxacum spp. 188, 228
Tincture Recipe, basic 4, 83
Townsend-Vennel, Robbie 5
Trailing Raspberry 27, 148, 165, 252, 271, 298
Trifolium hybridum 188, 192
Trifolium repens 192
Triglochin maritimum 28, 41
Triglochin palustris 41
Tsacrios, Nell v, 38, 52
Tundra Rose 56
Twisted Stalk 38, 141, 298

U

Ugyuun (Aleut) 197
Ungaayanaq (Aleut) 203
Urtica lyallii 188, 203, 245

V

Vaccinium ovalifolium 58, 62, 238, 296
Vaccinium uliginosum 58, 60, 61, 238, 296

Vaccinium uliginosum, ssp. *microphylum* 60
Vaccinium vitis-idaea 58, 67, 238, 297, 313
Vascular Plant, Principal Parts of a 218
Veratrum viride 58, 75, 242
Verba (Russian) 147
Veyniki (Russian) 117
Viburnum edule 114, 125, 147, 239, 297
Vierick, Dr. Eleanor 3
Viola spp. 114, 145, 256
Violet Family 145, 256

W

Wainiik (Aleut: banya or steam bath switches) 117
Walters, Bonnie K. 3, 218
Walters, Ozzie 38, 39
Water Lily Family 81, 257
Watermelon Berry 38, 141, 142, 271, 278, 284, 298
Wax Flower 166
Wax Myrtle Family 84, 258
Wild Alum 114, 139, 158, 253, 271, 279, 281, 289, 292, 293
Wild Celery 31, 32, 197
Wild Chamomile 207
Wild Chives 86, 93, 109, 242, 272, 301, 303
Wild Cucumber 54, 75, 114, 141, 142, 151, 242, 271, 278, 284, 298, 301, 303
Wild Flag 101, 241
Wild Geranium 86, 111, 235, 272, 279, 280, 282, 285, 286, 288, 290, 291, 292, 293
Wild Onion 93, 109
Wild Raspberry 99, 105, 297
Wild Rhubarb 211
Wild Rose 114, 143, 252, 272, 277, 278, 280, 285, 290, 292, 298

Wild Spinach 211
Wild Strawberry 181
Wild Sweet Potato 56
Wild Violet 54, 114, 145, 301, 302
Willow 91, 92, 114, 125, 147, 154, 183, 259, 271, 275, 280, 282, 283, 284, 285, 286, 287, 288, 289, 290, 293, 301, 303, 311, 317
Willow Family 91, 147, 259
Wineberry 105, 297
Wintergreen Family 134, 166, 260
Winterweed 190
Wiszinckas, Evelyn v, 3, 5
Wolfer, Greg (referred to in text by first name, Greg) v, 46, 48, 75, 141
Woodruff, Jim 201
Wormwood 188, 215, 216, 228, 271, 275, 276, 277, 280, 281, 282, 283, 284, 286, 288, 289, 292

Y

Yarrow 24, 86, 112, 113, 228, 271, 275, 277, 280, 281, 283, 284, 285, 287, 288, 289, 290, 291, 311
Yellow Pond Lily 81, 257, 303

Z

Zeine, Noreen 214
Zemlyanika (Russian) 181
Zholti golovnik (Russian) 24, 97
Zygadenus elegans 86, 93, 242

www.ingramcontent.com/pod-product-compliance
Lightning Source LLC
LaVergne TN
LVHW072116060526
838201LV00011B/256